The Campus History Series

STATE UNIVERSITY OF NEW YORK AT CANTON

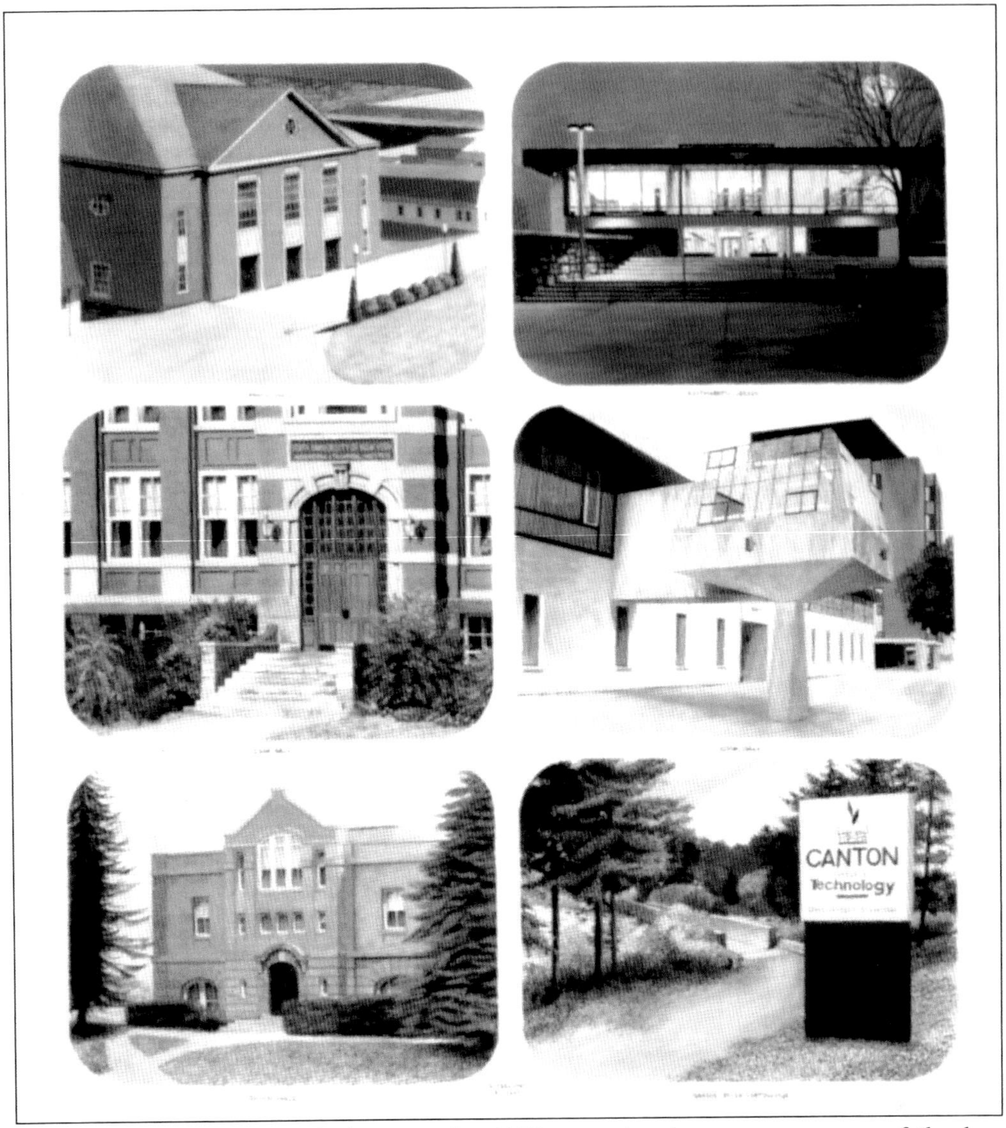

This painting by Hedlund, done in the 1970s, succinctly captures some of the key landmarks of both the old and new campuses. On the left are the images of the old campus: Madill Hall, the entrance to Cook Hall, and the dairy building, later known as Payson Hall. These buildings all became part of St. Lawrence University in 1968. The right column contains images of the new campus: Southworth Library, the greenhouse, and the sign and footbridge to the new campus on Riverside Drive. Only the tower greenhouse no longer exists.

The Campus History Series

STATE UNIVERSITY OF NEW YORK AT CANTON

Douglas Welch

ARCADIA
PUBLISHING

ISBN 978-0-7385-3907-2

Published by Arcadia Publishing
Charleston, South Carolina

Printed in the United States of America

Library of Congress Catalog Card Number: 2005928485

For all general information, contact Arcadia Publishing at:
Telephone 843-853-2070
Fax 843-853-0044
E-mail sales@arcadiapublishing.com
For customer service and orders:
Toll-Free 1-888-313-2665

Visit us on the internet at www.arcadiapublishing.com

CONTENTS

ACKNOWLEDGMENTS

The completion of *State University of New York: Canton* was made possible with the assistance of the following people and organizations: Trent Trulock, Stan Maine, and Jean Marie Martello of the St. Lawrence County Historical Association; Mark McMurray and Darlene Leonard of the Vance Archives at St. Lawrence University; and Canton town historian Linda Casserly. I also wish to thank Mary Bucher, Rich Fujita, Greg Kie, Alice Reed, Dave Gerlach, Scott Quinell, Anne Duncan, Janet Livingston, Peggy Levato, Terry Martin, Jerry Sawyer, Joanne Thornhill, Connie Bogart, and Stacey Basford. Rich Fujita and Greg Kie were particularly helpful with photographic and technical assistance. Writer David Martin of Ogdensburg shared his experience in doing the layout. I also wish to thank Pam O'Neil, our editor at Arcadia Publishing.

INTRODUCTION

This land, its people, their educational aspirations, and a small college—it isn't a complicated story, but it is an interesting and compelling one. The State University of New York at Canton is very much a product of the North Country, reflecting both the rugged landscape and the hardy character of its residents. For 100 years, the college has changed, adapted, and grown from its start in the farmhouse on outer Park Street to its present hillside location northwest of Canton.

The country was a far different place in 1906, being only 40 years removed from the Civil War and 15 years from the mythic closing of the frontier. In February of that year, the New York State Legislature approved the establishment of the School of Agriculture at St. Lawrence University. Elsewhere in 1906, Theodore Roosevelt was president of the United States, Zane Grey's first book, *Spirit of the Border*, was published, the National League New York team won the World Series, and the Army-Navy football game ended in a 6-6 tie.

St. Lawrence County was in its heyday, producing a marvelous variety of agricultural products and foodstuffs and providing a self-sufficiency befitting its independent-minded citizenry. Dairying was already an important industry, and the 100 butter and cheese factories that seemed to occupy every major intersection provided a steady source of cash to many of the county's residents. The village of Canton was a small and thriving farm community that had just marked the centennial of its settlement. In 1906, St. Lawrence University celebrated the golden anniversary of its founding in 1856, and E. J. Noble was writing home to his parents in Gouverneur about living through the San Francisco Earthquake.

The college known today as SUNY Canton was started as the School of Agriculture on land adjacent to St. Lawrence University in 1906. Over the years, the college has gone through several name changes. It has been known as the School of Agriculture, New York State Agricultural and Technical Institute at Canton (1941), State University of New York Agricultural and Technical Institute at Canton (1948), State University of New York Agricultural and Technical College at Canton (1965), State University of New York College of Technology at Canton (1987), and, since 1993, SUNY Canton.

There have been other, more substantive changes as well. During the first three decades, agriculture and home economics were the main emphasis, but starting in 1937, technical and engineering courses were added. In the past quarter century, the role of agricultural education has declined. Since 1997, the college has been adding four-year degree programs and making the gradual transition to a baccalaureate-granting institution. Currently, SUNY Canton is preparing to offer a variety of online courses that will bring more changes.

Over the past century, there have also been a number of construction projects that changed the appearance and ambiance of the college. Between 1907 and 1913, several buildings, including Cook Hall, the dairy building , the dairy barn, and various outbuildings, were constructed on the college grounds. The 360-foot long poultry building was added in 1926. In the 1940s, Madill Hall and the temporary buildings were added. Around 1960, the industrial lab, industrial classroom buildings, and Alumni Hall were built. The largest and most dramatic change was in 1968, when SUNY Canton moved from its original location to its newly built home on the other side of the village of Canton. Since the late 1980s, a major addition has been completed on Southworth Library, two campus centers have been built, and Newell Veterinary Technology Center, the veterinary science building, has been erected.

SUNY Canton has weathered rumors and hints of closure at various times in its history. In 1934, the School of Agriculture faced possible closure as the Great Depression wore on. Director Van Whittemore took a sizeable contingent to Albany to lobby, and the school stayed open. In 1960, when the industrial buildings and Alumni Hall were still new, St. Lawrence University announced that SUNY ATI at Canton would have to move. This decision created uncertainty about the future existence of SUNY Canton and its location. Some wanted to see the college moved from Canton. Local businessman and college council member Edson Martin donated the land where the college is now located. The events that led to SUNY Canton's relocation in the 1960s would not be the last time that uncertainty hung over the college's future. In the mid-1990s, reports of campus closings that included SUNY Canton circulated through Albany. Concerted effort by the college administration and staff, and broad support from the larger community, turned the tide.

There have also been times over the years when SUNY Canton's enrollment would peak, then decline or fluctuate for years. When classes started in 1907, there were only five students. In 1915, the enrollment hit 187 and did not surpass this level again until 1934, when there were 194 students. In the intervening years, World War I, an agricultural depression in the 1920s, and the Great Depression dampened college attendance. In the 1970s, enrollment reached 2800 students as the baby boom generation crested. While college registration numbers dwindled in the early 1990s to below 2000, enrollment has since increased to 2600. This trend is expected to continue over the next few years.

Through all these changes, SUNY Canton has endured. The life of the institution, including its academics, social activities, sports teams, and campus publications, has continued through all the challenges. There is something reassuring about how the college has continued to serve its students and the community of the North Country throughout the cycles of its history. Perhaps SUNY Canton's greatest asset is the people who have been a part of its first century. At critical times over the years, individuals have stepped up and made a difference in the college's development.

I hope you enjoy *SUNY Canton: A Pictorial History*, the story of the college's first century.

One

The Farmhouse Years 1906–1913

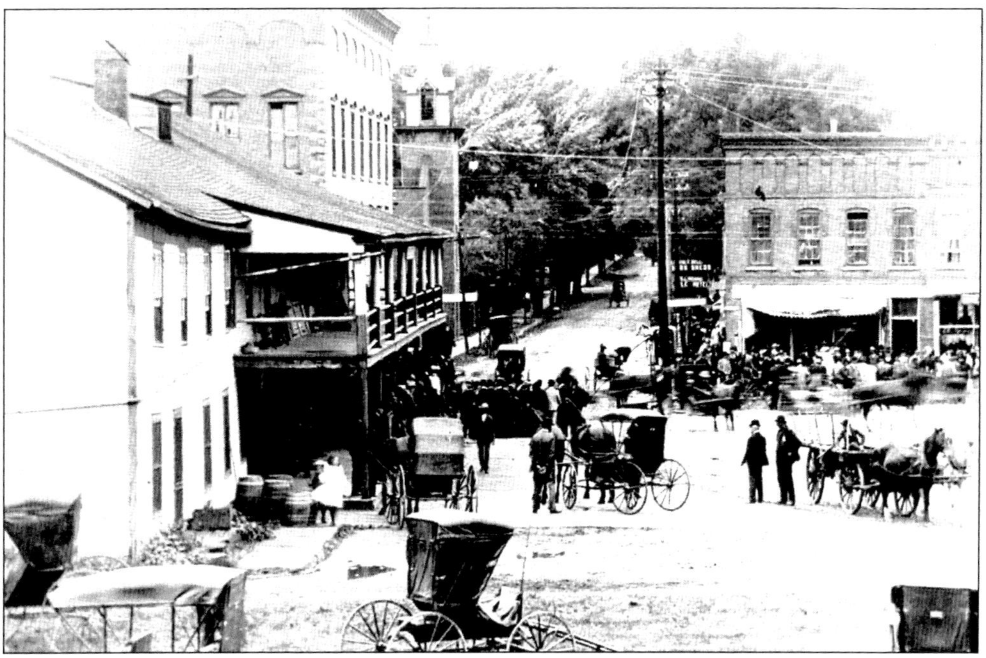

This is the central intersection of Canton, New York, where Court Street and Park Street meet Main Street, as it appeared in the late 19th and early 20th centuries. Around this time the School of Agriculture, later known as SUNY Canton, opened adjacent to St. Lawrence University on outer Park Street.

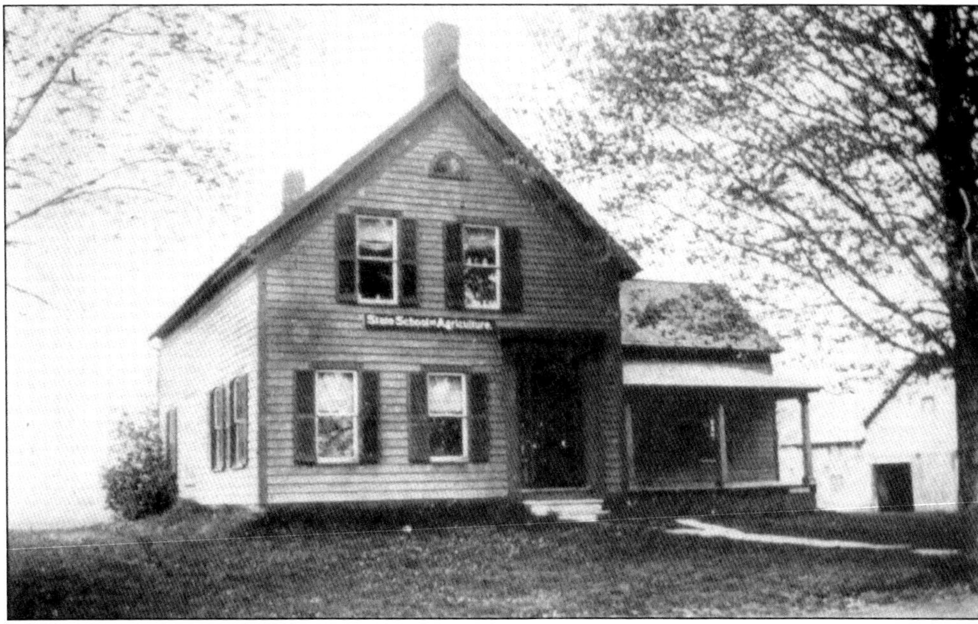

The farmhouse is where SUNY Canton began. It was the first building used by the School of Agriculture, and when classes started in 1907, there were five students. This was a temporary situation, as there would be a number of building projects, large and small, over the next several years.

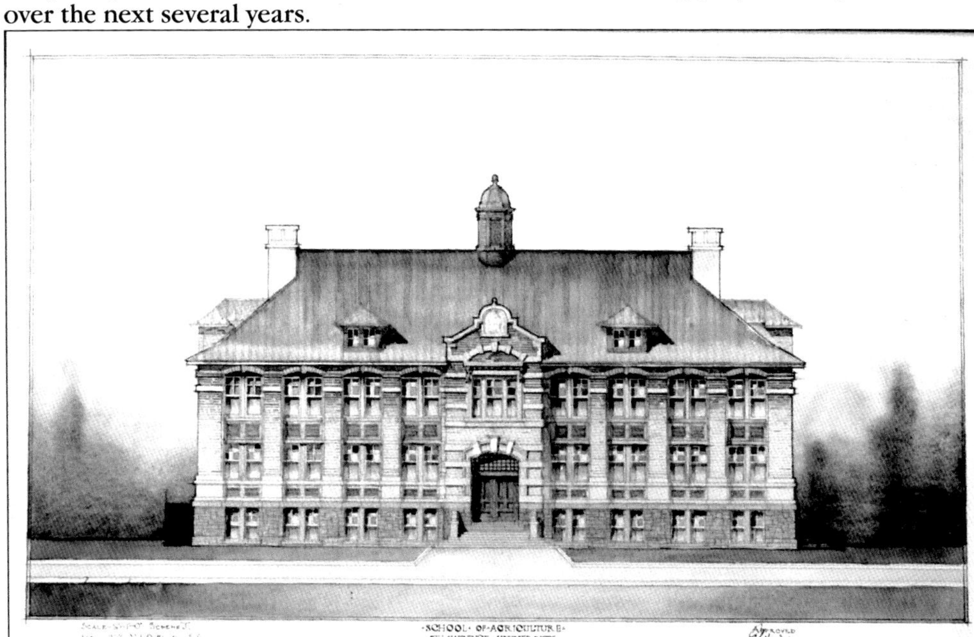

This drawing from the state architect's office depicts the first building to be erected for the School of Agriculture as a main classroom building. It was later named Cook Hall, after the director of the School of Agriculture from 1909 to 1917. Several decades later, it was renamed Piskor Hall. Students and school officials were frustrated by the slow progress on the part of the state in completing the drawings, and later by contractor problems that delayed use of the building until 1909.

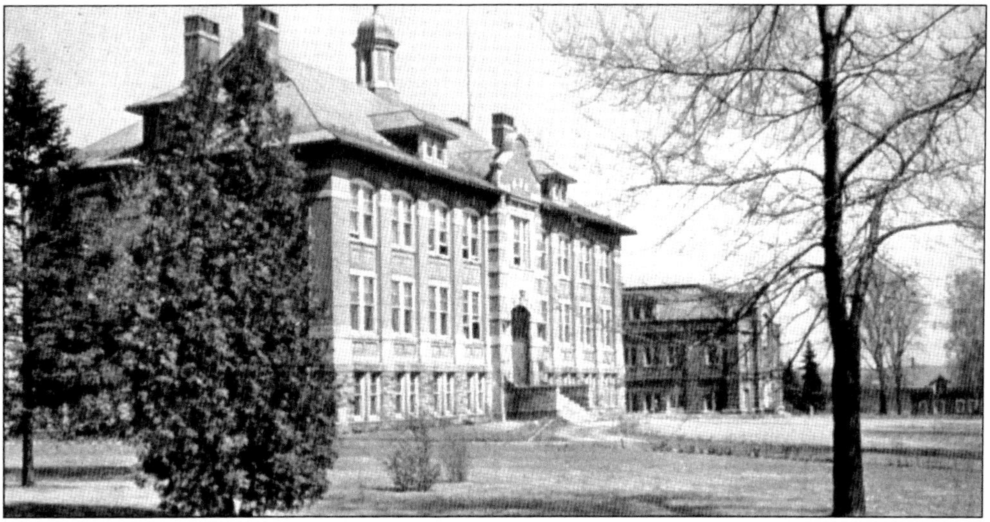

Cook Hall, in the foreground, and the dairy building were the main classroom buildings on campus. The dairy building was later named for another important person during SUNY Canton's early years, Dr. James Payson. A variety of other outbuildings were constructed between 1909 and 1913.

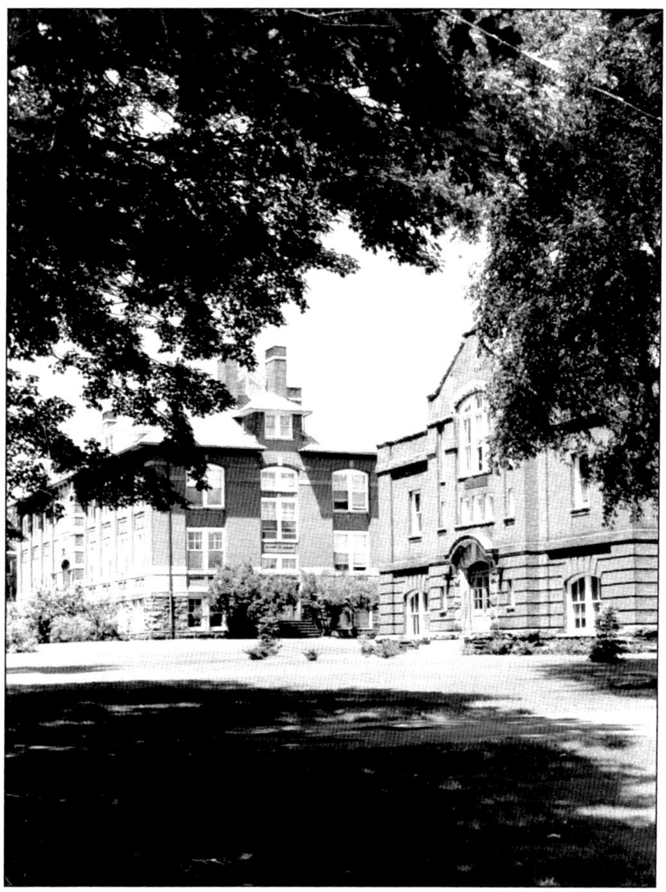

This later photograph highlights Payson Hall, with Cook Hall in the background on the east side of Park Street and facing northeast.

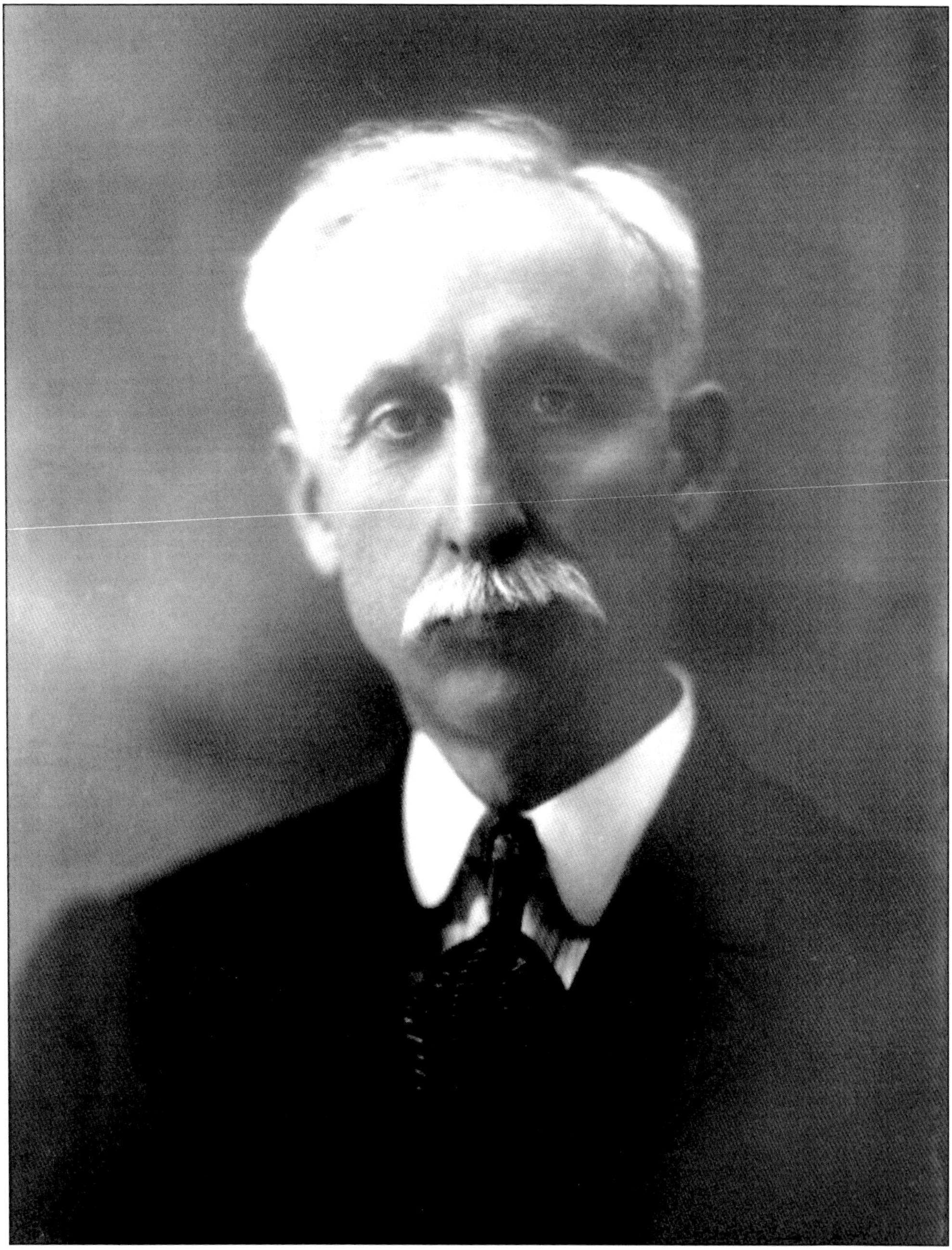

Herbert Cook's portrait hangs in a hallway gallery on the sixth floor of the faculty office building, along with other past and present leaders of the college. Cook is known for his steady leadership during the establishment of the School of Agriculture, the building phase, and the onset of World War I, when enrollment sagged. His important contributions were acknowledged again when a building on the new campus was named for him in the late 1960s.

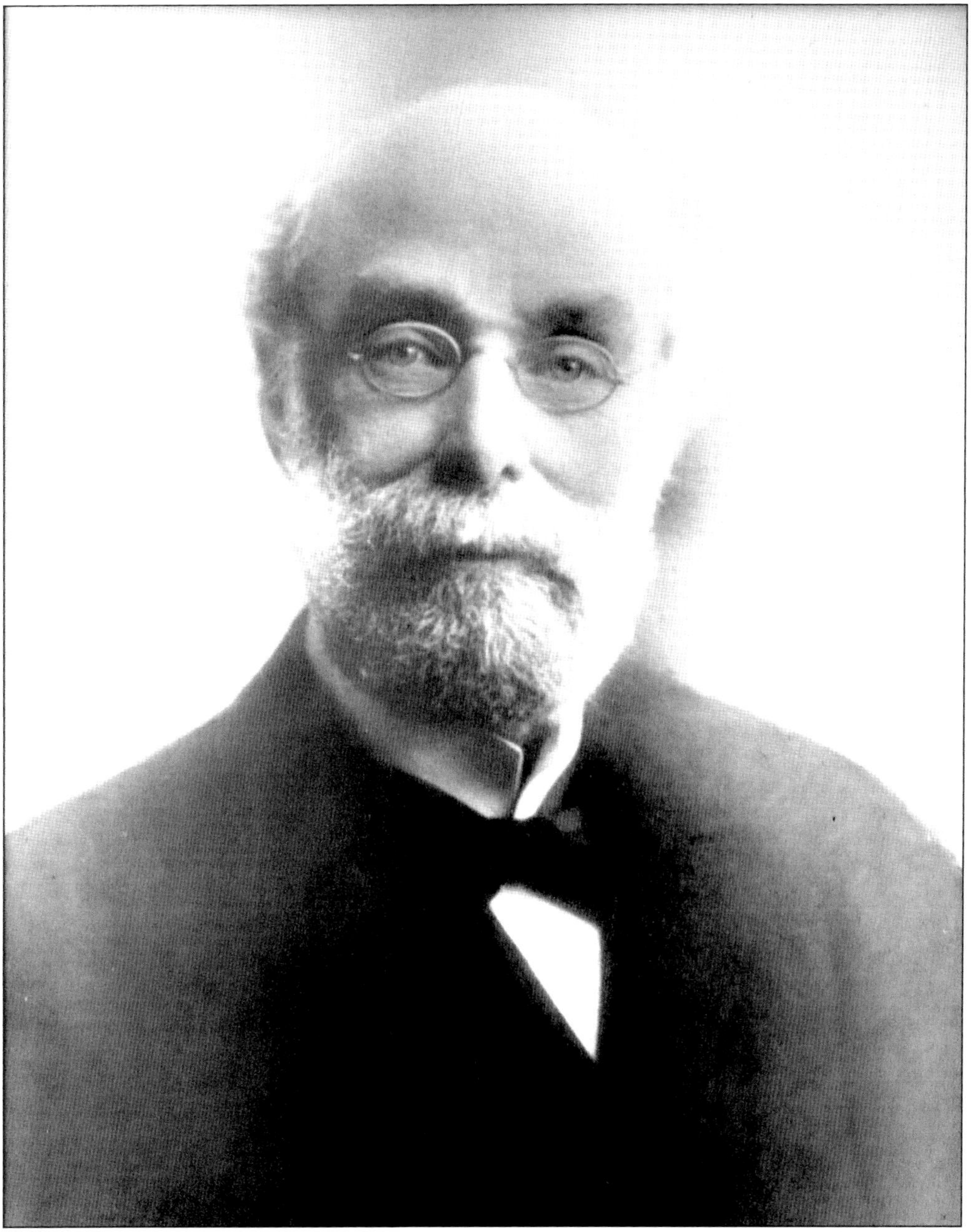

Dr. James Payson is perhaps the most beloved figure from the School of Agriculture's first two decades. Like Herbert Cook, he had buildings on both campuses named after him. Dr. Payson led the school only briefly in 1917–1918 on an interim basis. His contributions were in other areas. Between 1907 and his retirement at age 81 in 1929, he taught academic courses. He also was a strong advocate for the school, documenting those early years in a typescript work entitled *A Brief History of the State School of Agriculture*. It has been said of him that he was "founding father, venerable educator, revered friend."

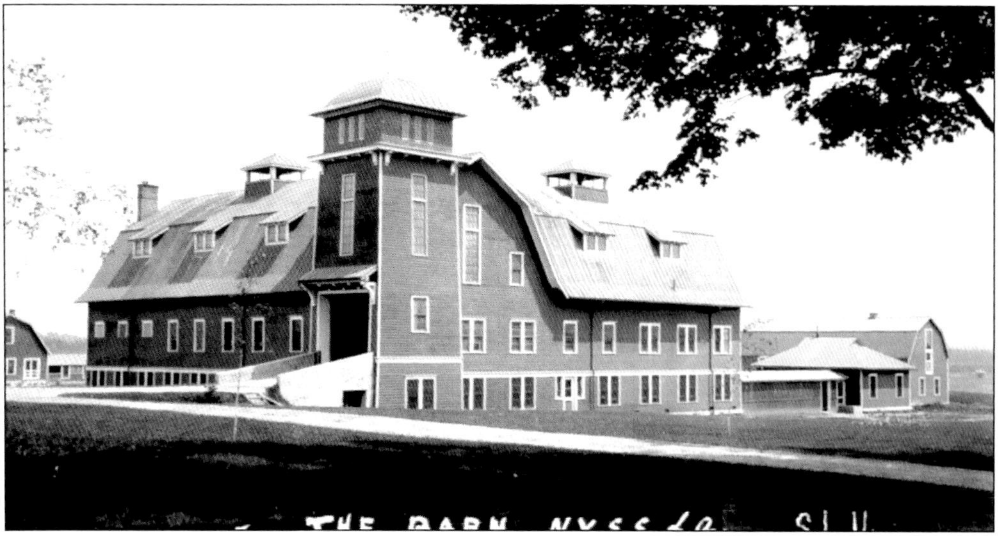

The dairy barn was built in 1909–1910 at a cost of $15,000. It had two wings, and its attractive lines made it an asset to both the school and the community. Other outbuildings pictured here, including the horse stables, granary, shop, and icehouse, were added later in 1910 and in 1911.

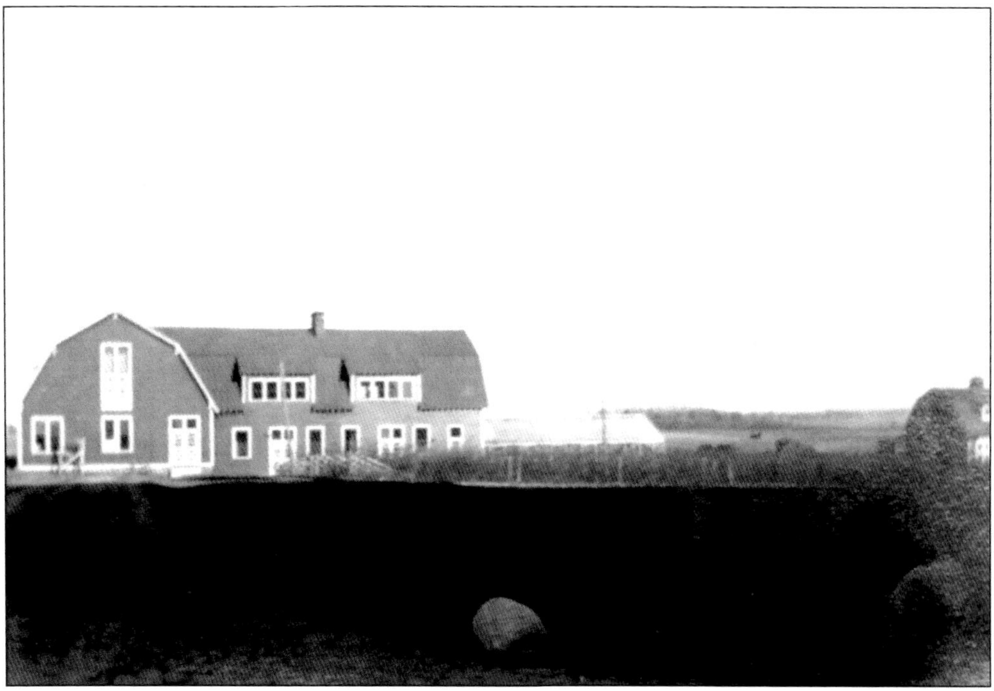

This view of the dairy barn is facing north, with outer Park Street to the left. Note the greenhouse in the center of the picture, off the end of the east-west wing of the dairy barn. It was built and finished in 1913.

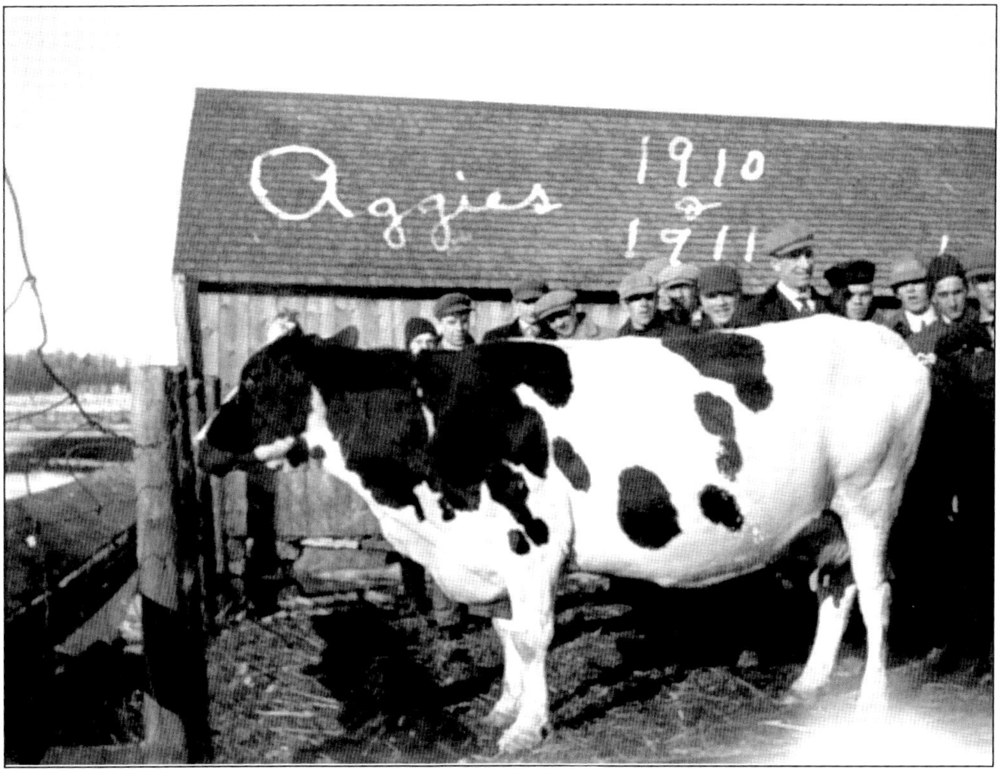

Things were happening fast at Canton's new School of Agriculture. There were suddenly people, buildings, and animals where there had not been any before. This *c.* 1910 photograph shows School of Agriculture students with one of their charges.

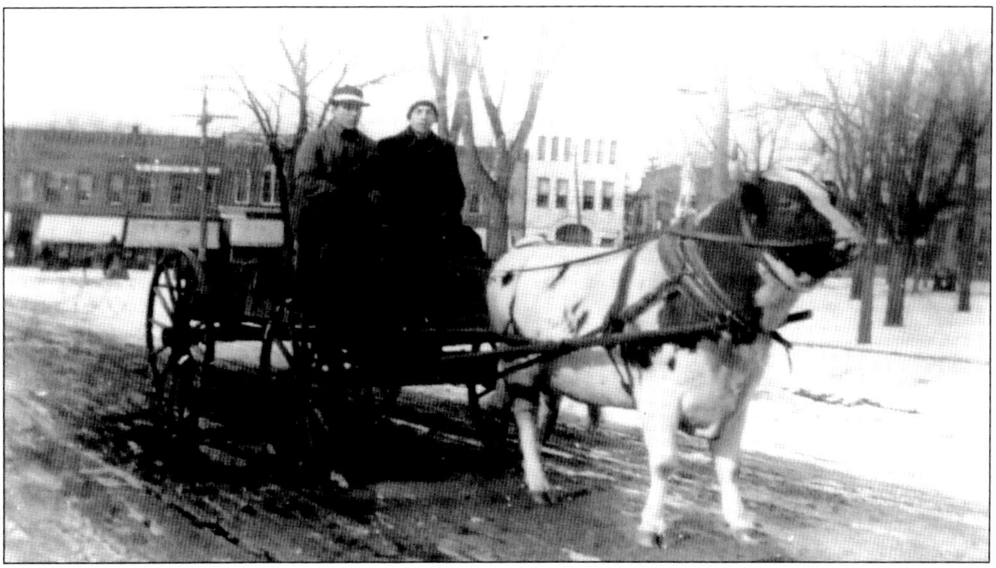

Driver Peron Kieckle and passenger Maynard Morrison, both of the class of 1911, are out for a ride on Park Street heading back to campus. White Star, an Ayrshire bull, is pulling them and their wagon. Notice the Canton Village Park and the East Main Street business block in the background.

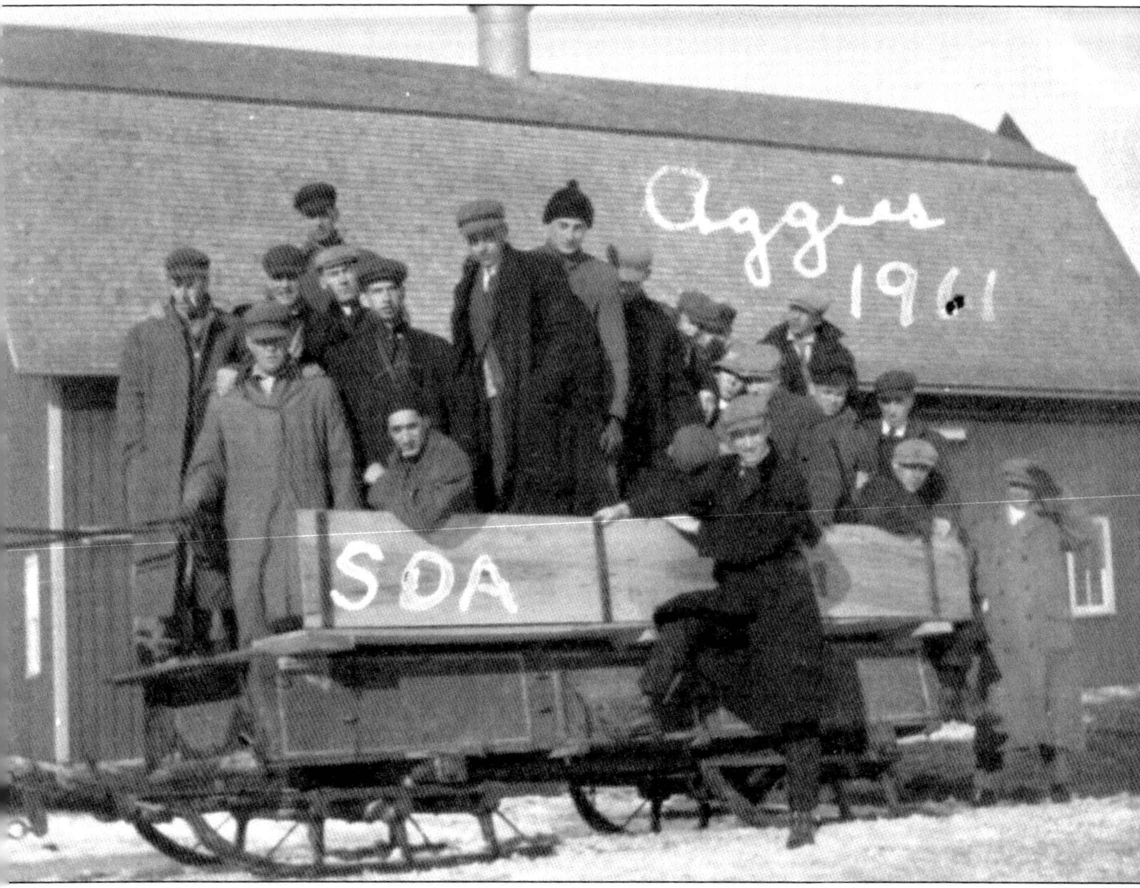

This group shot shows agriculture students in front of one of the school's outbuildings in 1911. Double bobsleds such as these were an important form of transportation in northern New York in the early 20th century. In winter, it was a convenient way to move wood, grain, and hay through the snow. Draft animals were able to move far heavier loads than they could on bare ground.

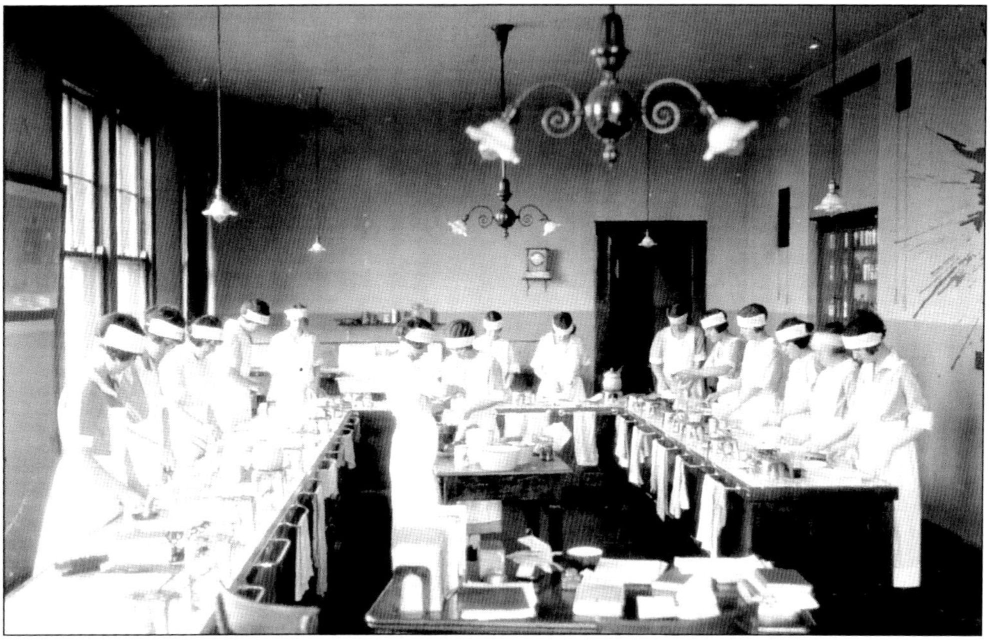

Domestic science was an important part of the curriculum at the School of Agriculture in the early part of the century. A well-run home was valued as much as a well-run farm. Female students made up a sizeable portion of the student body, and at times, their numbers exceeded those of male students.

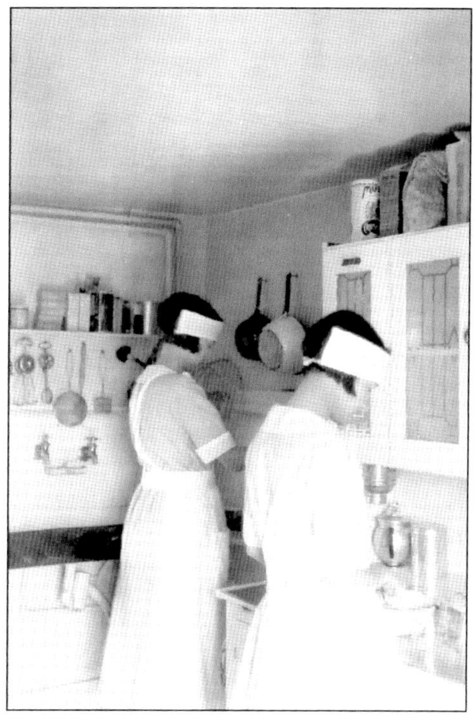

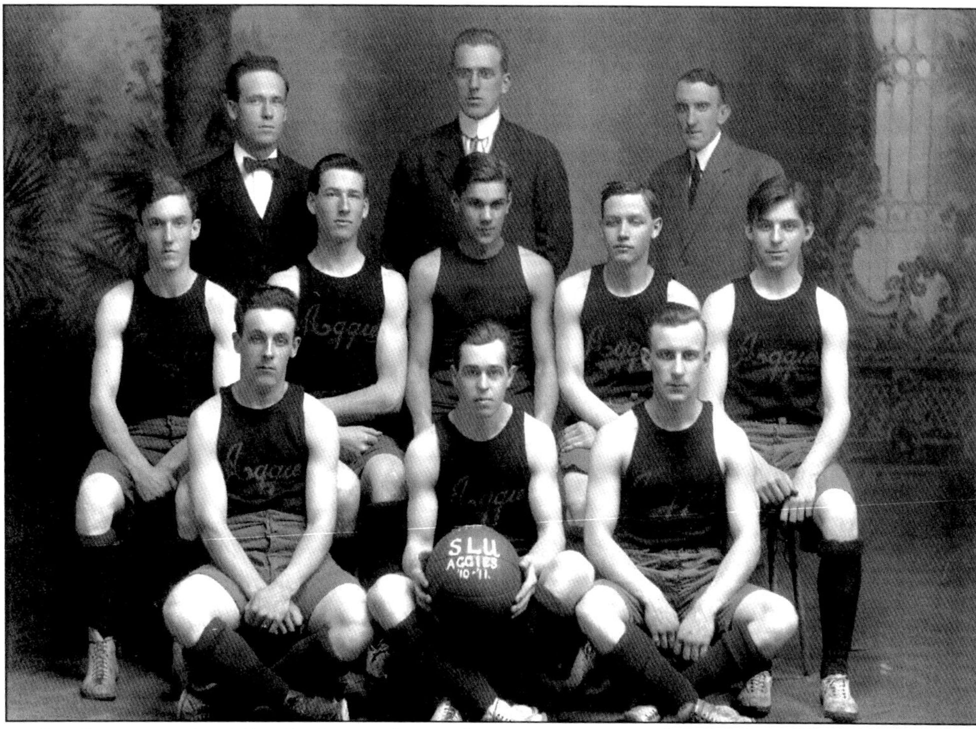

Within five years, the School of Agriculture, despite its small size, was taking on all the trappings of a well-established institution. As this photograph of the 1910–1911 Aggie basketball team attests, sports have been an important part of student life from the very beginning.

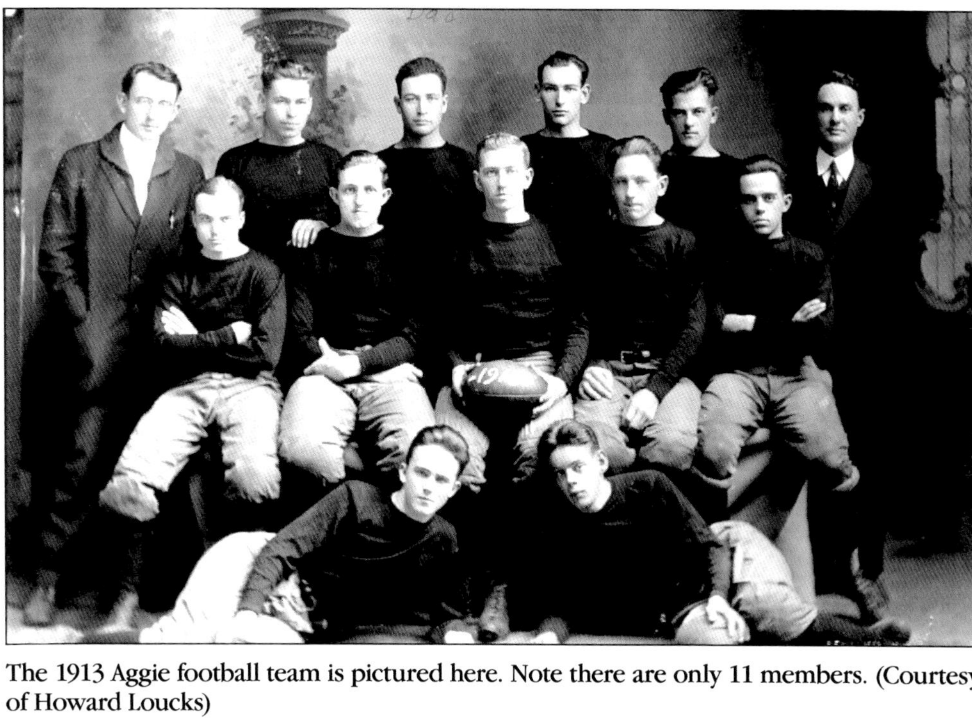

The 1913 Aggie football team is pictured here. Note there are only 11 members. (Courtesy of Howard Loucks)

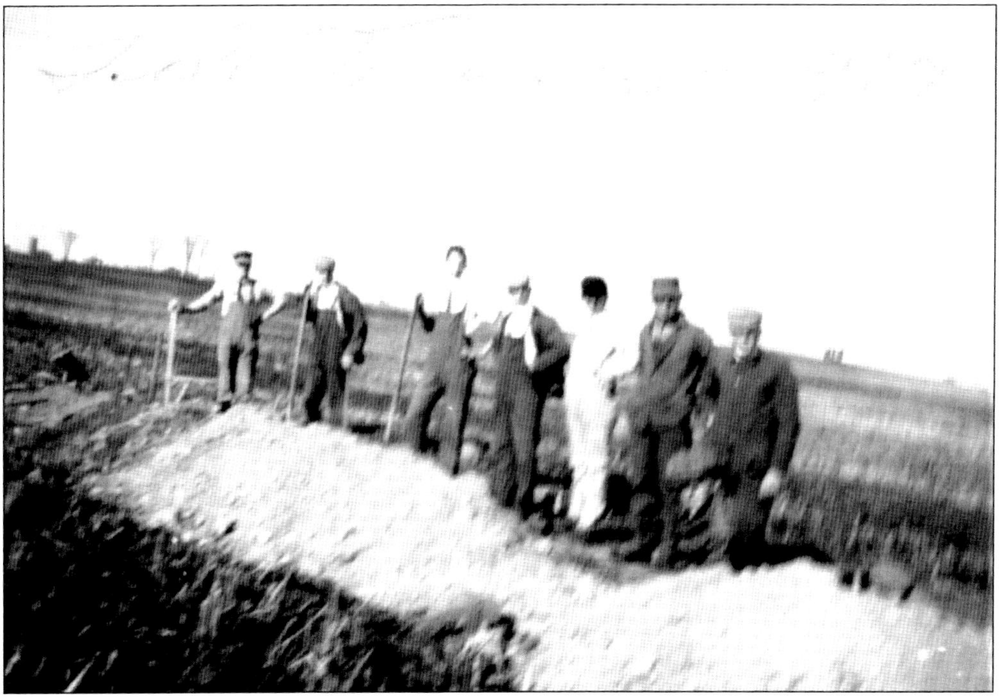

This 1912 photograph shows the installation of drainage tile in a farm field on campus. As the photographic record often shows, the education at the School of Agriculture was hands on and practical. Note the lack of trees. Land in St. Lawrence County was 70 to 80 percent open land in the early 1900s.

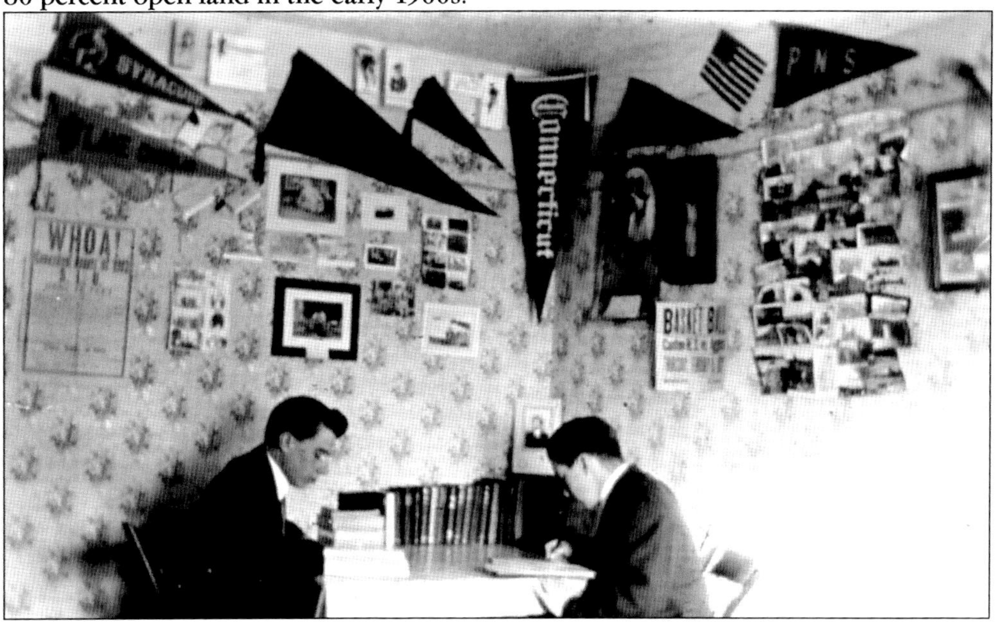

Arthur Harper (right) and an unidentified roommate study in their boardinghouse room in Canton Village. In those early years, students lived and boarded in the community, often in private homes. Evidently even a century ago students liked to decorate their college rooms with posters, pictures, and banners.

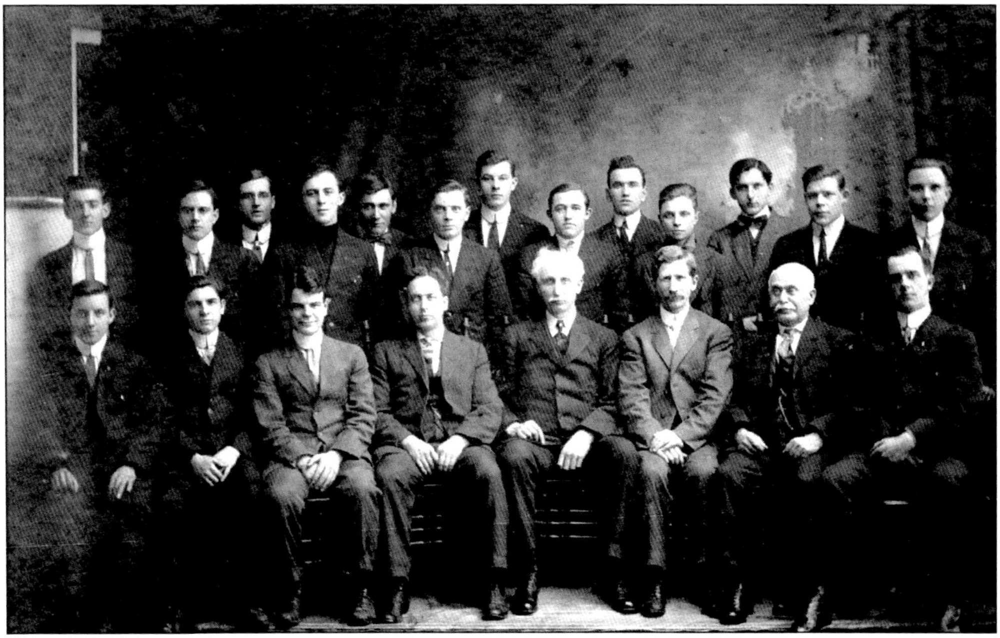

In this photograph of agriculture graduates from the class of 1912, only two students are identified. Floyd Holden is on the far left in the back row, and Larry Olmstead is sixth from the left in the back row. The four older gentlemen sitting on the right side of the photograph are faculty at the school. Dean Cook is fourth from the right; Homer Palmer, assistant in chemistry, is third from the right; Horace Rees, demonstrator in cheese making, is second from the right; and William Howe, engineer, is the last individual on the right in the front row. (Courtesy of Barbara Woodward.)

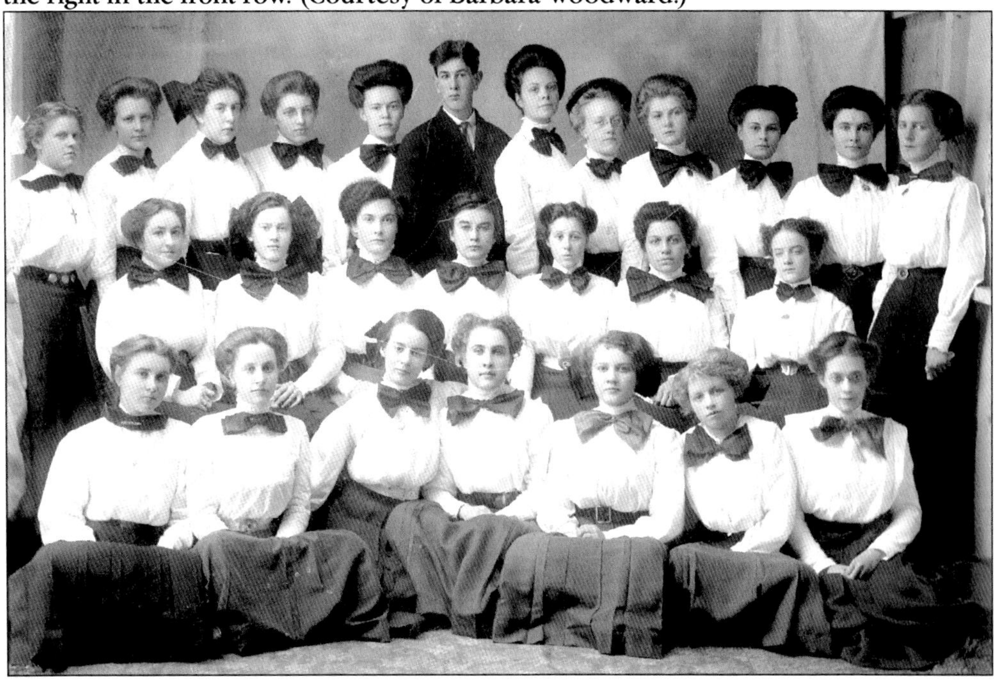

This photograph shows the domestic science class of 1912.

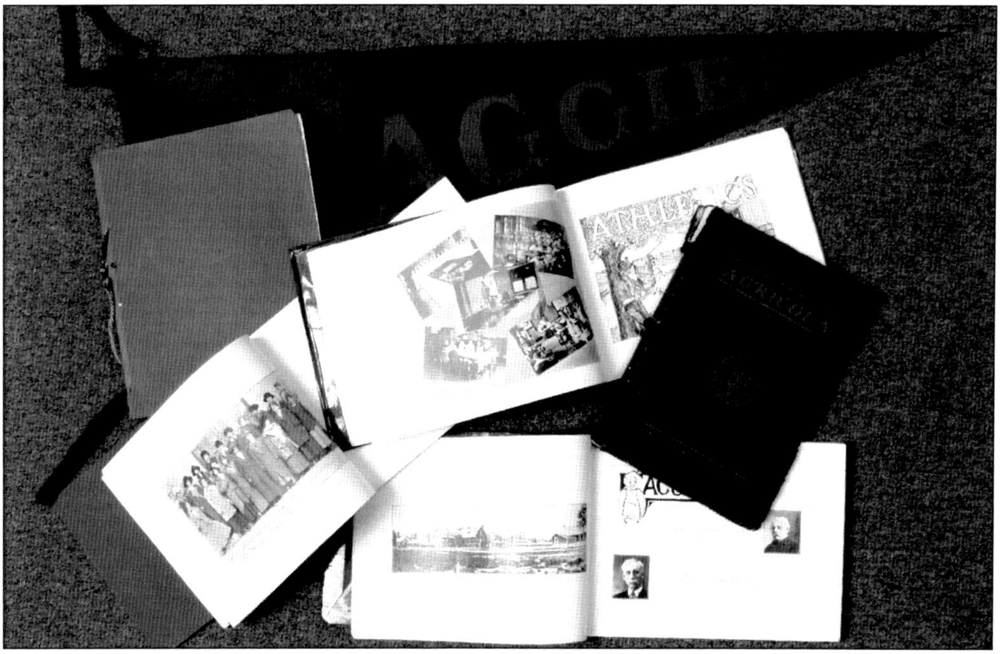

Agricola, the School of Agriculture yearbook, began in 1911. Pages from the 1912 *Agricola* are shown here. The yearbook was renamed *The Paysonian* in 1932. The yearbooks are a wonderful source of photographs from the school's early history. The photographs themselves no longer exist, and the ones in the yearbook are difficult to duplicate.

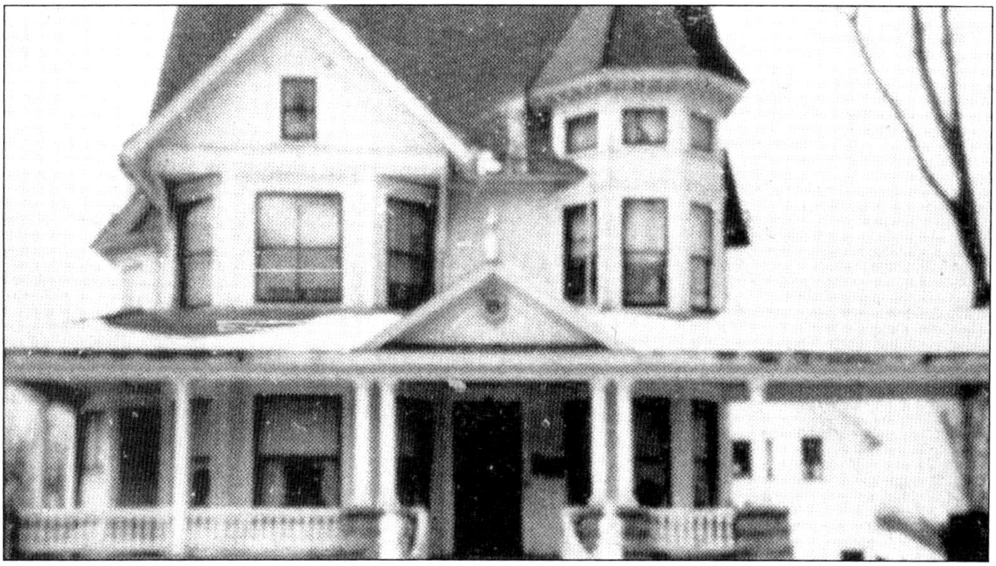

Theta Gamma Fraternity had existed for a number of years before it was recognized by the faculty in 1913. It has had a house at 53 Court Street for many years, which previously had been the residence of Dr. James Payson, so the building has a long SUNY Canton history. The fraternity Zeta Alpha Phi was recognized the following year, in 1914. Current SUNY Canton fraternities include Alpha Theta Gamma, Alpha Omega Chi, Delta Kappa Sigma, and Zeta Alpha Phi. Current sororities are Alpha Chi Omicron, Pi Nu Epsilon, Kappa Xi Omega, and Delta Sigma Tau.

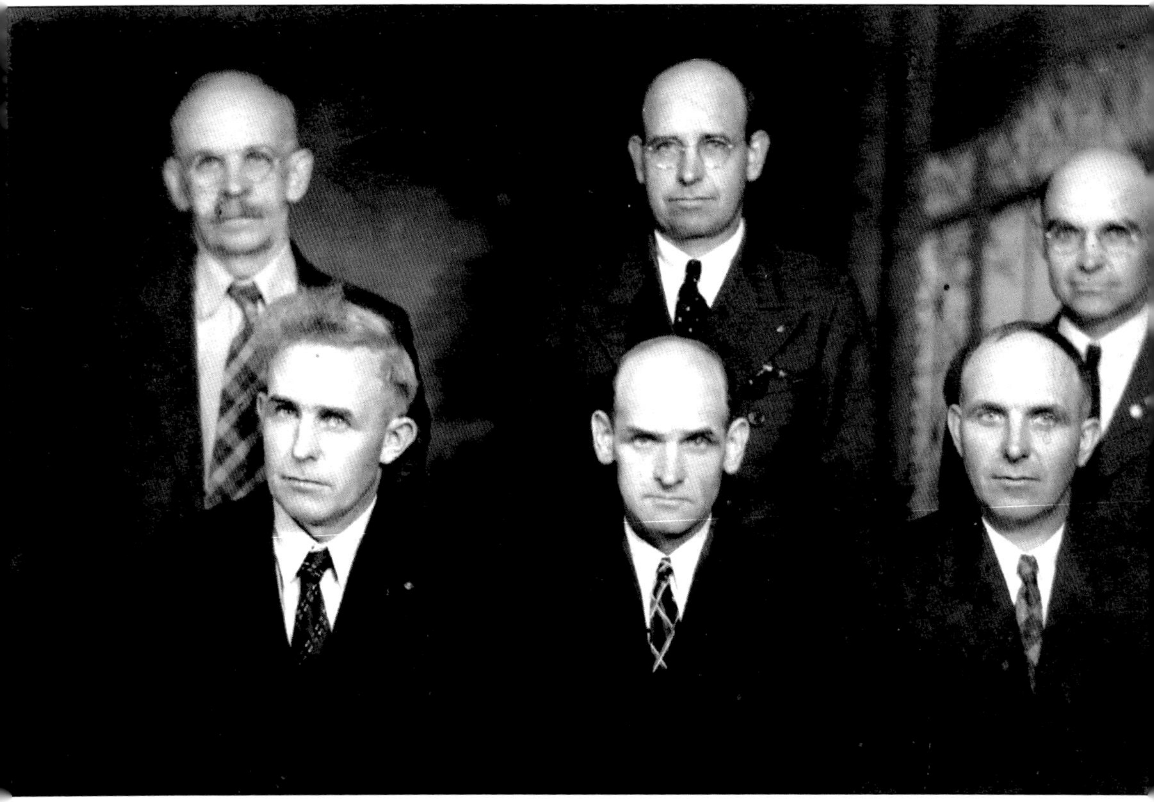

The Moulton family has ties to SUNY Canton, both as students and employees, that go back to the school's early years. This portrait was taken when the Moulton brothers were in middle age. Seated in the first row are, from left to right, Ivan (class of 1915), Earl (class of 1913), and Rex (class of 1911). Standing in the back row are, from left to right, Levi Hunt, a half-brother, Ray (class of 1911), and Asa (class of 1910). Asa was an instructor of poultry science in 1910. His grandson Harry Moulton worked at the college for 34 years and was an instructional support assistant in building construction when he retired in 2003. Alice Reed, a granddaughter of Earl, taught math at SUNY Canton.

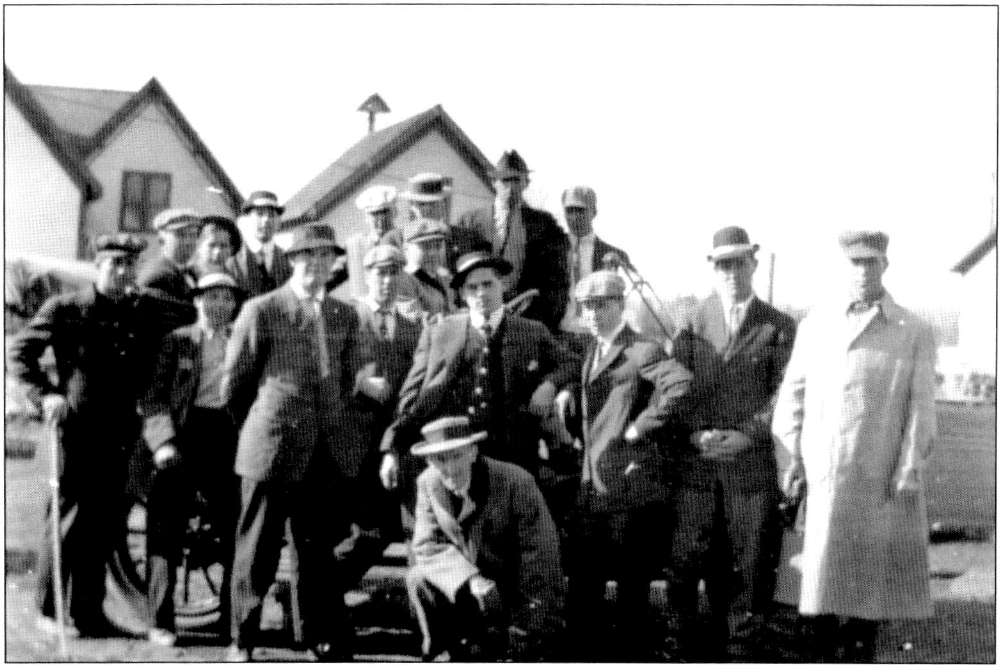

Rex Moulton (class of 1911) appears in this photograph from an agricultural class field trip to E. H. Dollar's farm. Moulton is the young man with his hat pushed back on his head, second from the left, in the second row.

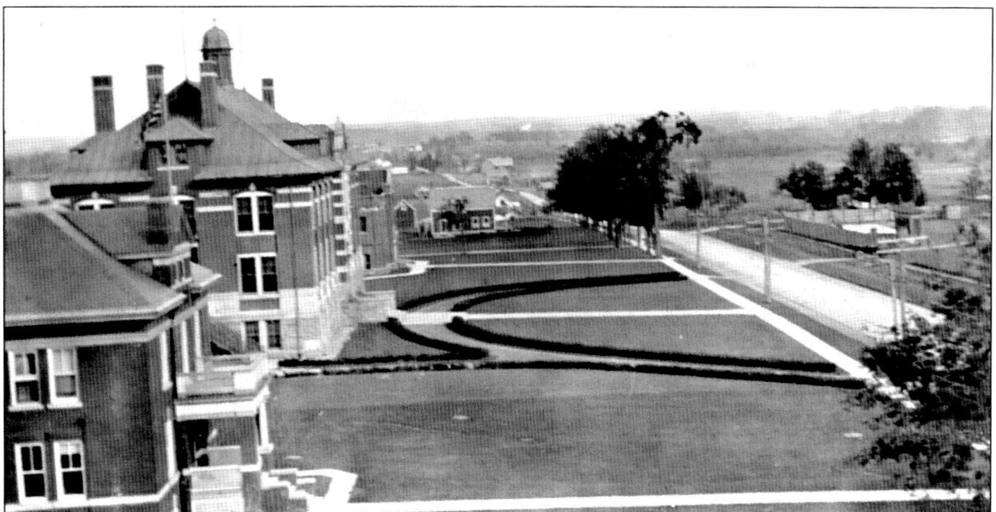

This early photograph of the campus was taken around 1913. Note the semicircular driveway in front of Cook Hall. The building in the front left foreground is the weather bureau, later known as Memorial Hall.

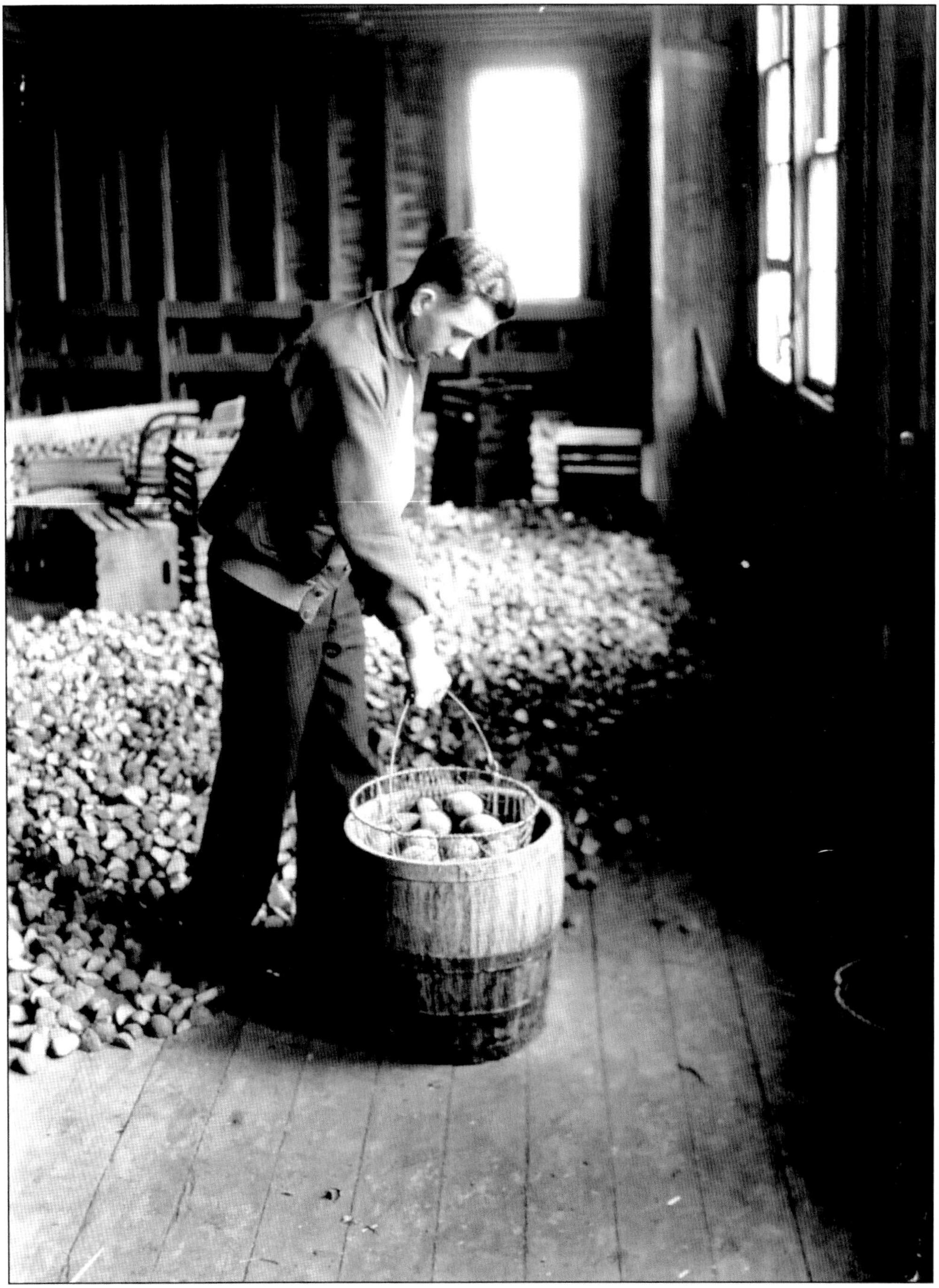

In this evocative early photograph, a lone, unidentified School of Agriculture student sorts potatoes in one of the school's outbuildings.

Two

YEARS OF CHALLENGE 1914–1936

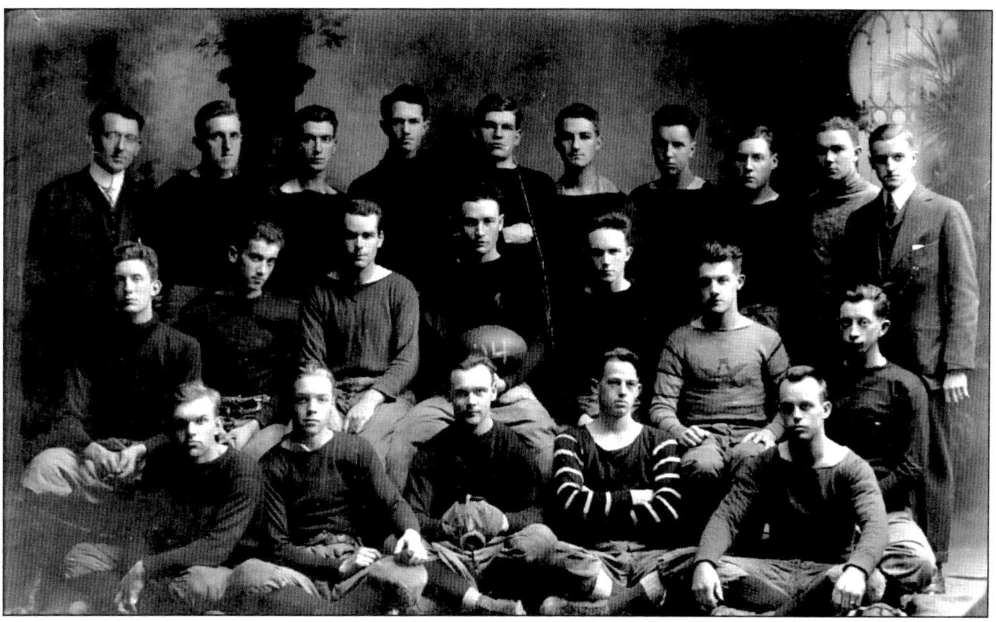

The 1914 football team had almost twice as many members than the previous year's football team, and overall enrollment, at 181 students, was the highest to that point. Football has been an intermittent part of the college's student life. It was discontinued in 1919 so money could be reallocated to the basketball team, then returned in 1995 for several years.

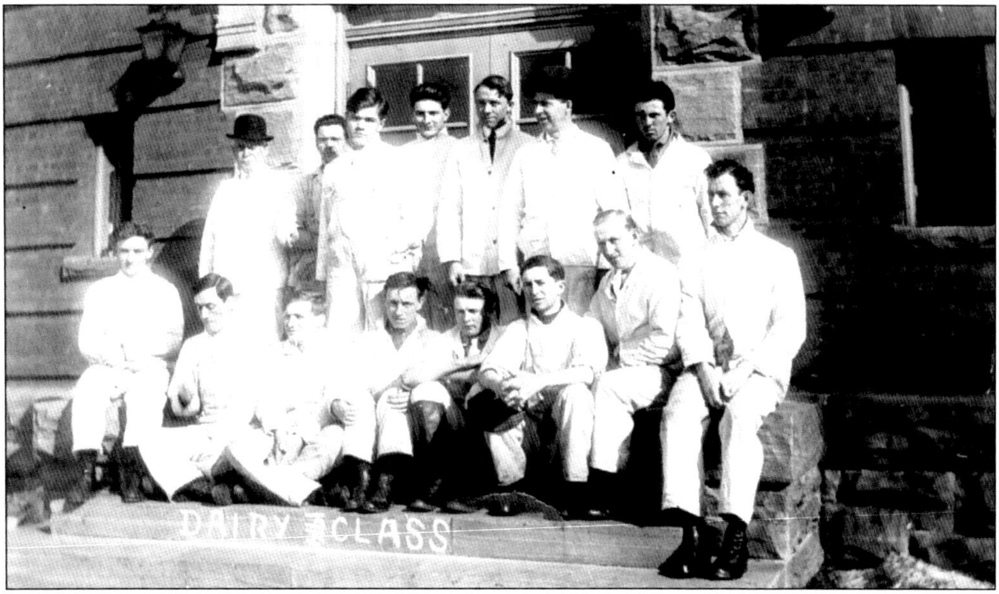

The 1914 dairy class takes a break from barn chores and classes to pose on the steps of the dairy building . At this time, the program was still very much focused on butter and cheese making. Later, in the mid-1920s, these two activities were discontinued due to the industry's shift toward the production of fluid milk.

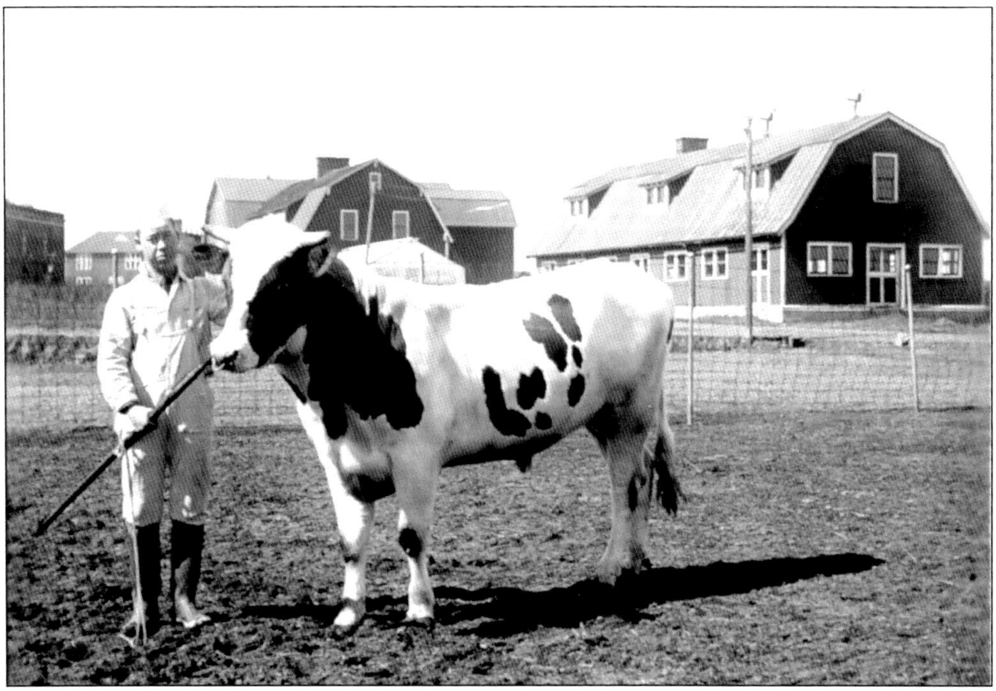

Managing the farm bull was never an easy task. An unidentified School of Agriculture student has this one under control long enough for a photograph. Note the ring in the bull's nose. This picture was taken in back of the dairy barn, and the greenhouse is visible. Both the dairy building and Cook Hall can be seen in the background.

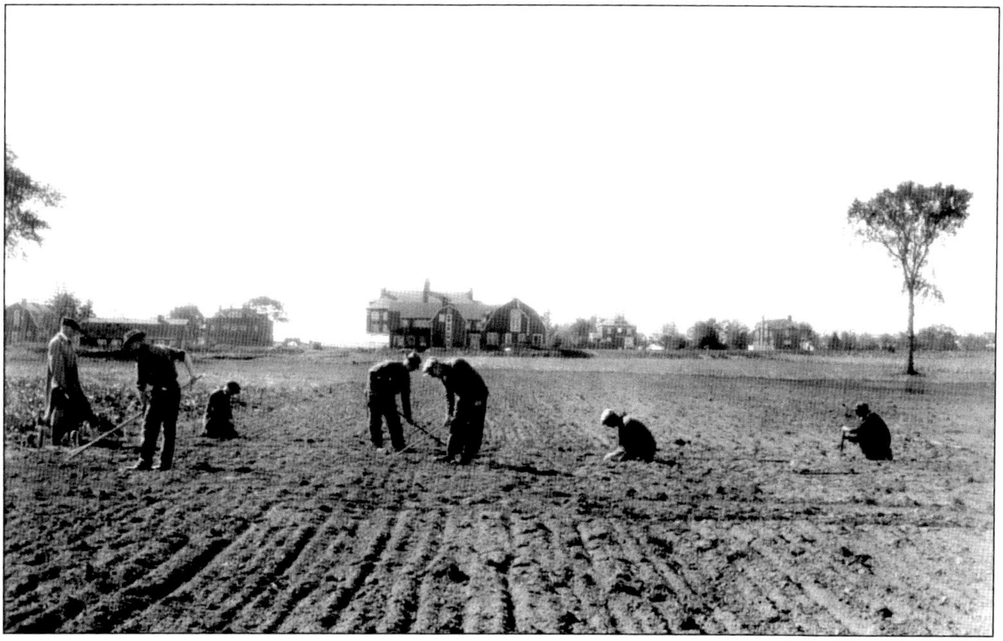

Agriculture students work in the fields behind the campus buildings on the east side of Park Street. This photograph is a rare shot in that it faces west. The tree on the right is an elm tree, which was far more common in northern New York in the early 20th century than it is today due to Dutch Elm disease.

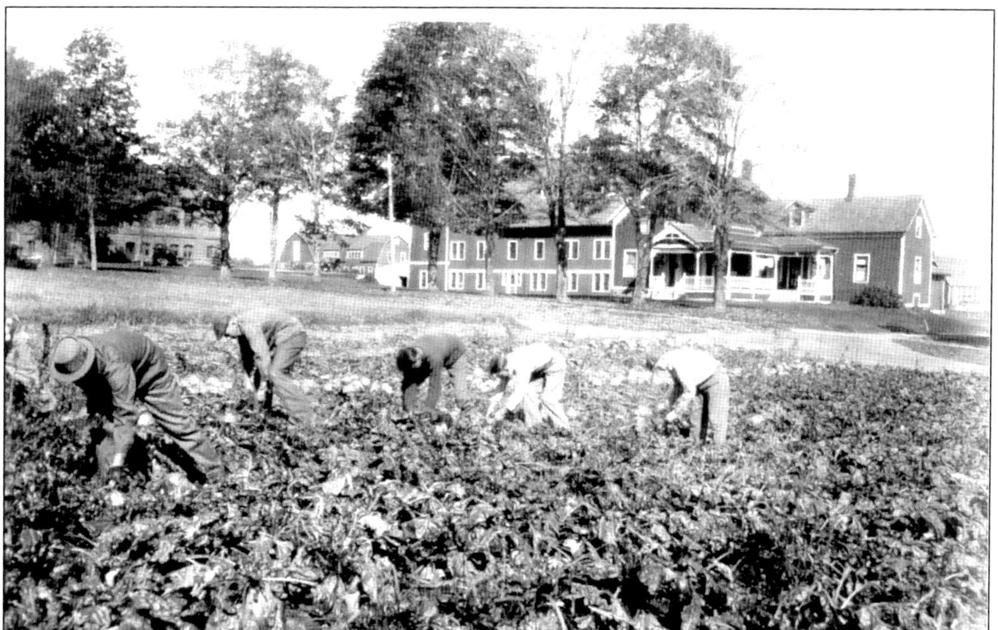

Students harvest vegetables across the road from the farmhouse and the rest of campus. The trees have already started dropping their leaves. The barn and other school buildings are in the background.

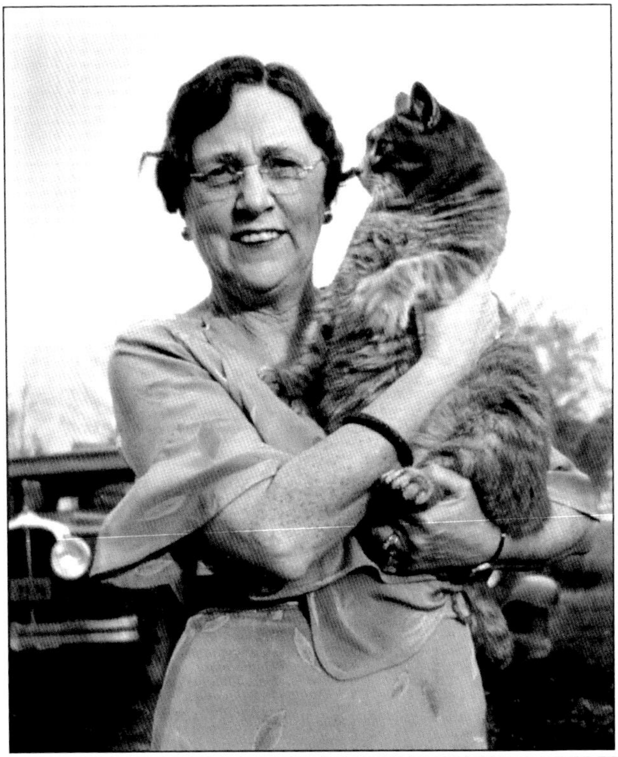

Women played an important role in the early days of SUNY Canton, both as students and as staff. Mary Adele Chaney was one such woman. Chaney joined the School of Agriculture as second assistant in domestic science and became first assistant in 1914. Two years later, in 1916, she became head of the domestic science program. Here she is pictured with her cat. Chaney Dining Center on the new campus is named in her honor.

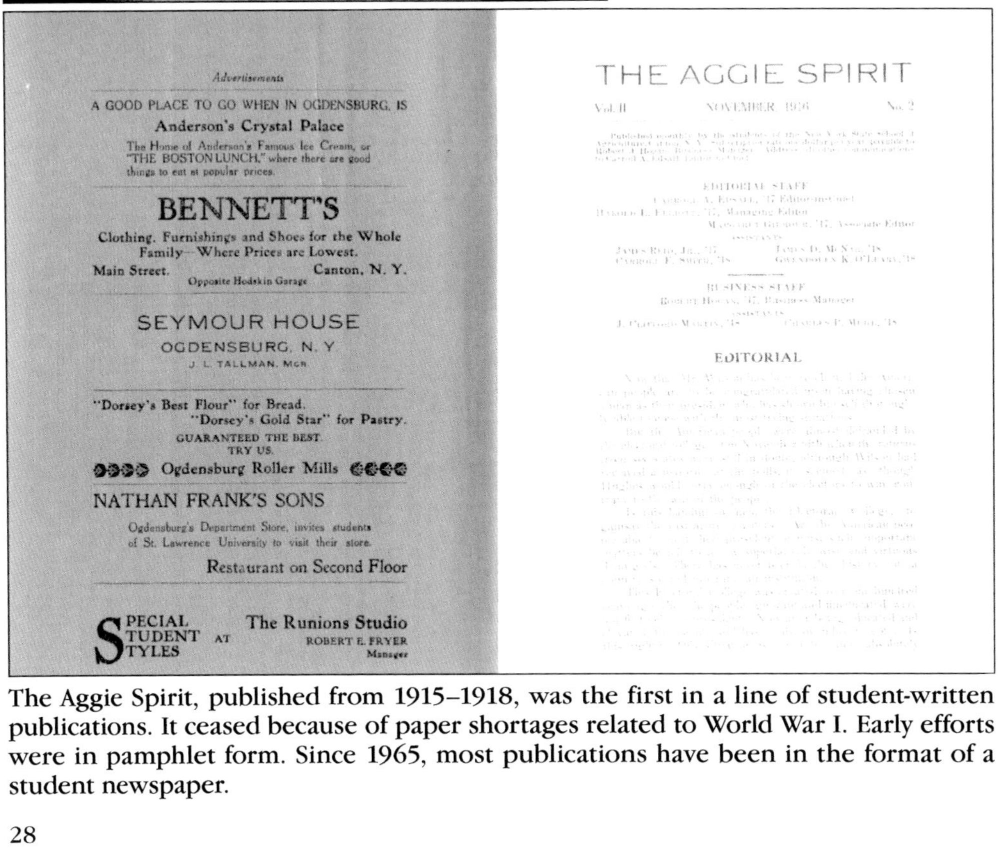

Advertisements

A GOOD PLACE TO GO WHEN IN OGDENSBURG, IS

Anderson's Crystal Palace

The Home of Anderson's Famous Ice Cream, or "THE BOSTON LUNCH," where there are good things to eat at popular prices.

BENNETT'S

Clothing, Furnishings and Shoes for the Whole Family—Where Prices are Lowest.

Main Street. Opposite Hodskin Garage Canton, N. Y.

SEYMOUR HOUSE

OGDENSBURG, N. Y

J. L. TALLMAN, Mgr.

"Dorsey's Best Flour" for Bread.
"Dorsey's Gold Star" for Pastry.
GUARANTEED THE BEST.
TRY US.

Ogdensburg Roller Mills

NATHAN FRANK'S SONS

Ogdensburg's Department Store, invites students of St. Lawrence University to visit their store.

Restaurant on Second Floor

SPECIAL STUDENT STYLES AT The Runions Studio
ROBERT E. FRYER
Manager

THE AGGIE SPIRIT

Vol. II NOVEMBER, 1916 No. 2

EDITORIAL

The Aggie Spirit, published from 1915–1918, was the first in a line of student-written publications. It ceased because of paper shortages related to World War I. Early efforts were in pamphlet form. Since 1965, most publications have been in the format of a student newspaper.

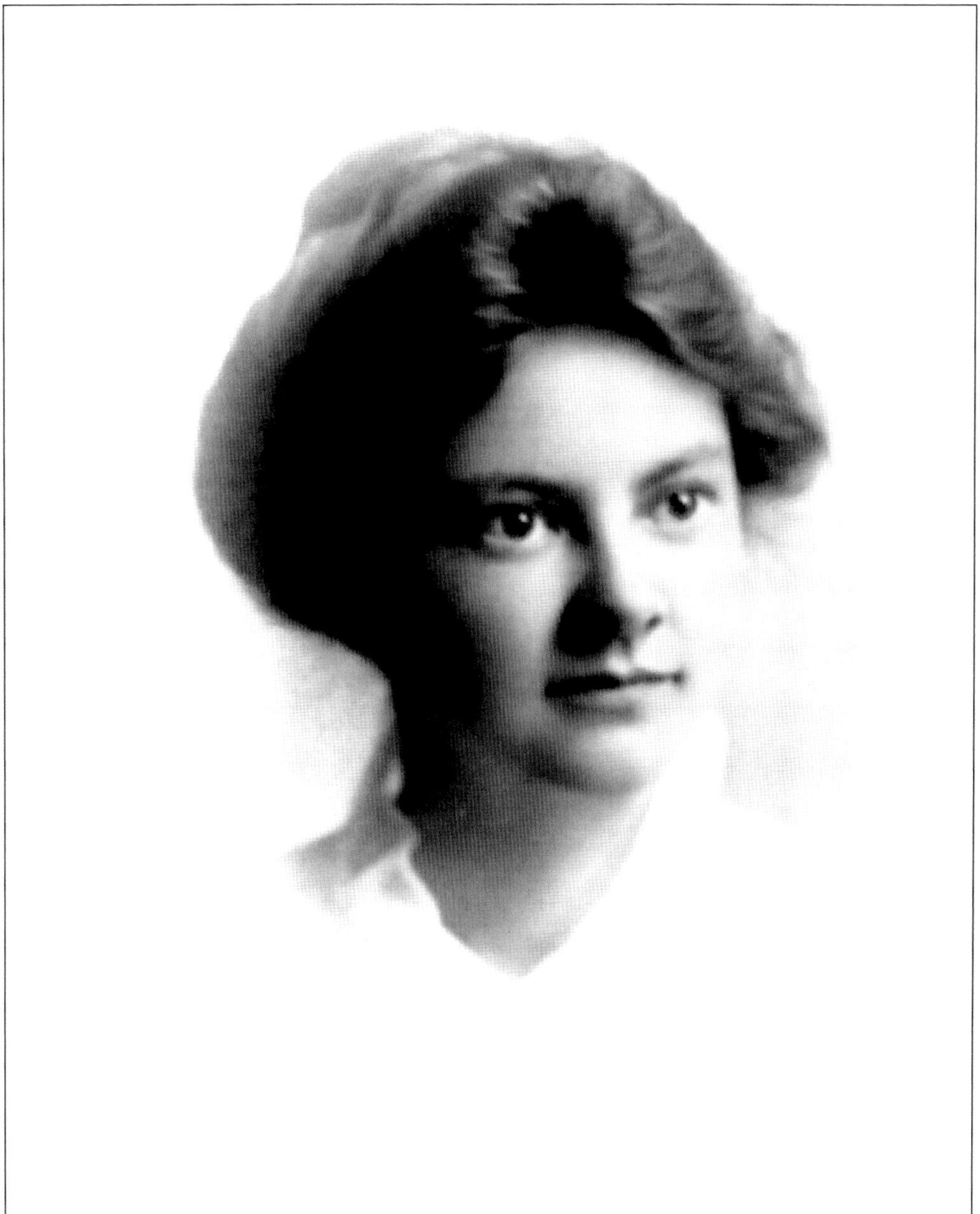

Another prominent woman in college history is Lottie Southworth, who attended St. Lawrence University in 1914 and the School of Agriculture in 1918. She taught in Colton and Canton public schools until 1924, when she joined the school's staff. Starting as an assistant to an instructor in domestic arts, she later taught academic subjects. She worked at the college until 1945. Southworth Library on the new campus was named in her honor.

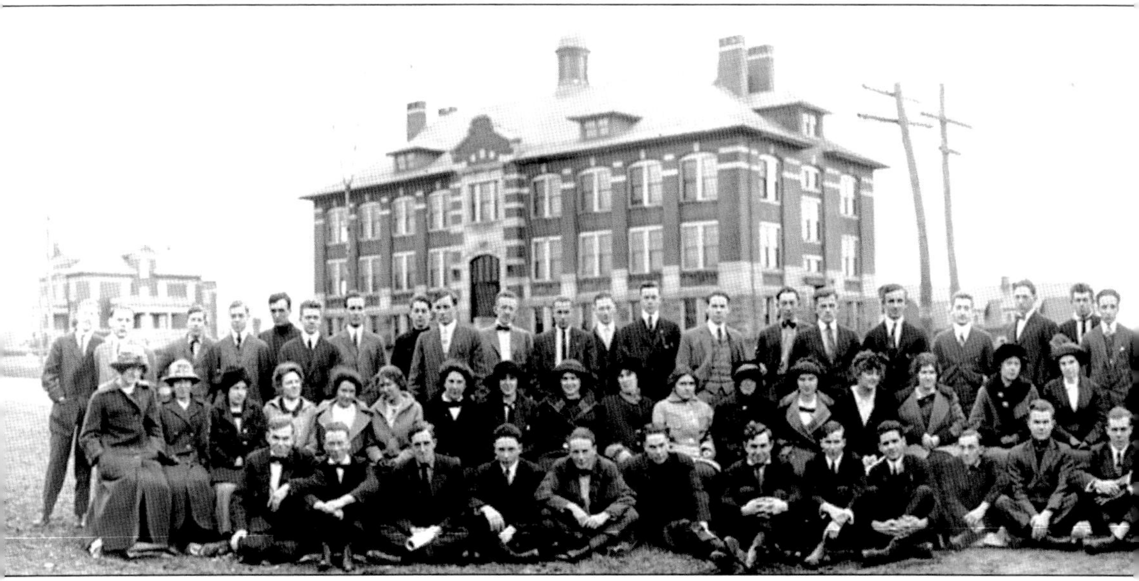

This class photograph, a gift from Ivan Moulton, a 1915 graduate, was taken in front of Cook Hall. Memorial Hall, on the St. Lawrence campus, is in the background. Enrollment in 1915 was 187, with 115 agriculture students and 72 home economics students. The School of Agriculture did not enjoy this level of enrollment again until 1934. A farm

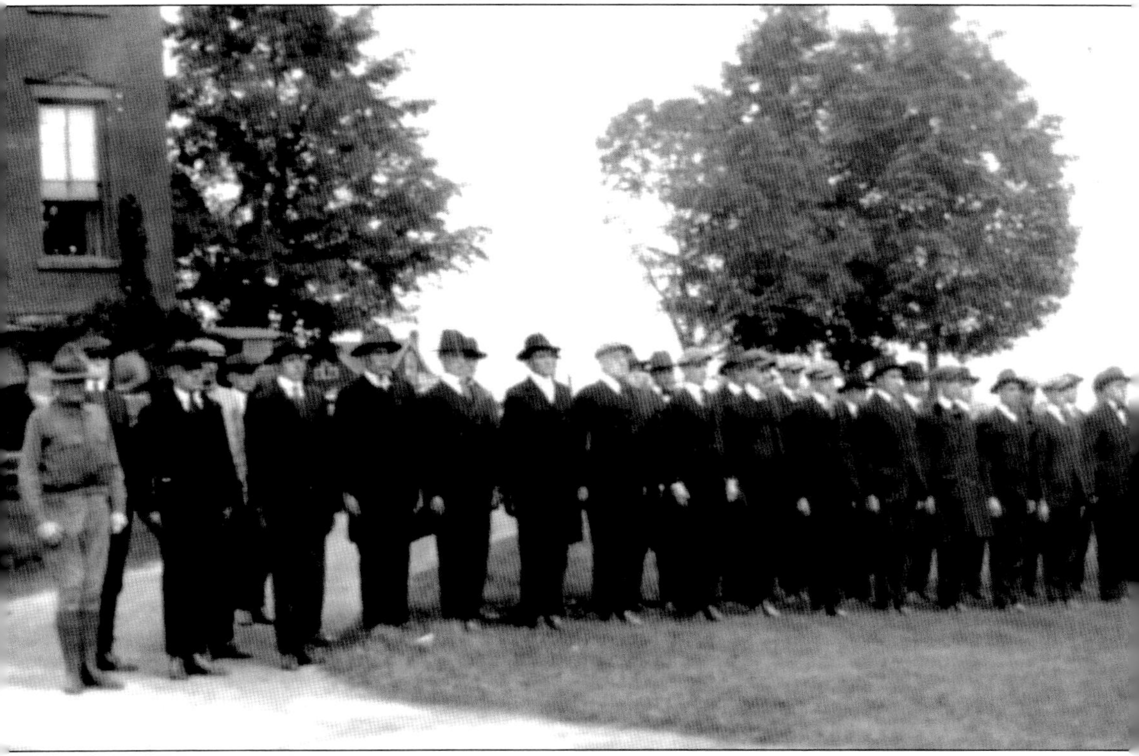

According to the writings of Dr. James Payson, World War I had a disruptive effect on the School of Agriculture. Not only did many students go to fight in the war, but those who remained behind were preoccupied by its course. The establishment

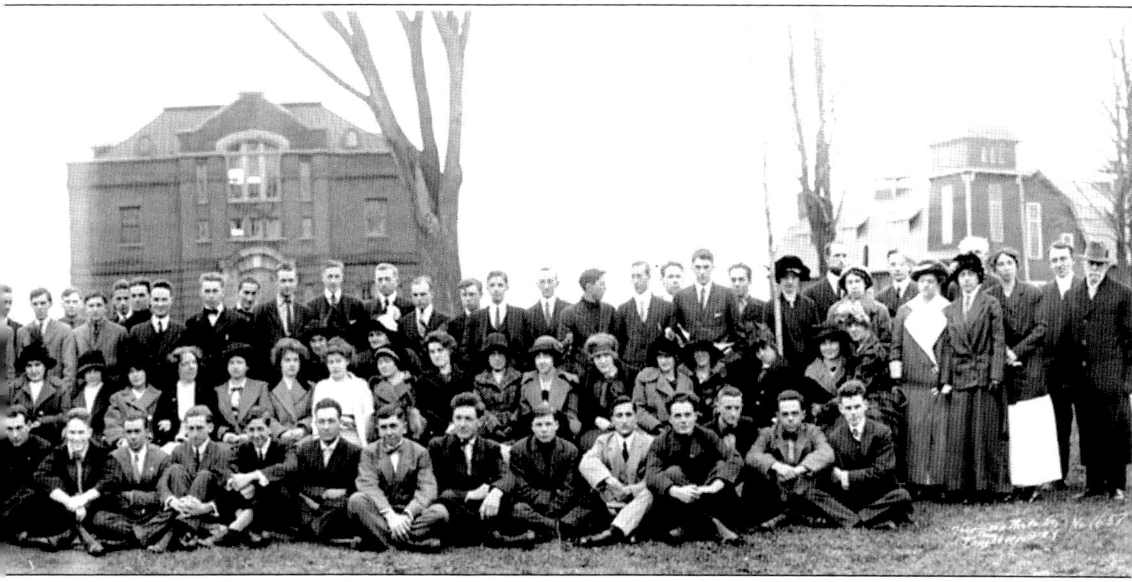

depression in the 1920s, the Great Depression, and World War I all played a role in dampening the numbers who attended the school over the next 20 years. The number of agriculture students dropped by 30 to 85 in 1916.

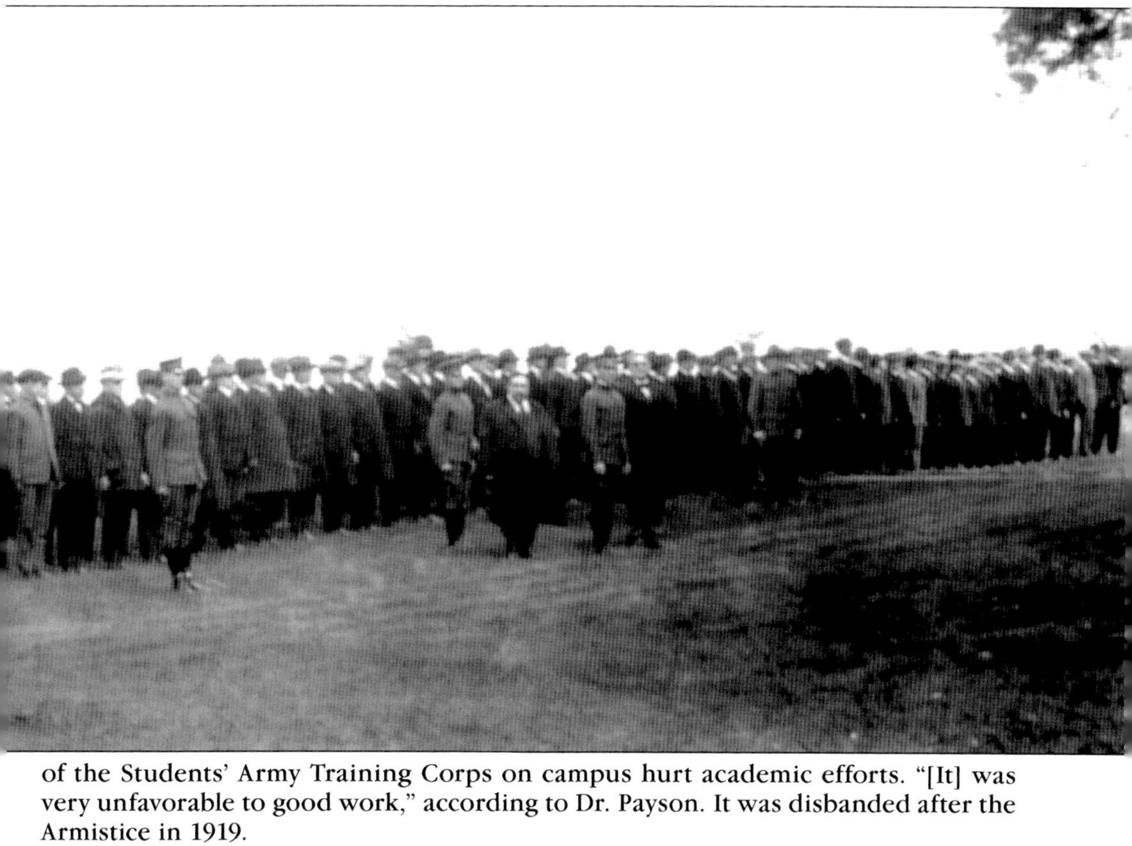

of the Students' Army Training Corps on campus hurt academic efforts. "[It] was very unfavorable to good work," according to Dr. Payson. It was disbanded after the Armistice in 1919.

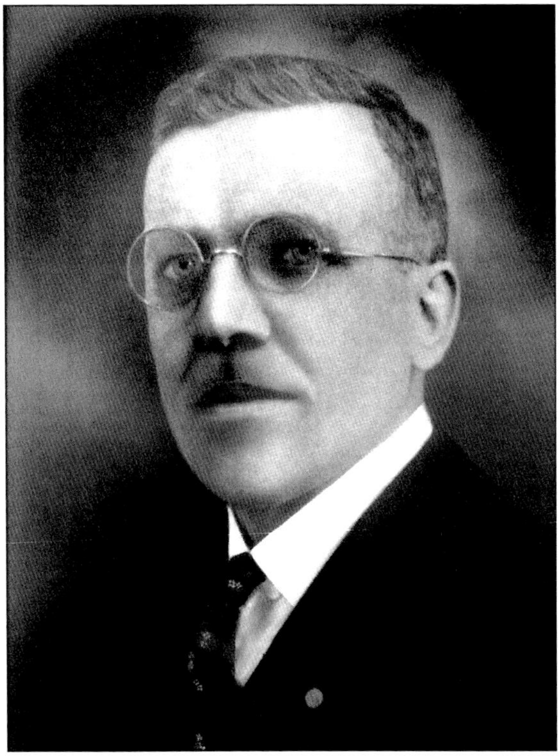

Dean Herbert Cook resigned in 1917, and after Dr. James Payson's service in the interim, Roland Verbeck became director of the School of Agriculture in 1919. Verbeck had to contend with declining enrollment, tight budgets, and inadequate salaries for instructors—all problems that have recurred at various times in SUNY Canton's history. Verbeck left for Stockbridge School of Agriculture in 1924 and remained there for 30 years.

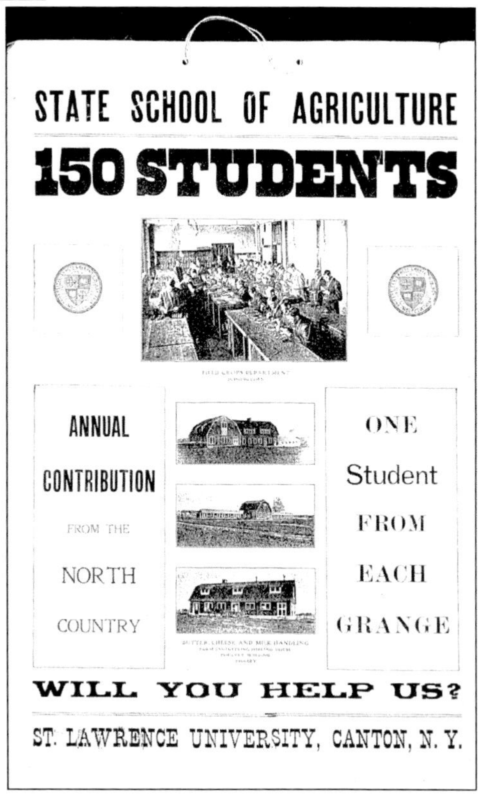

A decline in the number of students due to war and a continuing agricultural depression resulted in the school's first ad campaign. By 1921, enrollment numbered 112, and half of these students were women. In 1924, the balance had shifted even further, with 77 women among the 121 students.

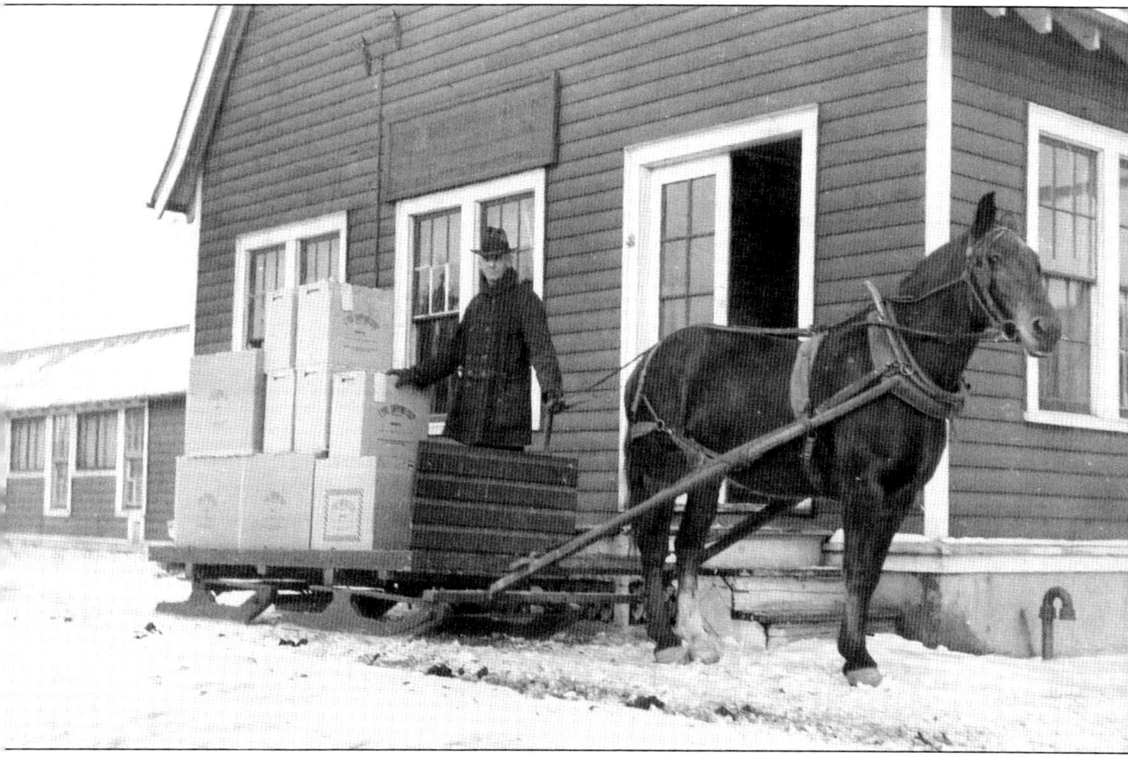

Chickens are being loaded for shipment at the poultry building on the School of Agriculture campus. Horsepower and this type of flat sled without a box and on two sets of runners was still in use in 1922, when this photograph was taken.

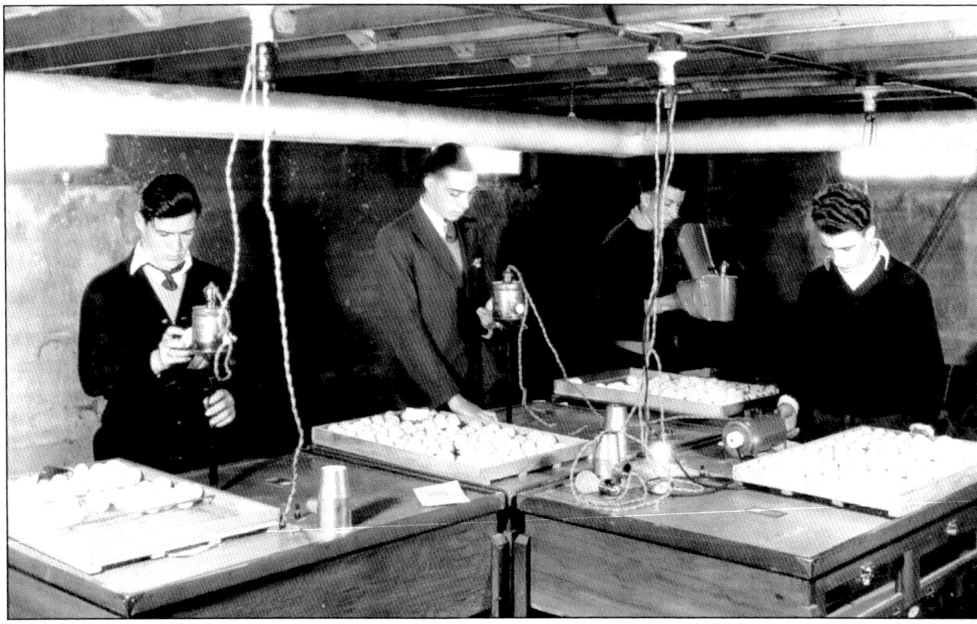

The School of Agriculture's poultry program was one of its most important programs. A new poultry building was built in 1925. Here students work in the incubator room sorting eggs for hatching. Well into the 1950s, small family poultry operations were common throughout rural New York State, and the school met the need for skilled, knowledgeable poultry producers.

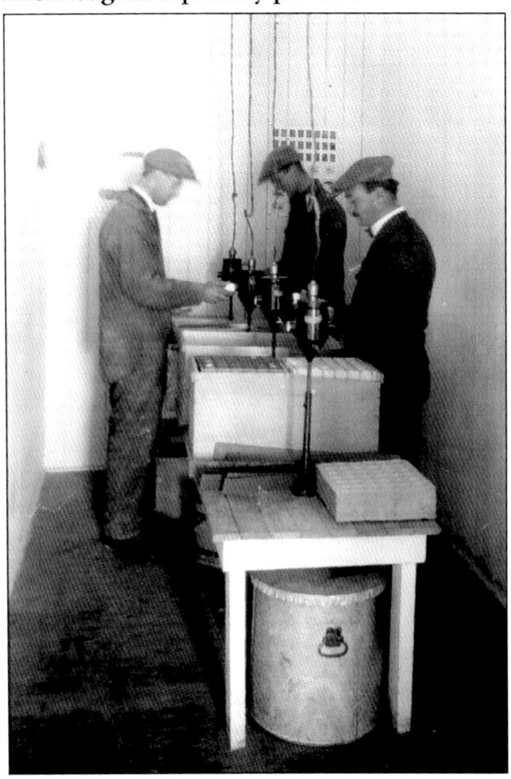

This later photograph shows School of Agriculture students preparing eggs to ship to market.

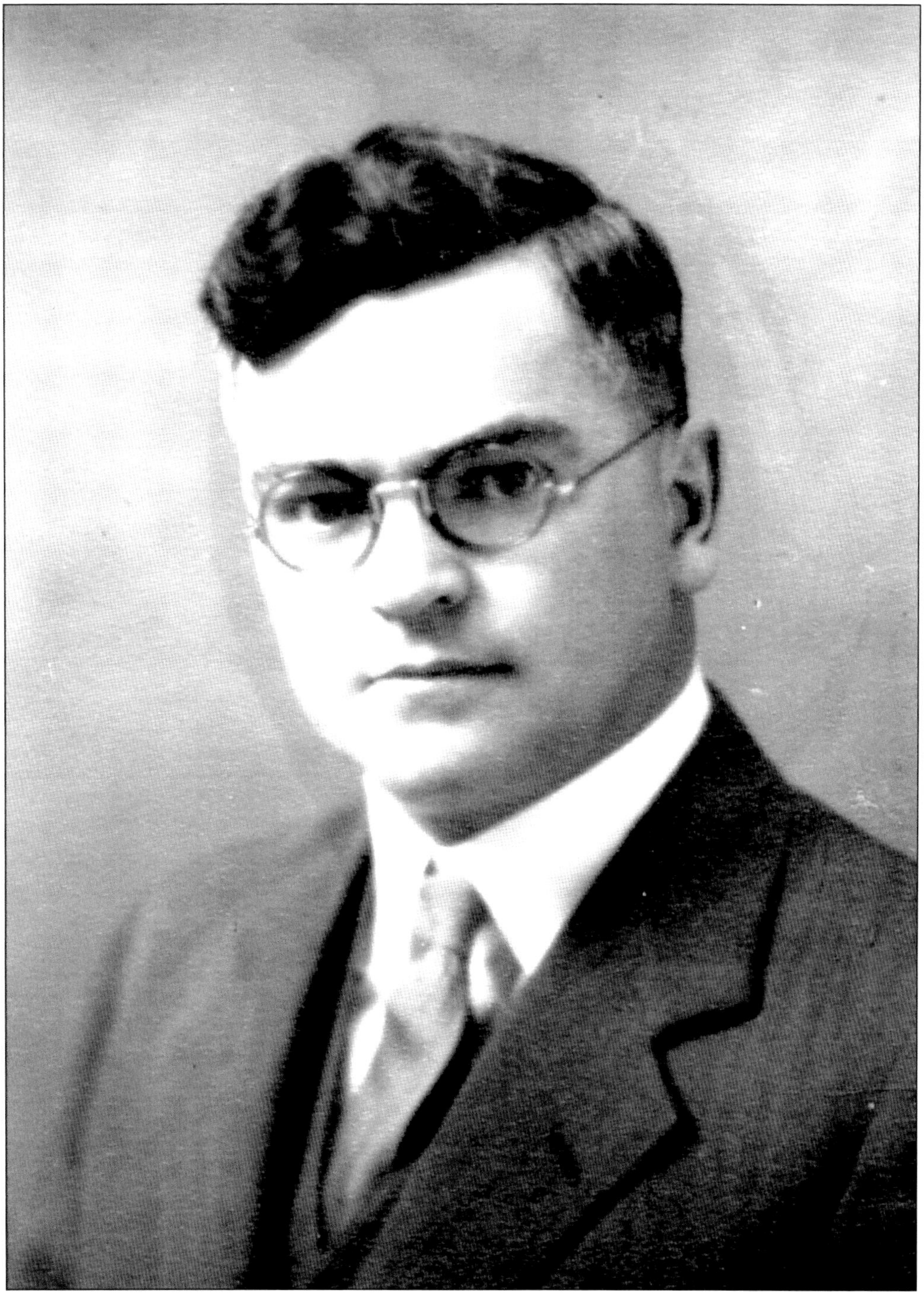

Van C. Whittemore served as director of the School of Agriculture for 24 years, nearly one quarter of the institution's existence, from 1924 to 1948. During his tenure, he faced many challenges, including the Great Depression, the threat of the school closing in 1934, and World War II. He saw the campus through a name change and the transition to more technology-based curriculum and programs.

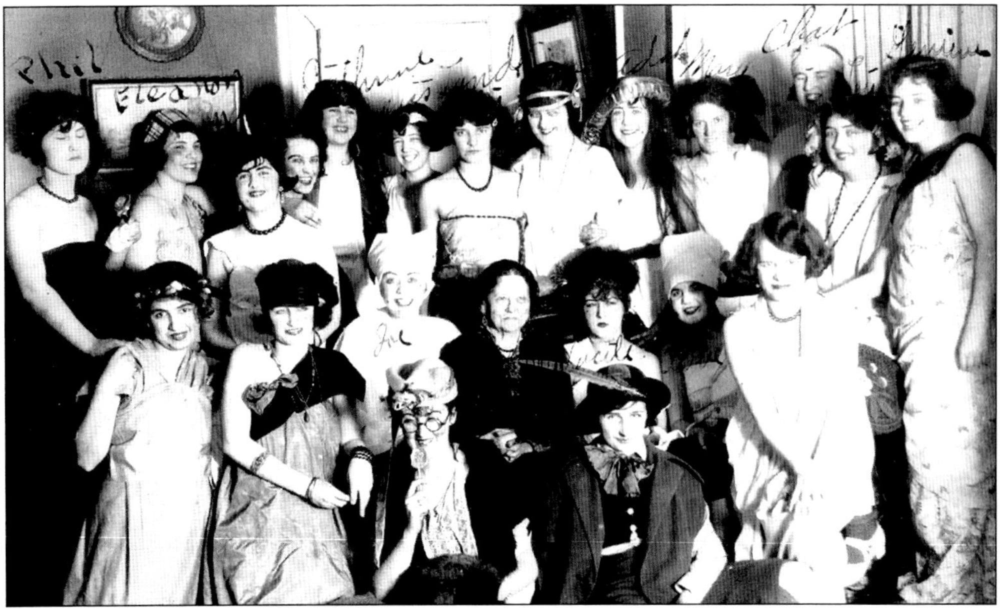

Students in the 1920s knew how to have a good time. The Unlucky Love Party pictured here was held at a boardinghouse in Canton. Female students and a couple of their instructors attended this event on February 3, 1924.

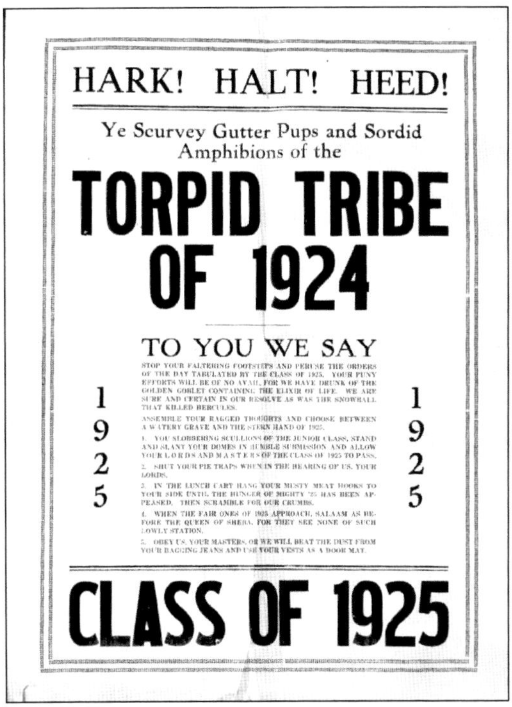

HARK! HALT! HEED!

Ye Scurvey Gutter Pups and Sordid Amphibions of the

TORPID TRIBE OF 1924

TO YOU WE SAY

1925 STOP YOUR FALTERING FOOTSTEPS AND PERUSE THE ORDERS OF THE DAY TABULATED BY THE CLASS OF 1925. YOUR PUNY EFFORTS WILL BE OF NO AVAIL, FOR WE HAVE DRUNK OF THE GOLDEN GOBLET CONTAINING THE ELIXIR OF LIFE. WE ARE SURE AND CERTAIN IN OUR RESOLVE AS WAS THE SNOWBALL THAT KILLED HERCULES. 1925

ASSEMBLE YOUR RAGGED THOUGHTS AND CHOOSE BETWEEN A WATERY GRAVE AND THE STERN HAND OF 1925.

1. YOU SLOBBERING SCULLIONS OF THE JUNIOR CLASS, STAND AND SLANT YOUR DOMES IN HUMBLE SUBMISSION AND ALLOW YOUR LORDS AND MASTERS OF THE CLASS OF 1925 TO PASS.

2. SHUT YOUR PIE TRAPS WHEN IN THE HEARING OF US, YOUR LORDS.

3. IN THE LUNCH CART HANG YOUR MISTY MEAT HOOKS TO YOUR SIDE UNTIL THE HUNGER OF MIGHTY '25 HAS BEEN APPEASED. THEN SCRAMBLE FOR OUR CRUMBS.

4. WHEN THE FAIR ONES OF 1925 APPROACH, SALAAM AS BEFORE THE QUEEN OF SHEBA, FOR THEY SEE NONE OF SUCH LOWLY STATION.

5. OBEY US, YOUR MASTERS, OR WE WILL BEAT THE DUST FROM YOUR BAGGING JEANS AND USE YOUR VESTS AS A DOOR MAT.

CLASS OF 1925

In this humorous broadside, the class of 1925 makes the case that their time has come and puts the upperclassmen on notice. Understandably, and perhaps wisely, the author remains unknown. In any case, the poster is a unique piece of college lore and memorabilia that still brings a smile 80 years after it was written.

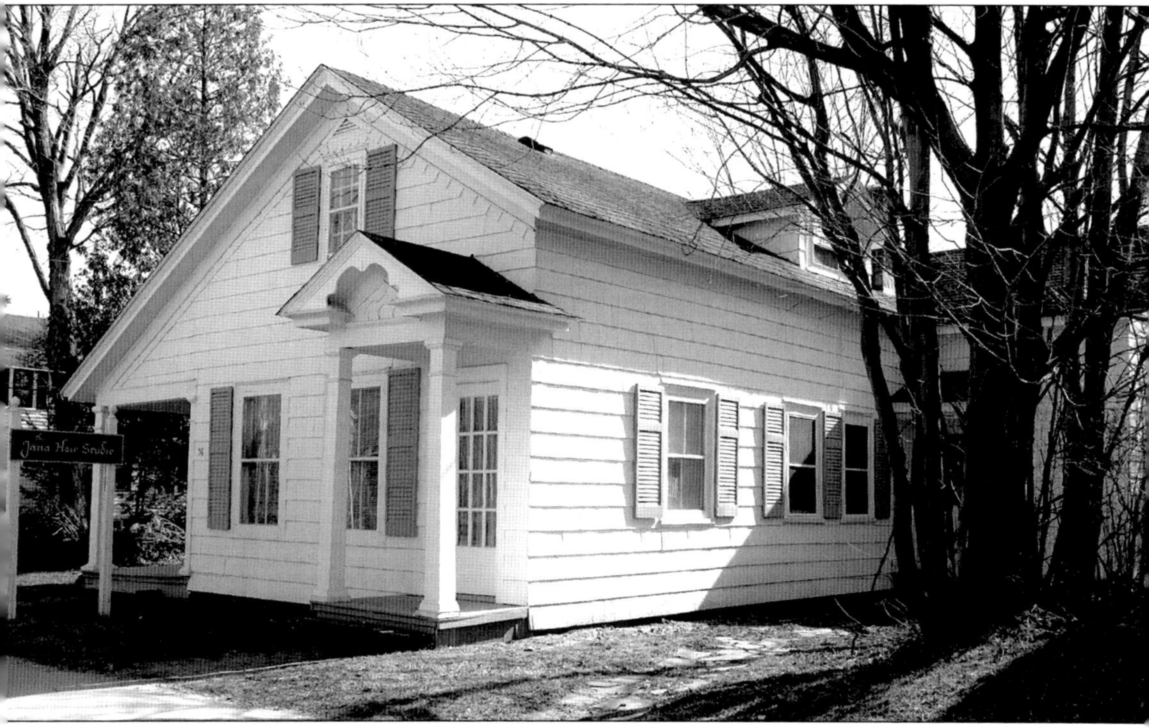

This building at 36 Park Street on the corner of West Street was the site of the Old Lantern, a coffeehouse that served as a training venue in management for female students. While this is a current picture, the lines of the building are the same as they were in 1926 when the coffeehouse opened. The coffeehouse was a financial success and provided a source of valuable training.

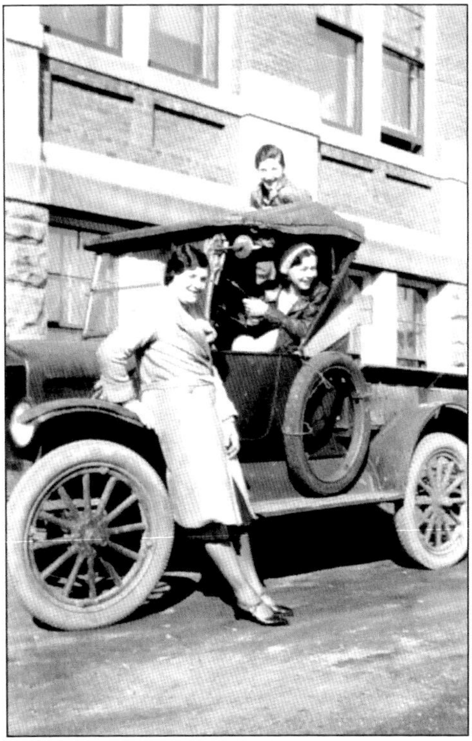

From left to right, students Helen Balaniz and Helen Backus, both class of 1931, and Adelaide Lefevre, class of 1932, pose with their car on a campus road near Cook Hall.

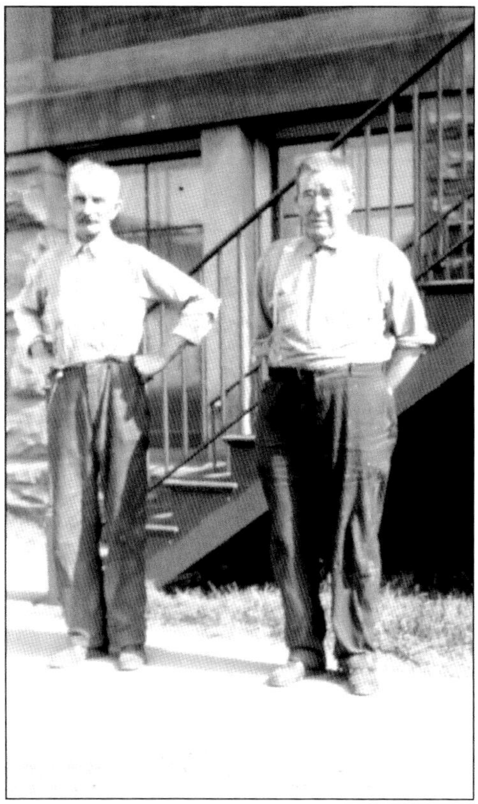

Dedicated staff members have always been a part of the SUNY Canton tradition. Here two janitors, Mr. Gaffney and Mr. Howe, are pictured outside Cook Hall in 1932.

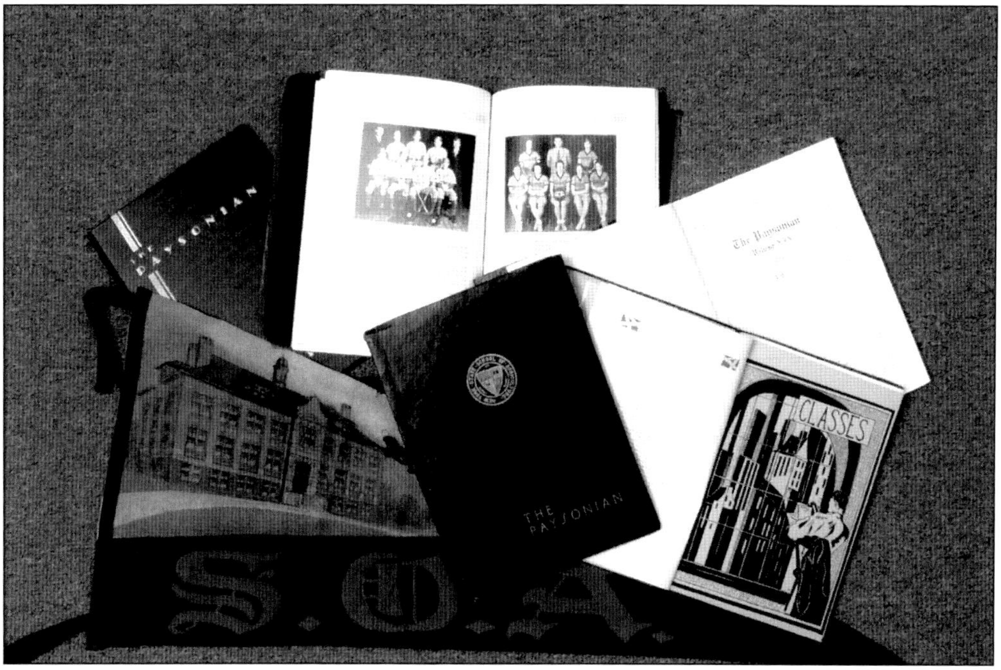

After 21 years, the name of the college yearbook was changed from *Agricola* to *The Paysonian* in honor of Dr. James Payson, who had retired three years earlier in 1929. The name continues to be used seven decades later.

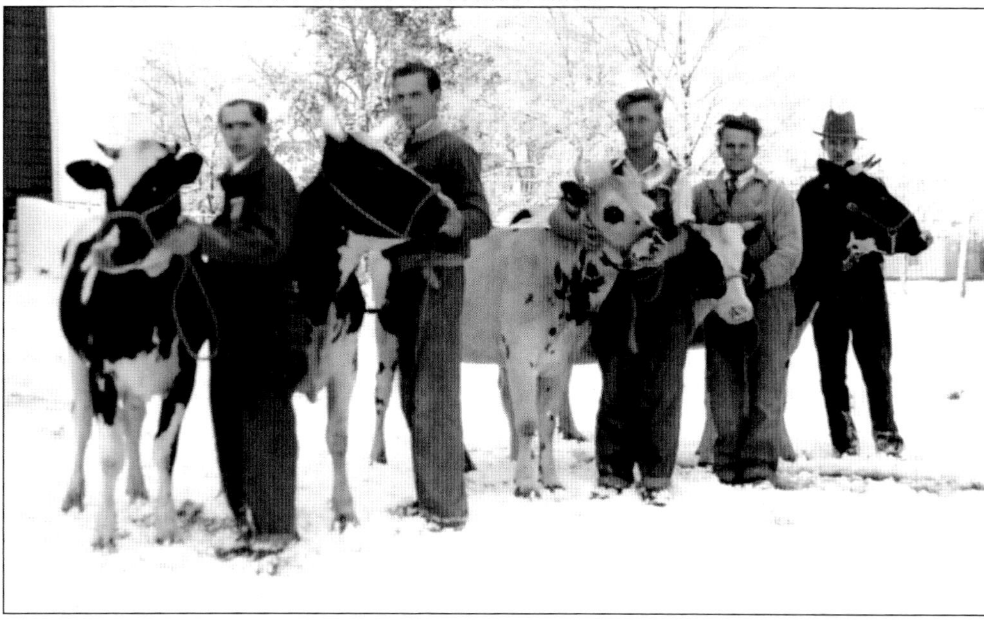

Bovine livestock remained a part of the School of Agriculture in the 1930s. The butter and cheese making ended in 1925, when the refrigerated rail tank car made the shipping of fluid milk possible. Pictured here with their animals in 1934, from left to right, are Claude Moulton, Howard Andrus, Herbert Hatch, Homer Chapin, and Robert Simpson. Claude Moulton, whose father, Asa, was graduated from the School of Agriculture in 1910, was the first child of a School of Agriculture graduate to attend the school.

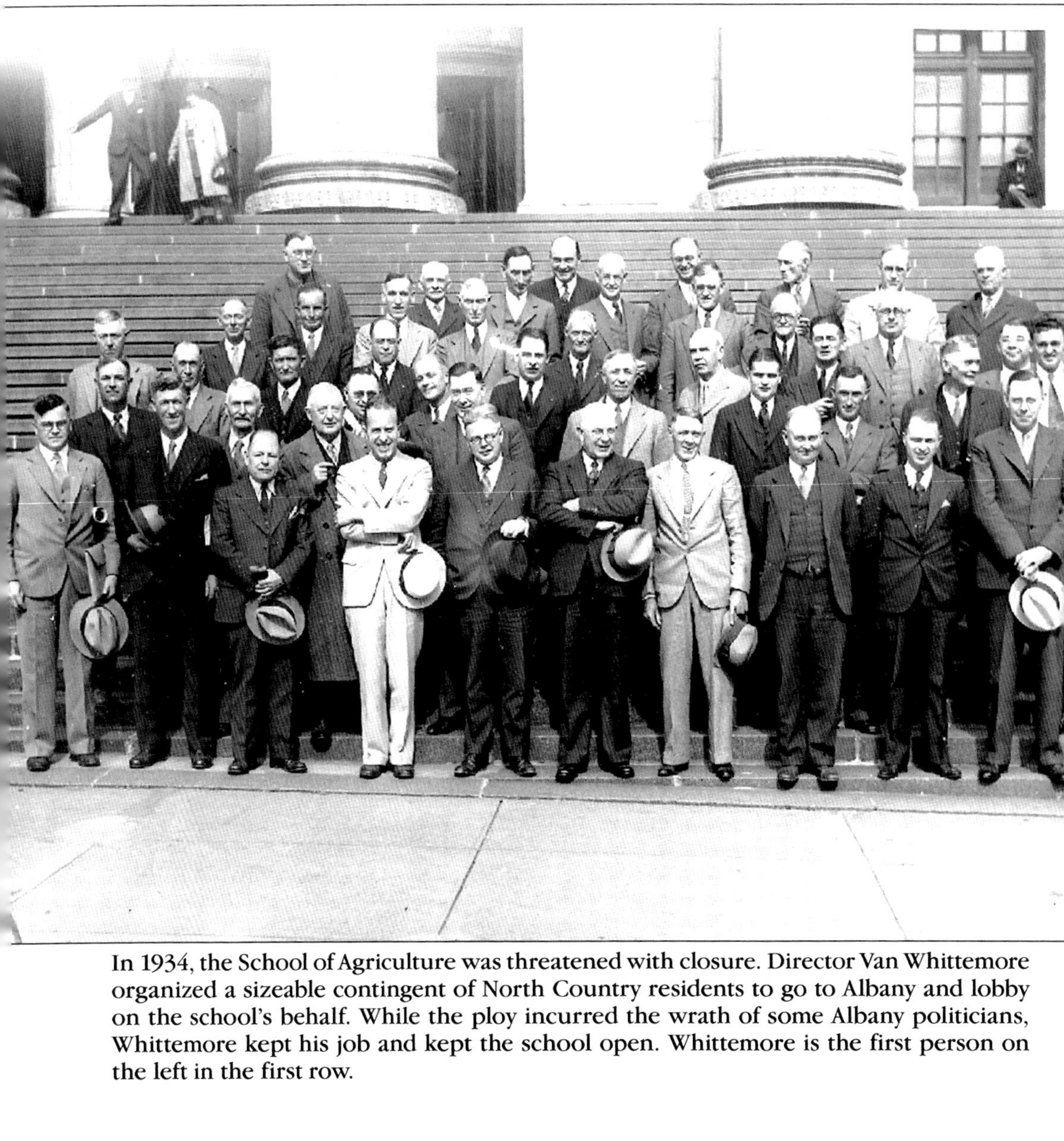

In 1934, the School of Agriculture was threatened with closure. Director Van Whittemore organized a sizeable contingent of North Country residents to go to Albany and lobby on the school's behalf. While the ploy incurred the wrath of some Albany politicians, Whittemore kept his job and kept the school open. Whittemore is the first person on the left in the first row.

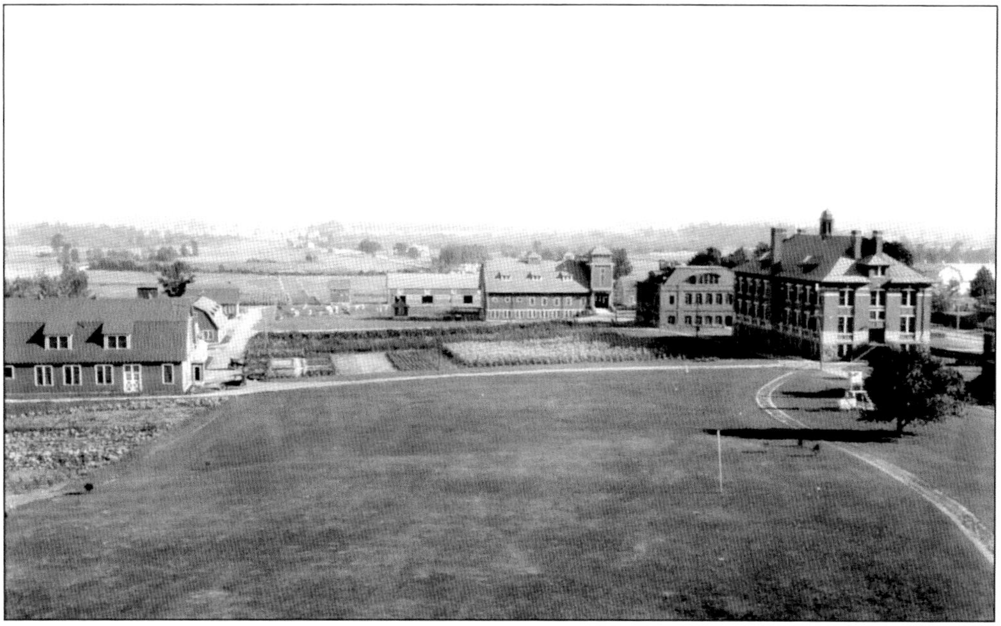

The campus, as pictured in 1935, appears orderly, well-maintained, bucolic, and almost idyllic. Looking at such a lovely pastoral scene, it is hard to imagine that a year earlier the school had faced possible closure, as well as all the other challenges of the previous 20 years.

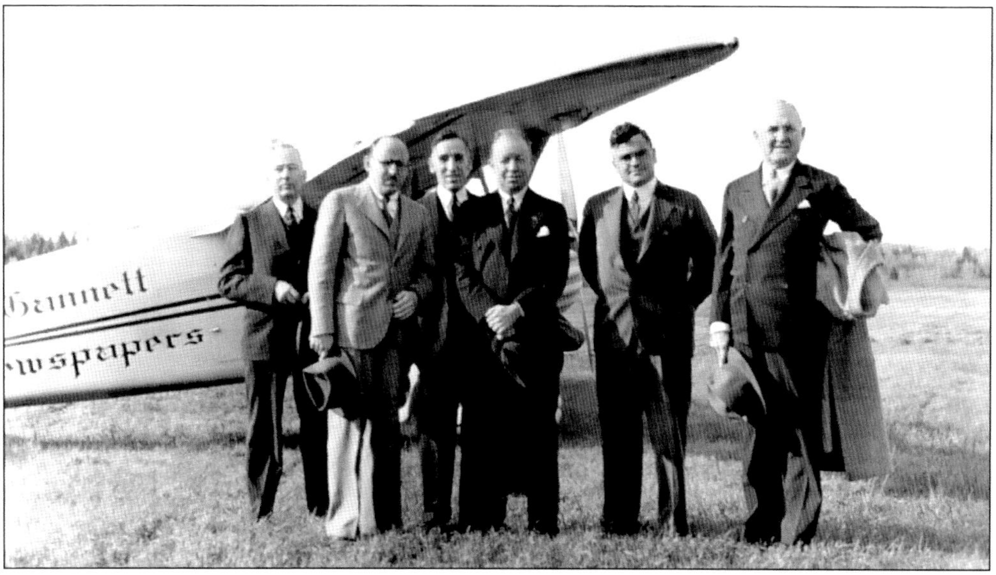

The School of Agriculture was instrumental in a number of farm-related activities and events, such as the Farm Bureau, and was the forerunner of Cooperative Extension. Here Director Whittemore greets dignitaries arriving for Farm Week events in 1935. Notice the Gannett Newspapers airplane in the background.

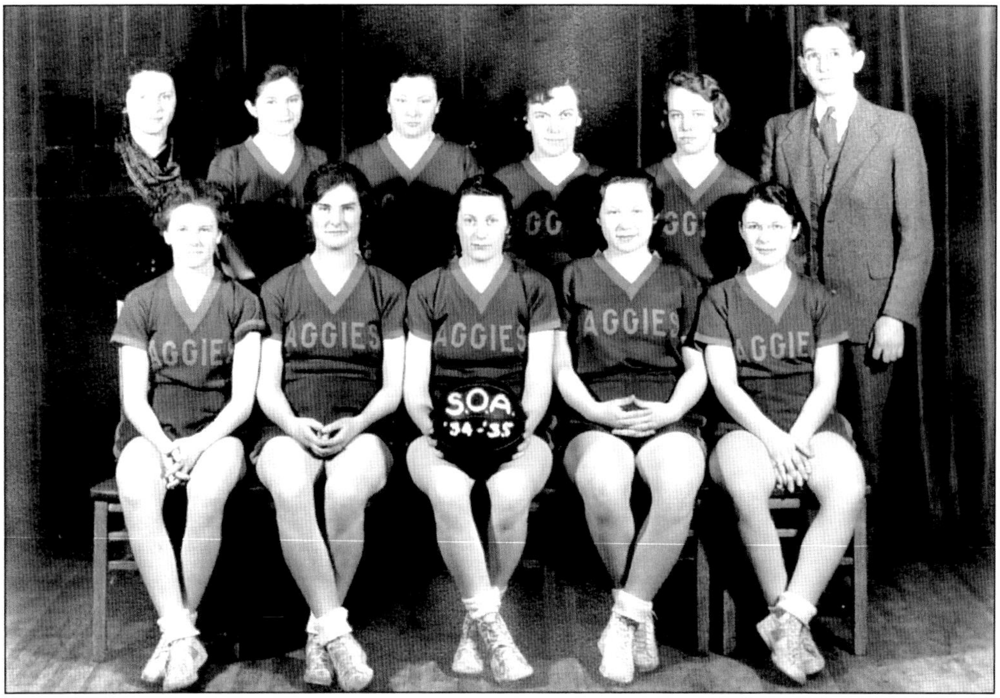

Coach Lester Rawlins is shown with the 1934–1935 women's basketball team.

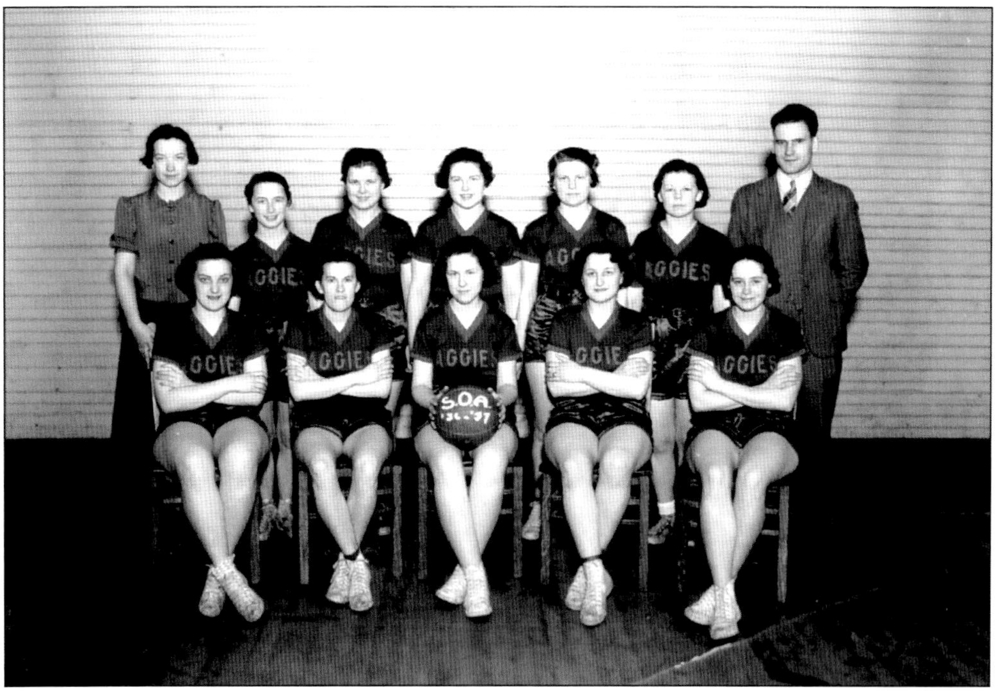

The 1936–1937 women's Aggie basketball team pose for their yearbook photograph. While some people considered the term "Aggie" a negative one, many at the school and in the community embraced it with a certain amount of pride. Both men's and women's teams were known as Aggies at that time.

Students George Grathier, E. Lyle Richardson, Irwin Frary, Daniel Fitzgerald, Lynn Drake, and Allan Woodward pose on campus in 1936 or 1937. (Courtesy of John Burns.)

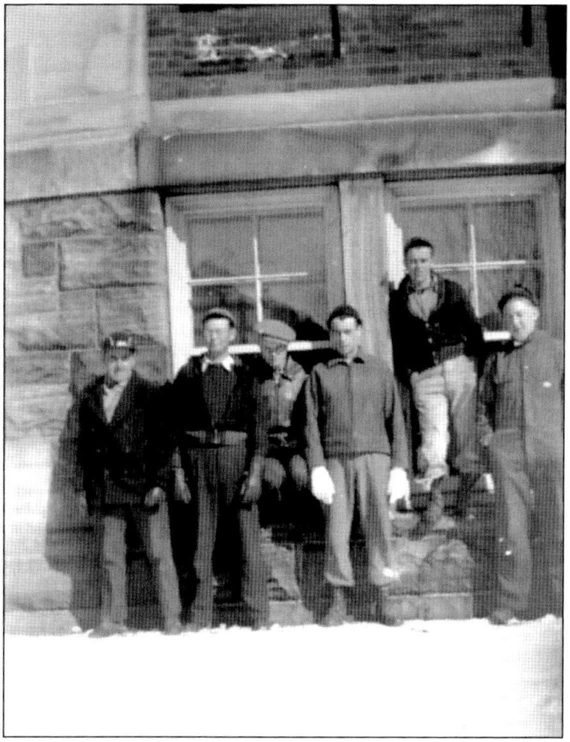

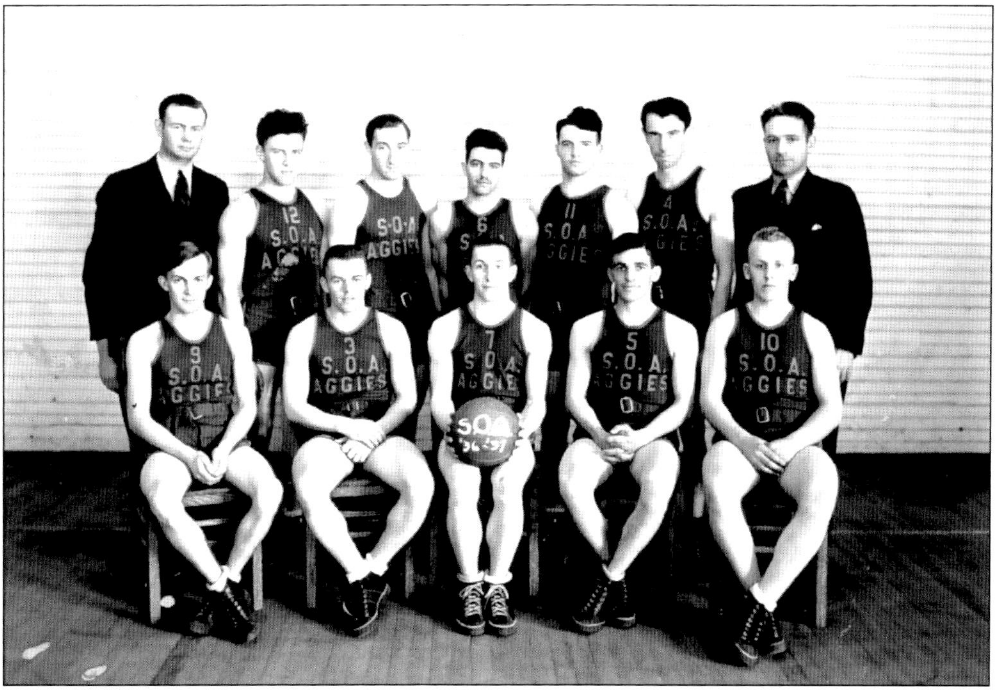

The 1936–1937 men's basketball team and their coaches are shown in this team photograph.

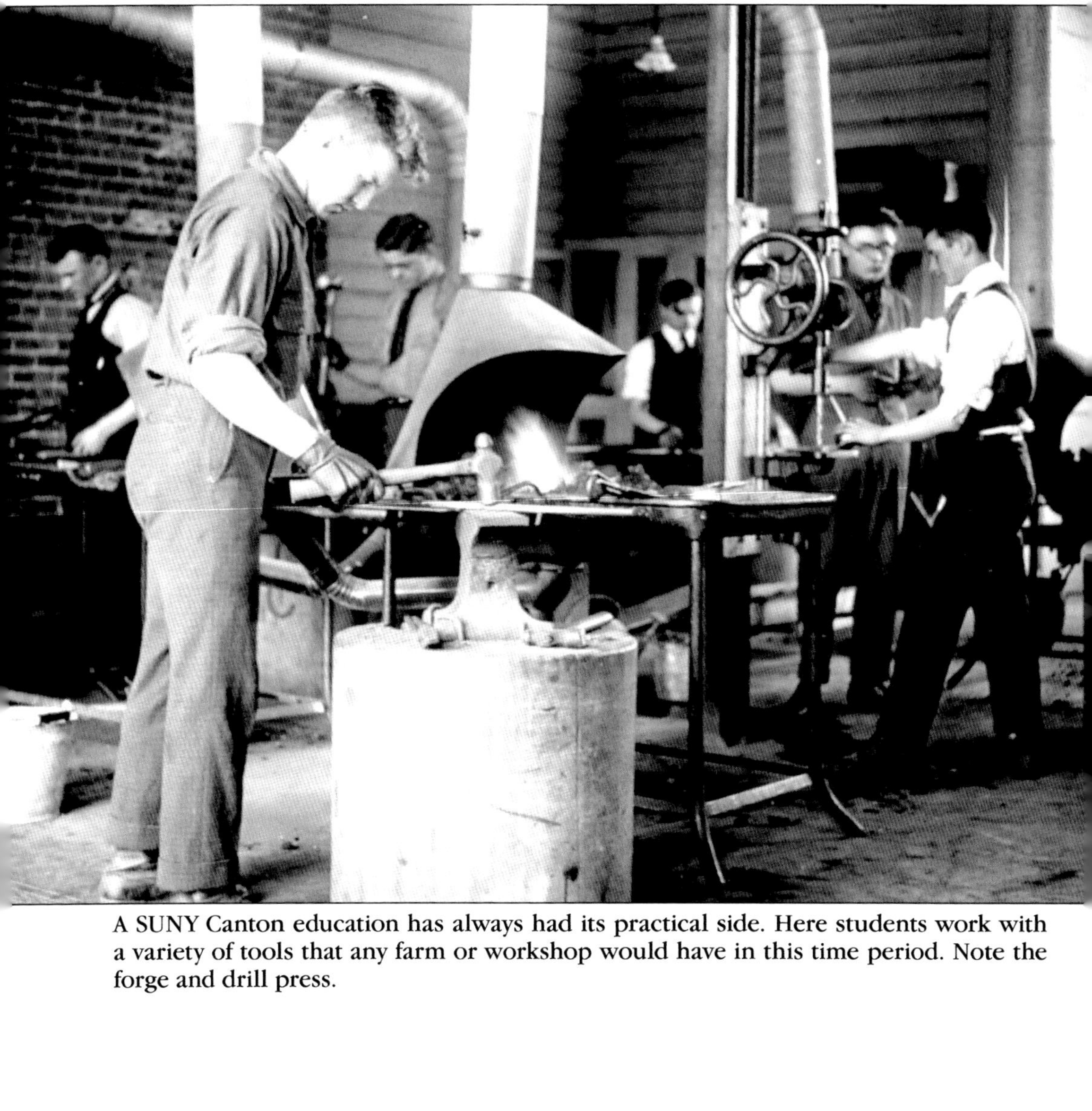

A SUNY Canton education has always had its practical side. Here students work with a variety of tools that any farm or workshop would have in this time period. Note the forge and drill press.

Three

An Opportunity in Technology 1937–1947

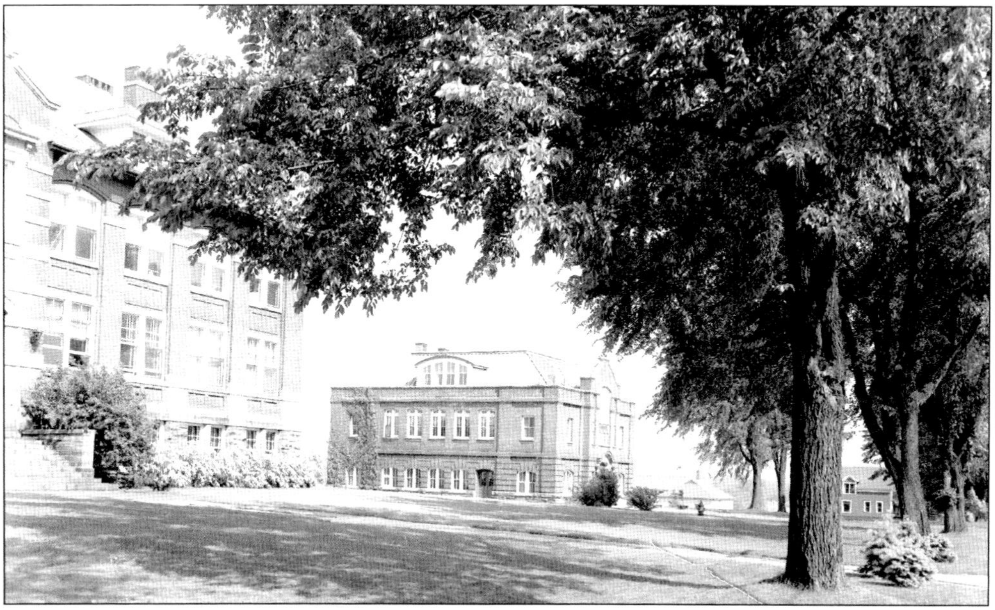

The close call of school closure in 1934 jarred Director Whittemore and his staff into action. By 1937, a new curriculum was developed with an increasing emphasis on technology and engineering. These changes were to shape the college's future development for the next six decades. (Courtesy of W. Kingston.)

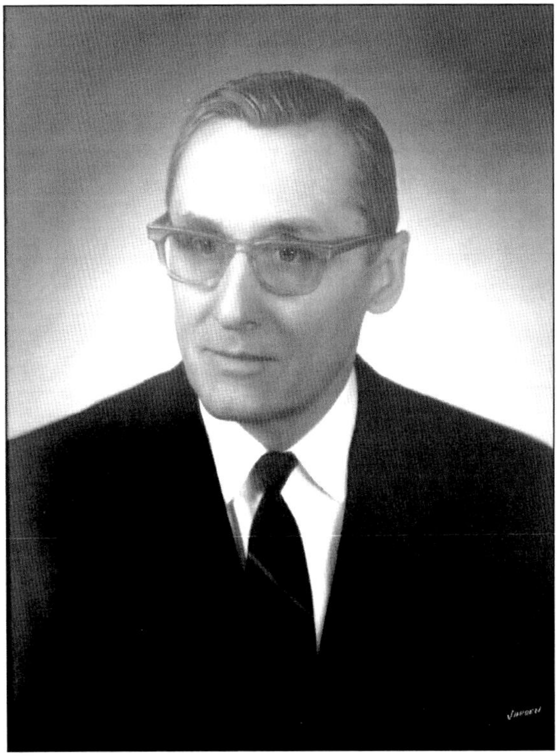

Professor Peter Nevaldine joined the faculty in 1937, and during his years of service, which lasted until 1973, he was instrumental in carrying forward the school's educational mission in technology. His numerous contributions were the reason that the expansive engineering and technology building on the new campus carries his name.

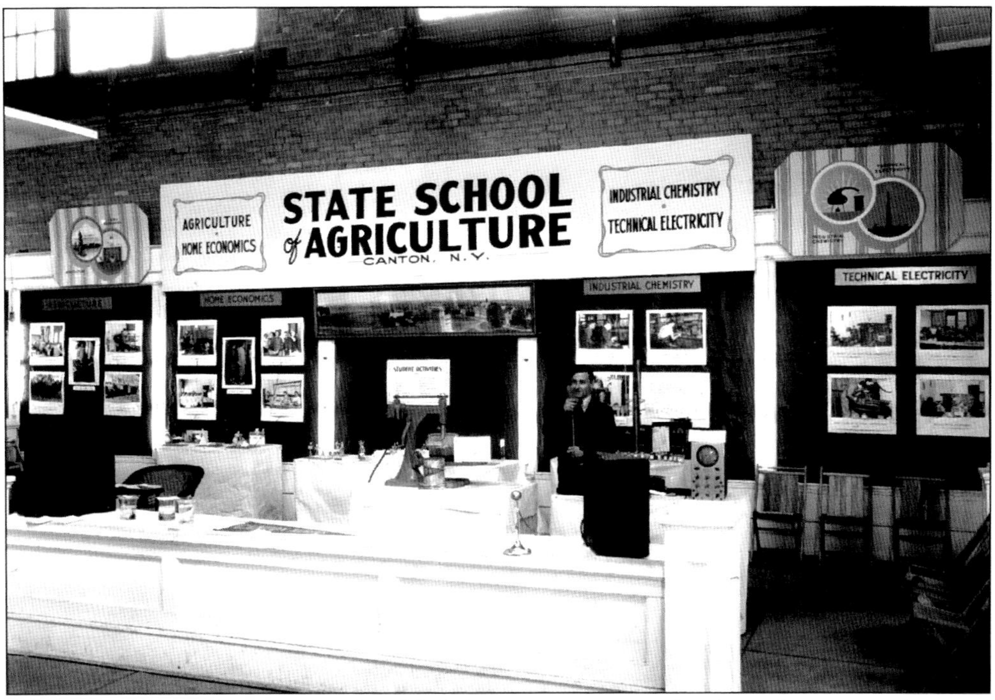

Peter Nevaldine, who organized and led the engineering technology division at the State School of Agriculture at Canton, attended the New York State Fair for several years as an exhibitor for the college. Here he is shown at the 1938 fair.

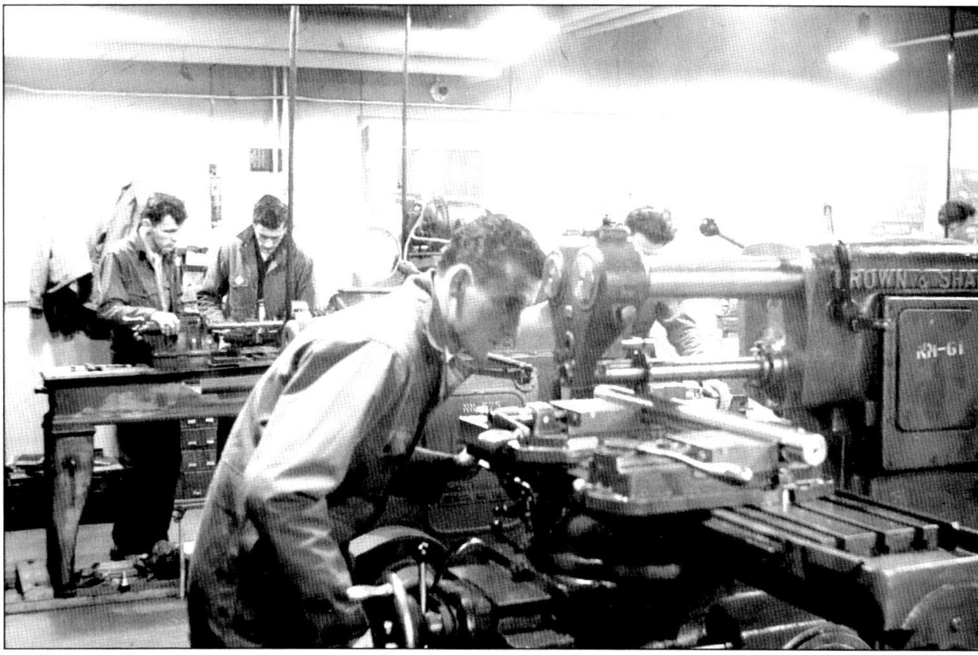

This photograph was taken in the machine shop, where tolerances were in the thousandths and challenged both the patience and the skill of students.

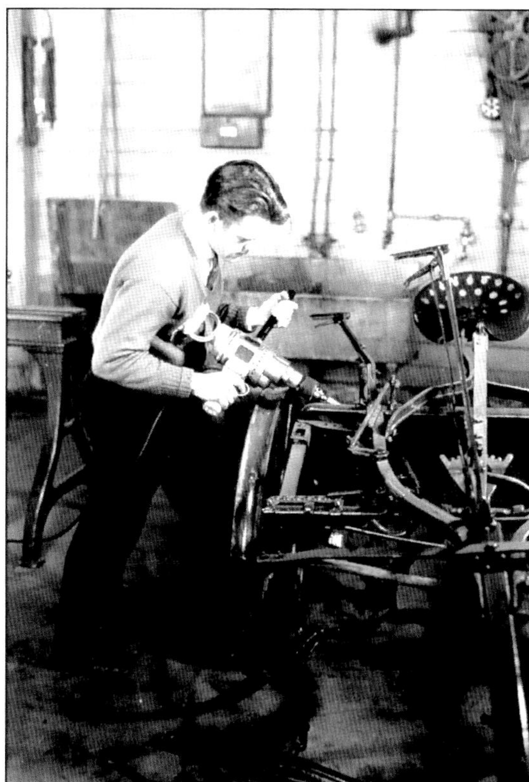

The school's farm shop taught students the skills necessary to repair and maintain farm equipment.

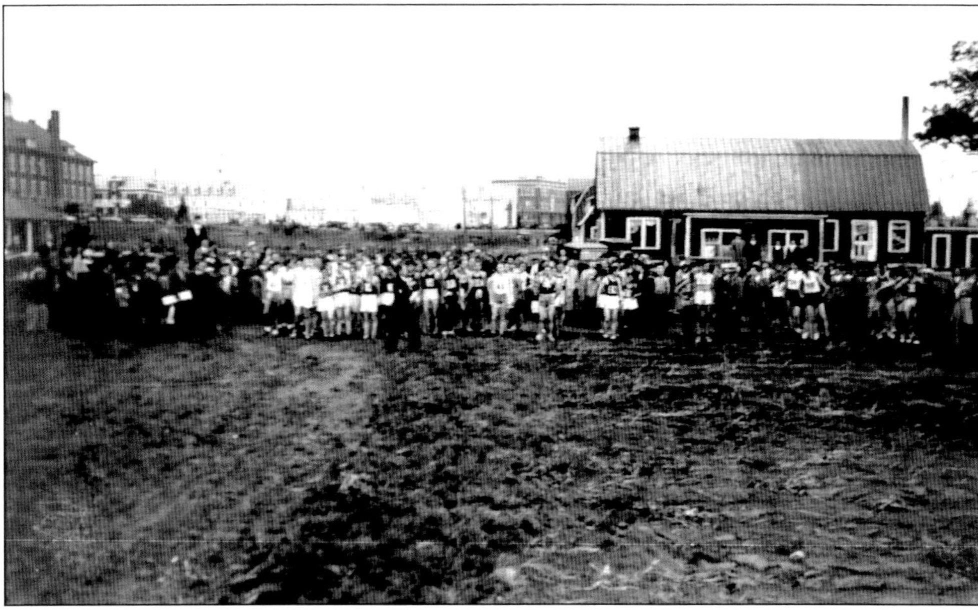

This 1938 photograph shows the annual cross country running event hosted by the State School of Agriculture for regional high school students. The background view is the St. Lawrence University campus with Cook Hall on the left. (Courtesy of W. Kingston.)

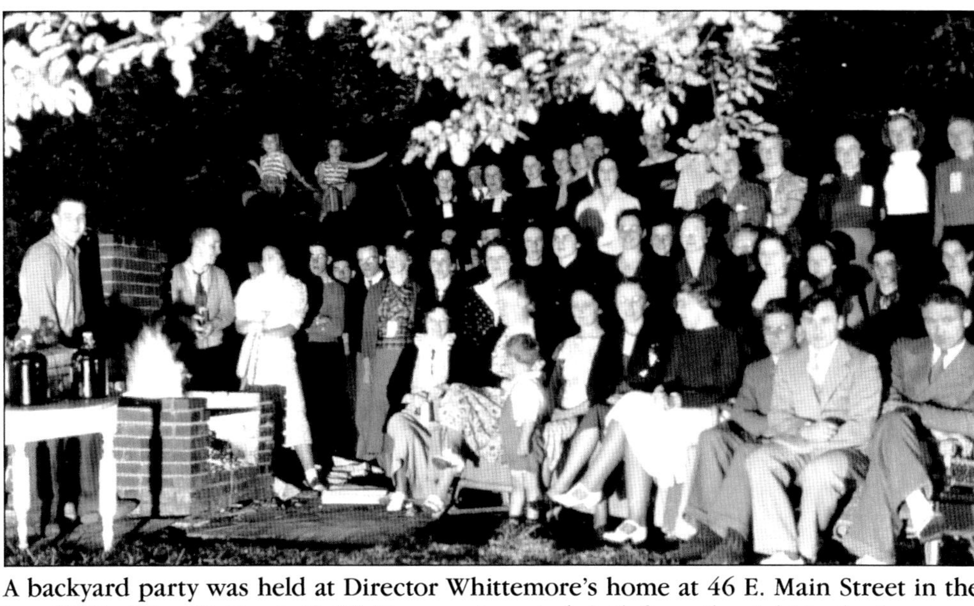

A backyard party was held at Director Whittemore's home at 46 E. Main Street in the late 1930s. His wife Bessie G. Whittemore is seated sixth from the right in the front row with their son Winston. Twin daughters Aela and Alma are in the striped shirts, perched in their favorite tree. Guests are from the School of Agriculture. In the first row, left to right, are Evan Dana, Peter Nevaldine, and William Long.

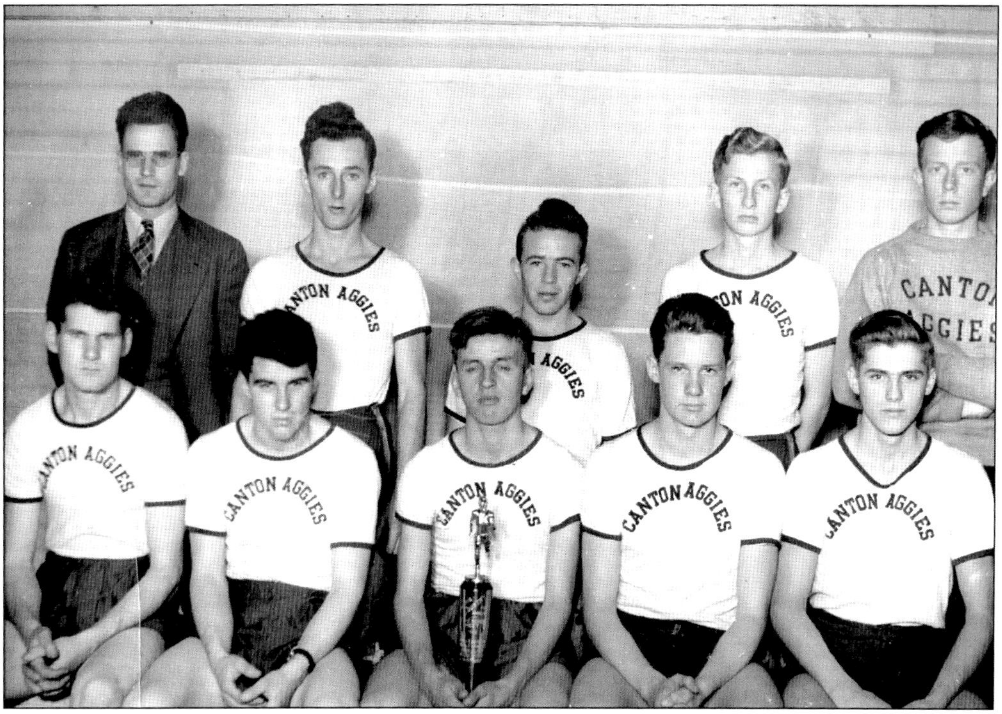

The Aggies men's track team won the state championship in 1939.

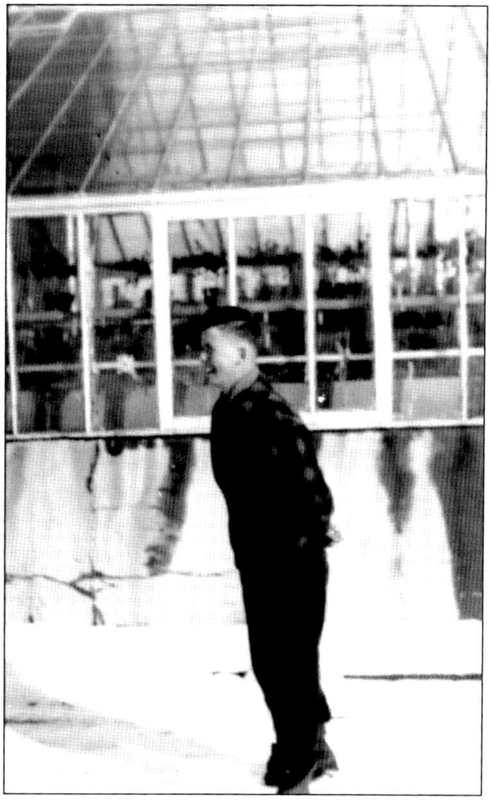

The greenhouse off the back of the dairy barn was still very much in use in 1939. Student Clinton Thompson is in the foreground. (Courtesy of Sally Thompson.)

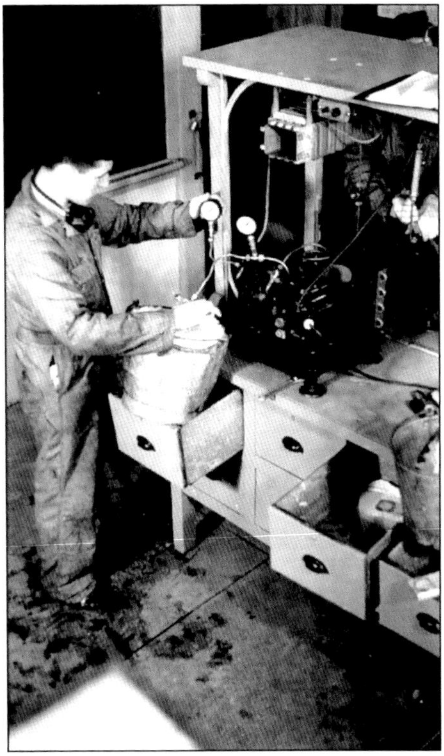

Student Howard Plumb learns about refrigeration in the electrical technology lab in Payson Hall.

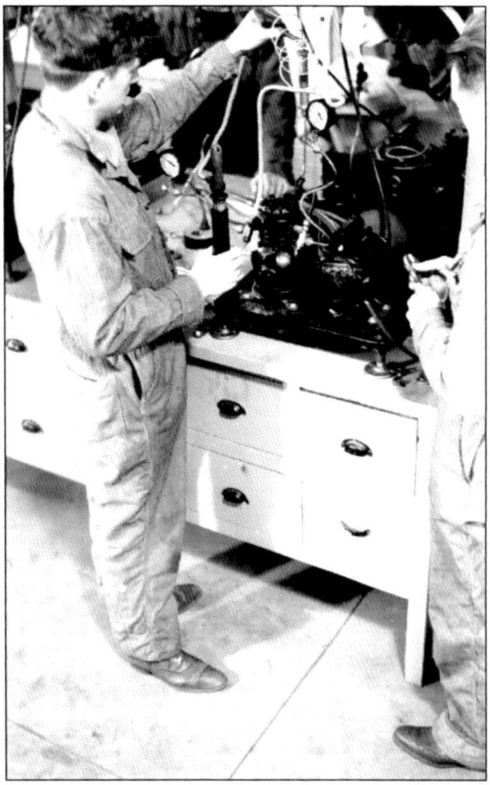

In this 1939 photograph, Howard Bauter works in the refrigeration lab. Refrigeration was a new technology at that time and required new skills for a growing demand.

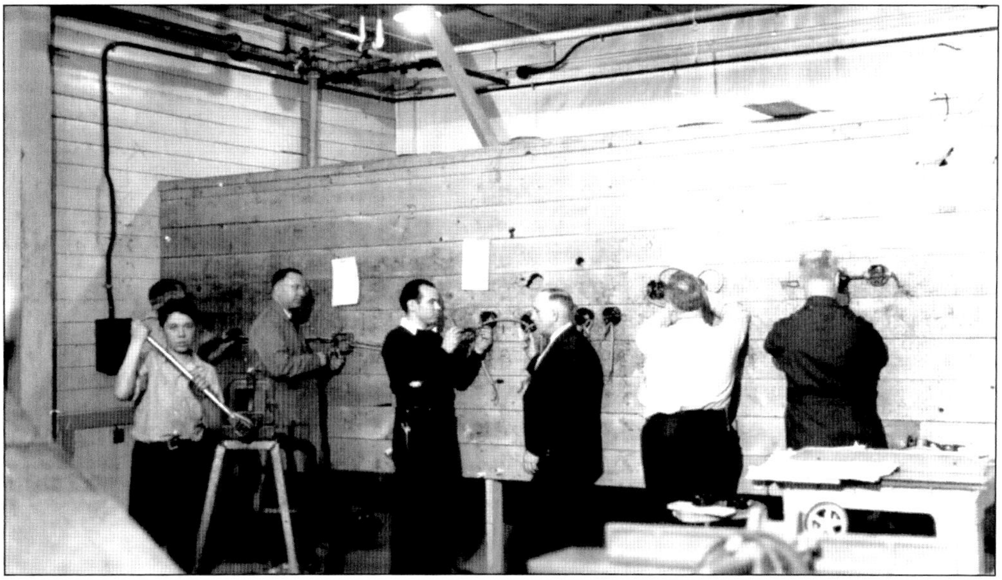

SUNY Canton has always had continuing education programs. This evening class, a national defense training program for electricians, was part of the World War II effort.

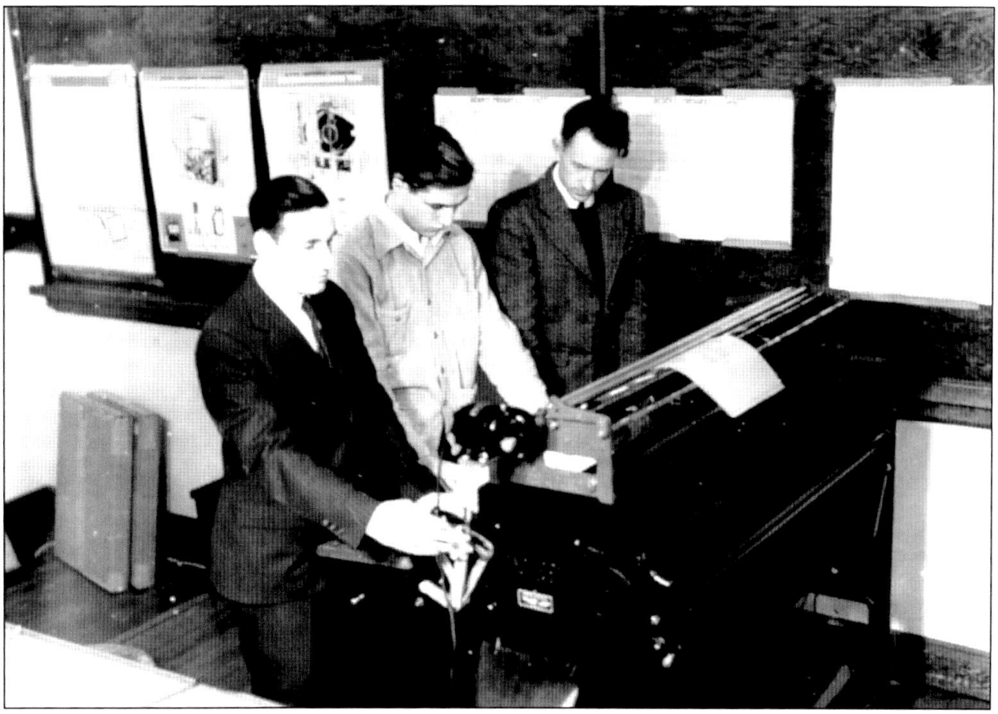

Instructor Peter Nevaldine, on the left, shows students Howard Plumb and Phillip Rogers how to use a blueprint machine in the Cook Hall drafting room.

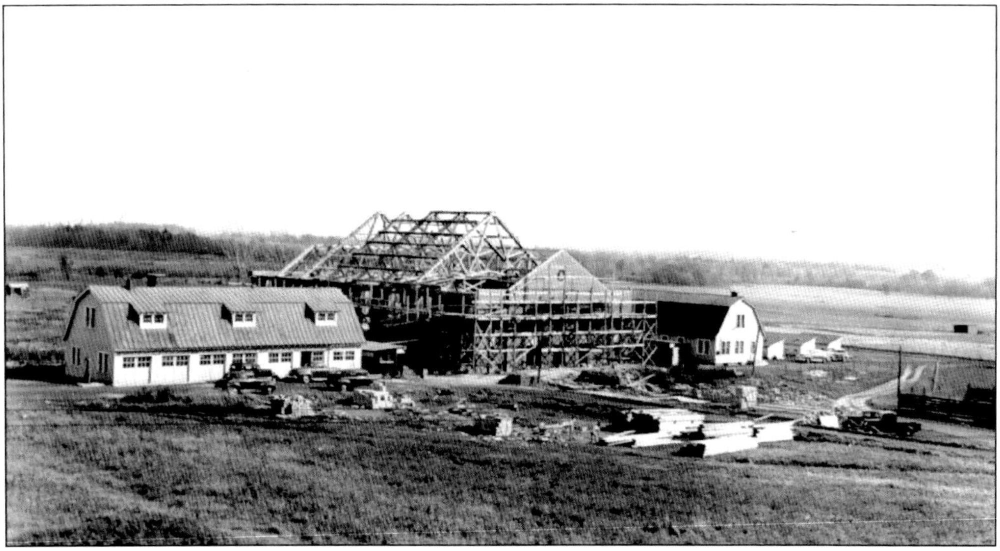

Madill Hall was under construction on the old campus in the early 1940s. The farm shop is to the left, and the poultry building is to the right.

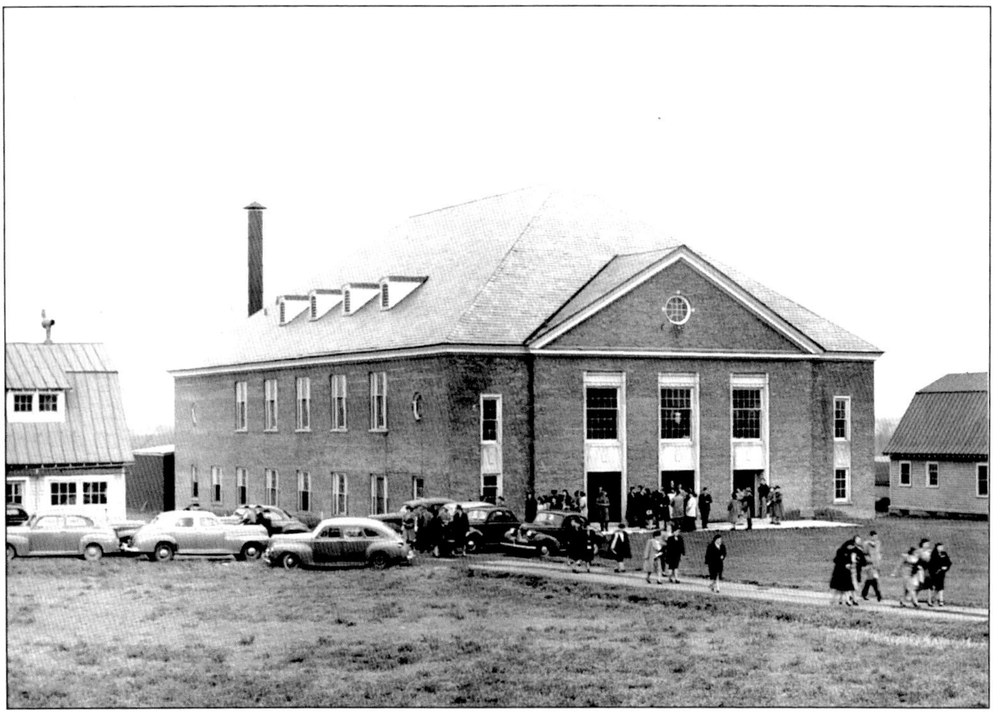

Madill Hall is pictured at its completion. Construction was a drawn-out affair, with completion in 1943 and the dedication in November 1945.

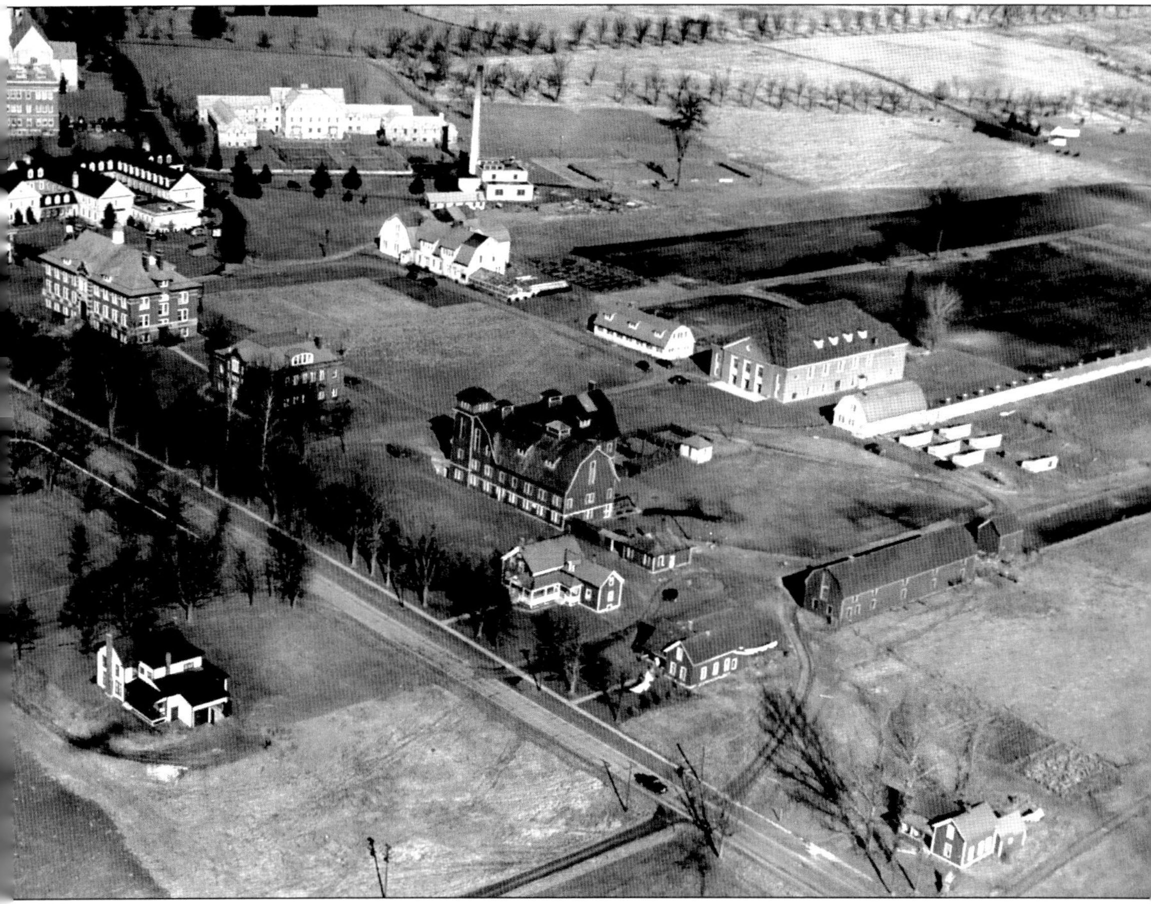

This aerial photograph provides a bird's-eye view of the campus in the mid-1940s with Cook Hall, the dairy building, the dairy barn, and the farmhouse along Park Street from left to right. Recently finished Madill Hall is to the left of the poultry building and its 360-foot extension.

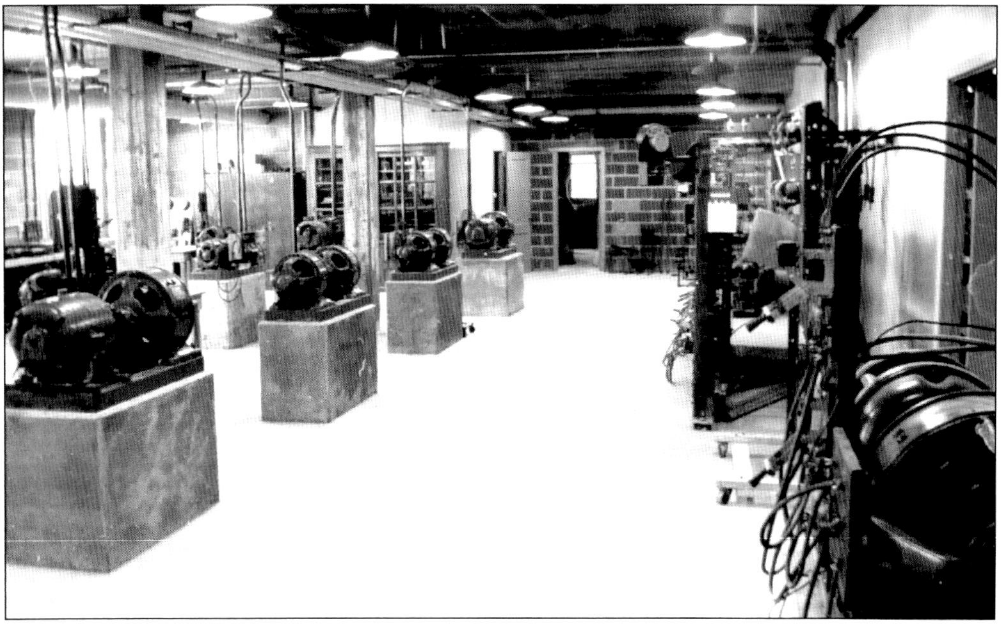

Pictured here are workstations in the electrical lab located in the basement of Madill Hall in the 1940s, shortly after Madill had been finished and dedicated.

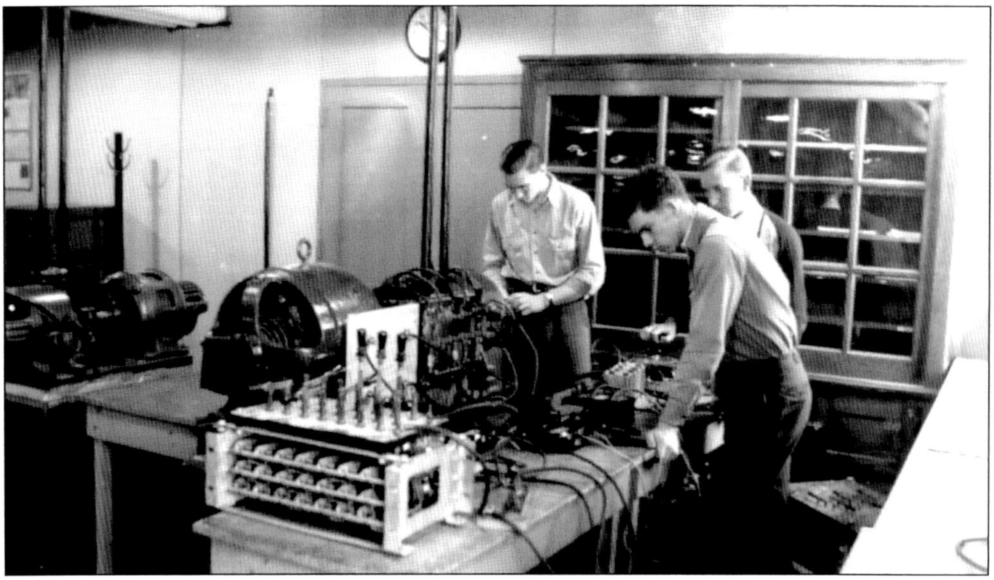

In this *c.* 1944 photograph, students Bob Gould, Herb Catlin, and Everett Flint are shown working on motors in the electrical lab.

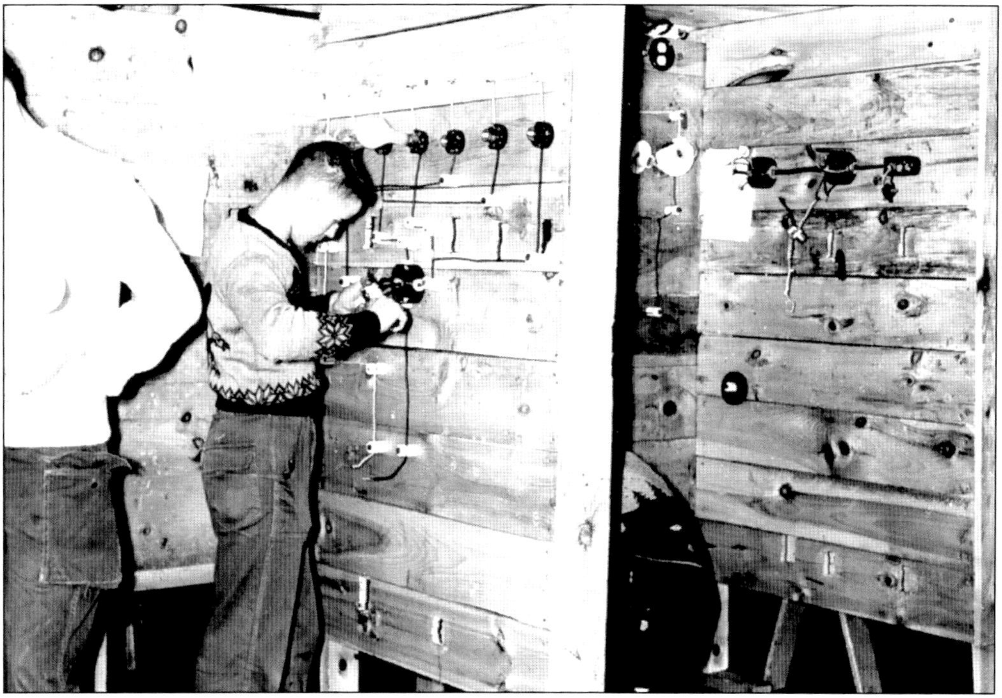

Unidentified students practice what they have learned about wiring buildings in the electrical construction shop in Madill Hall around 1944.

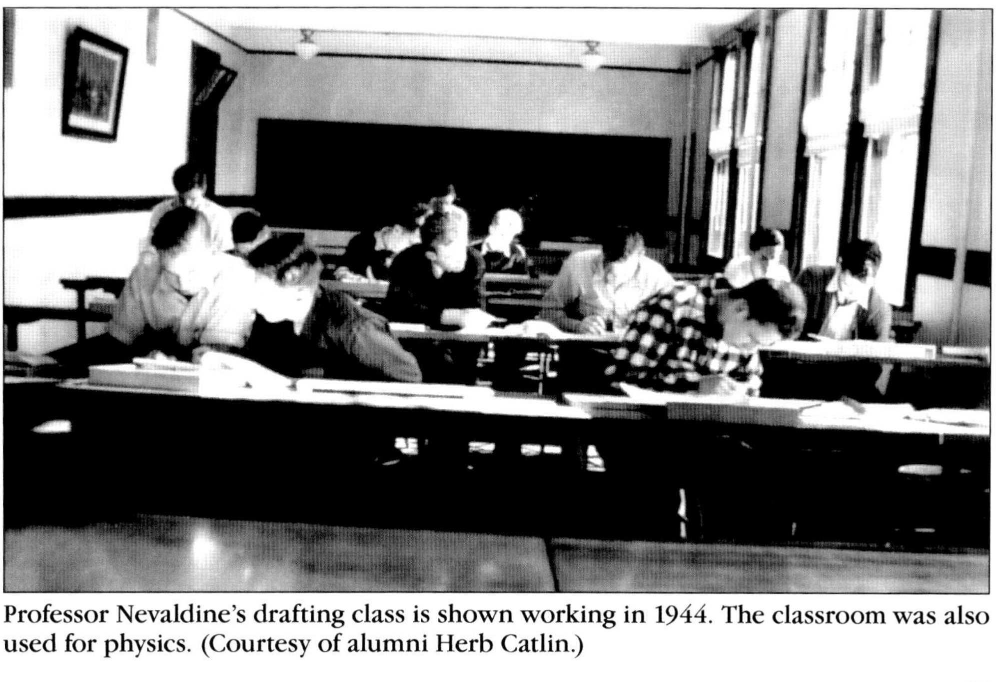

Professor Nevaldine's drafting class is shown working in 1944. The classroom was also used for physics. (Courtesy of alumni Herb Catlin.)

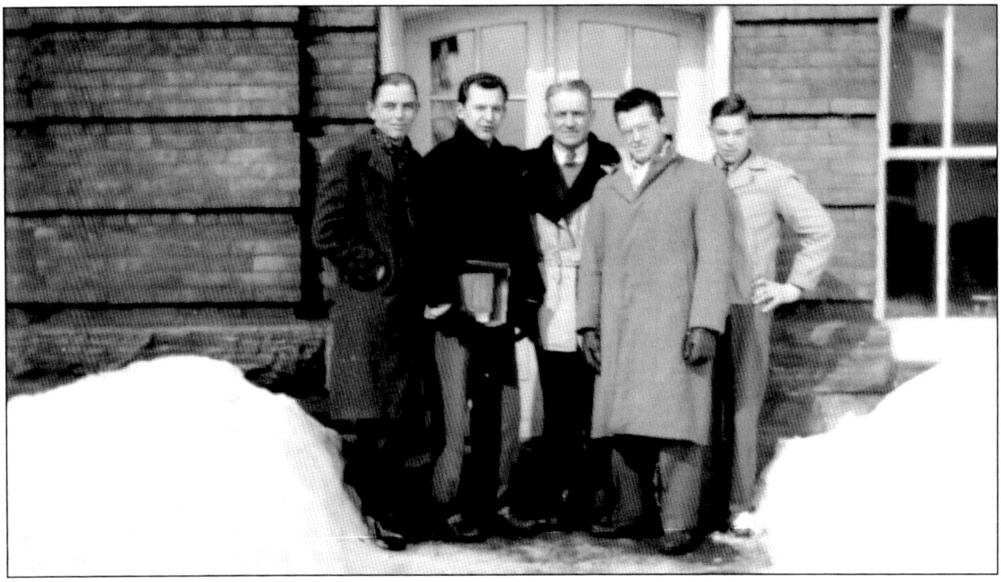

Professor Long and some of his agriculture students are pictured in February 1945. Long is in the center, with Ray Strack and Bill Trowbridge to his left and Don Edgar and Merrill Whitmore to his right. (Courtesy of Sally Thompson.)

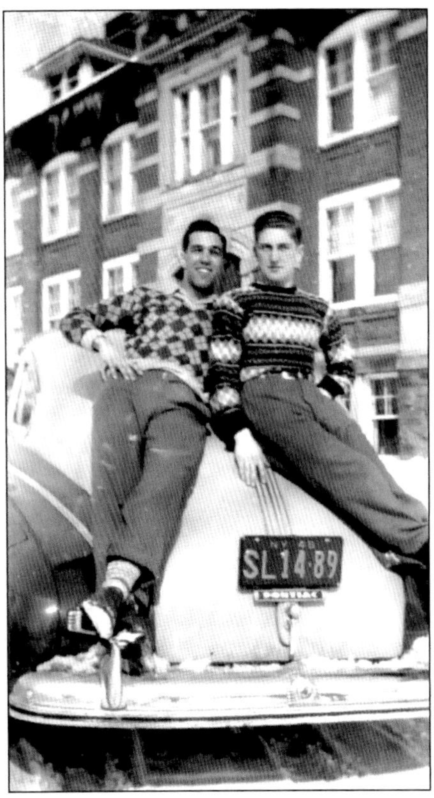

Electrical students Bob Meyers and Jerry Boyer pose with a car in 1945. (Courtesy of Sally Thompson.)

Pictured here are student actors from the 1945 play *Boos in the Night* before their performance. In front are Sally Yandeau (left) and Edith Weaver. In back, from left to right, are Ellen Signor, Martha Young, Elma O'Connor, and Marion Whitmore. (Courtesy of Sally Thompson.)

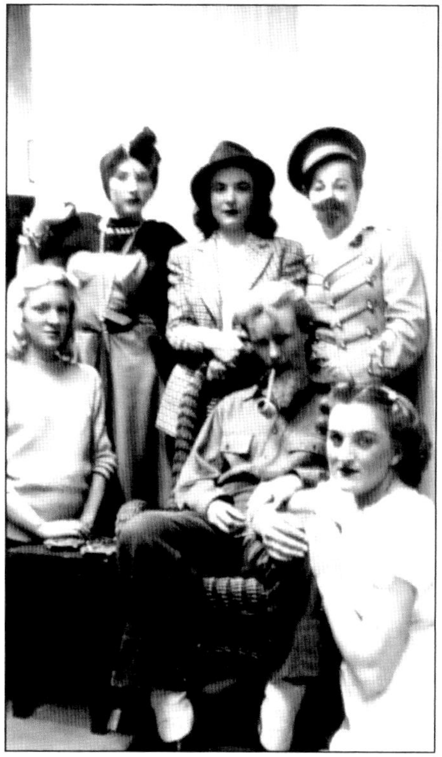

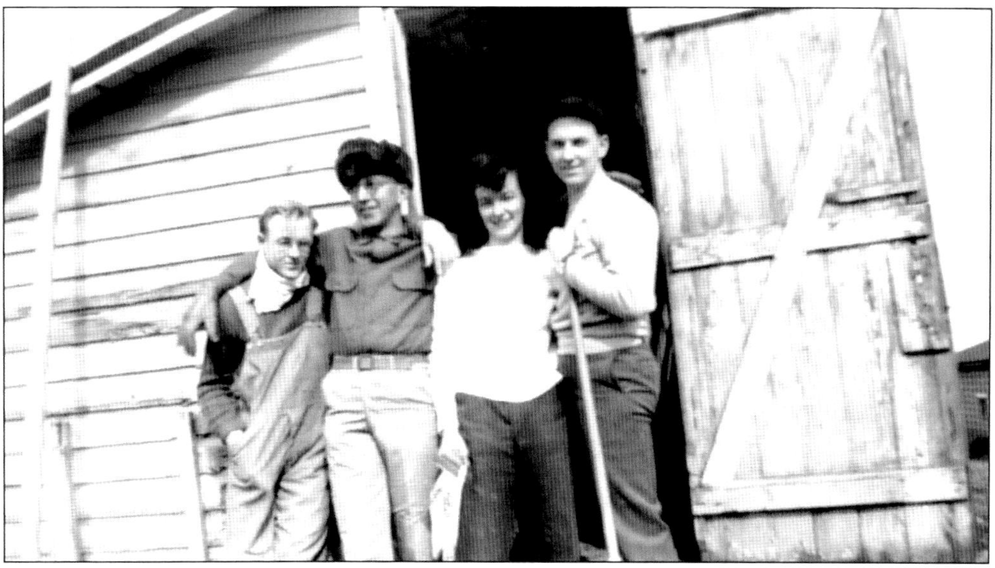

Agriculture students Dean Hutchins, John Dean, Sally Yandeau Thompson, and Chuck Costello pause from cleaning out the poultry house in 1946 and even manage a little smile. (Photo courtesy of Sally Thompson.)

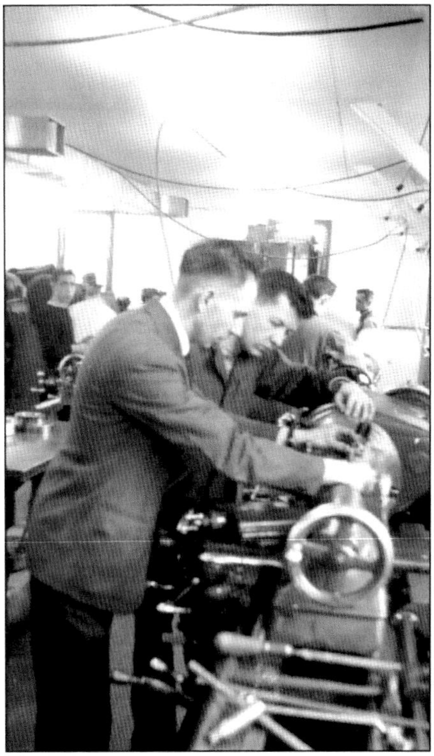

Professor Walter Kingston helps an unidentified student adjust the lathe in the ATI lab on May 1, 1947.

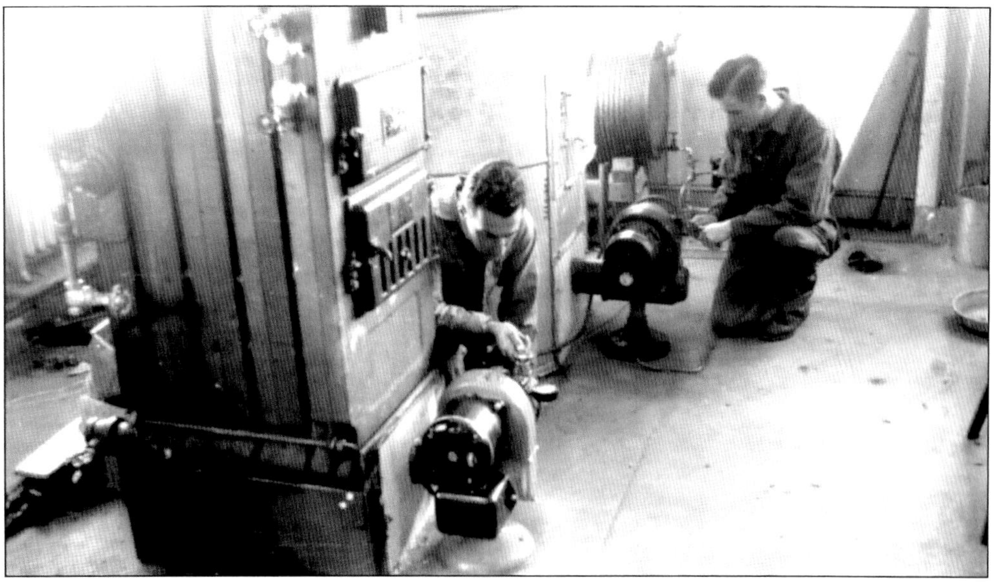

Two students in the heating curriculum adjust furnace motors in the ATI lab. This photograph dates from December 1946.

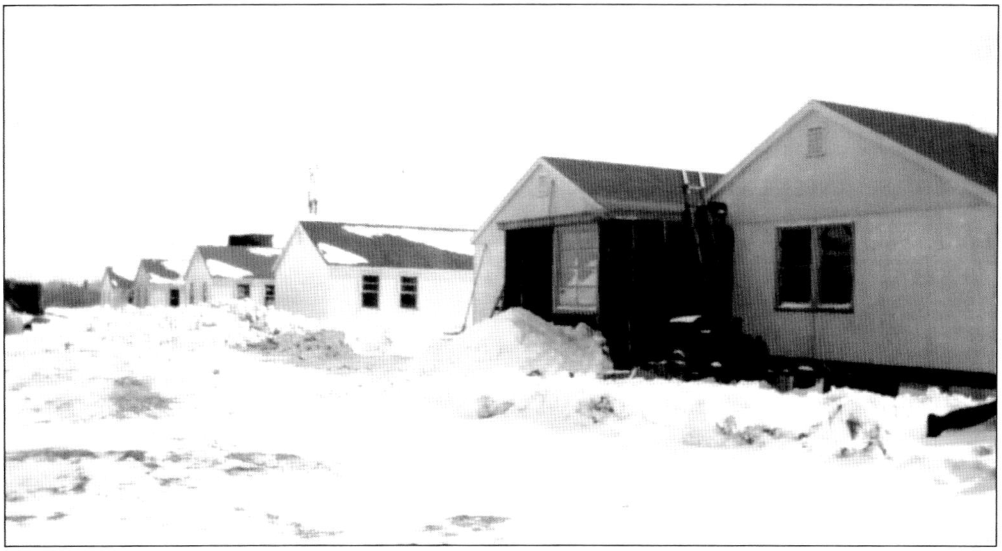

To meet ATI's growing space needs, temporary buildings were constructed on campus to house the heating lab, refrigeration lab, machine tools lab, drafting rooms, and more classroom space. This February 1947 photograph shows the buildings under construction.

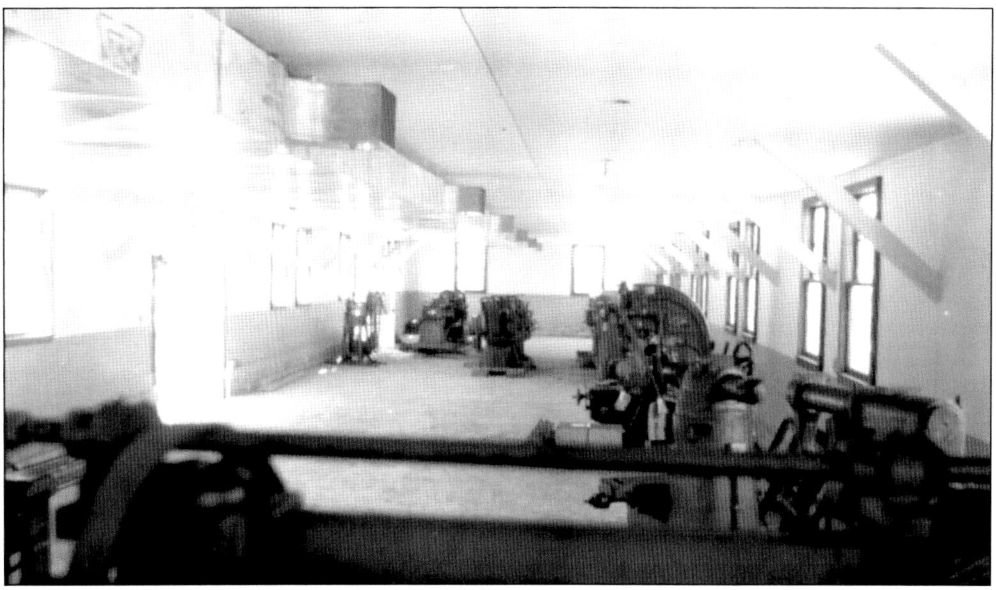

Later, in April 1947, the temporary buildings were ready for occupancy. Here one of the labs is being set up for future student use.

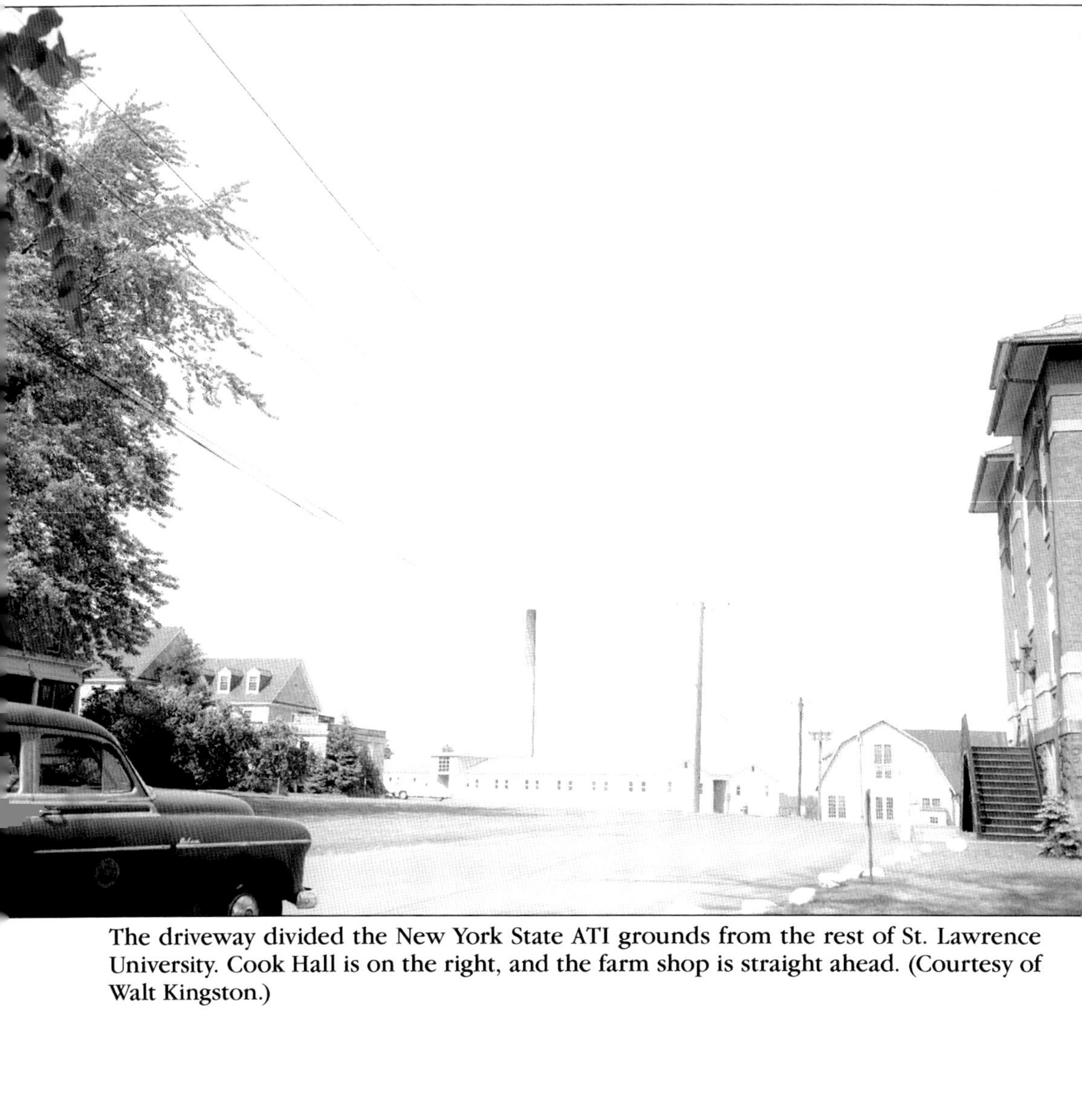

The driveway divided the New York State ATI grounds from the rest of St. Lawrence University. Cook Hall is on the right, and the farm shop is straight ahead. (Courtesy of Walt Kingston.)

Four

Technology, Growth, and New Buildings 1948–1967

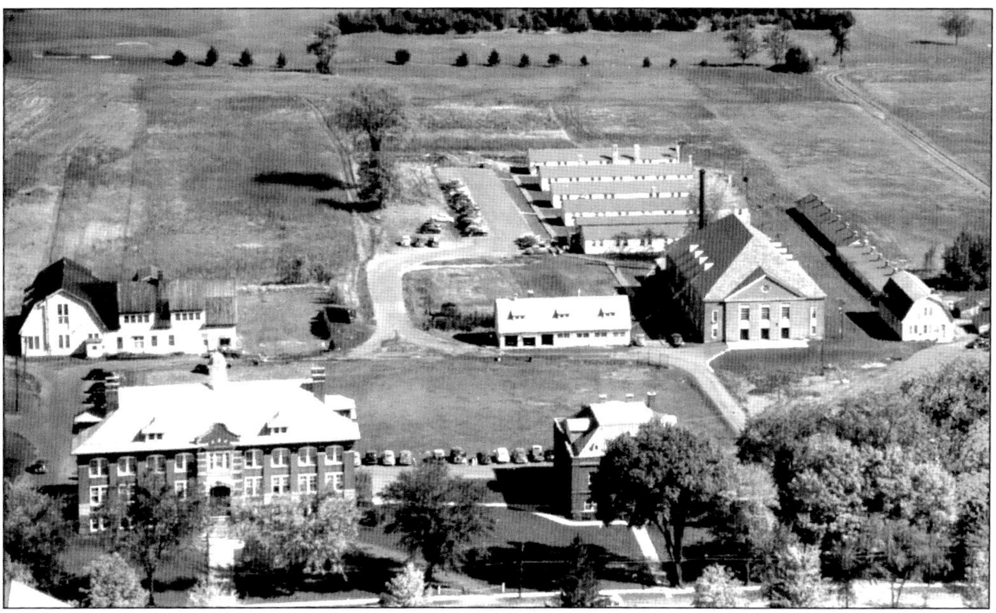

This aerial photograph shows the ATI campus as it looked in the late 1940s. Madill Hall and the temporary buildings have been completed. The grounds would look very much the same for nearly a decade. Other changes were about to happen, but none quite as visible as a major building initiative. (Skyview by Dwight Church.)

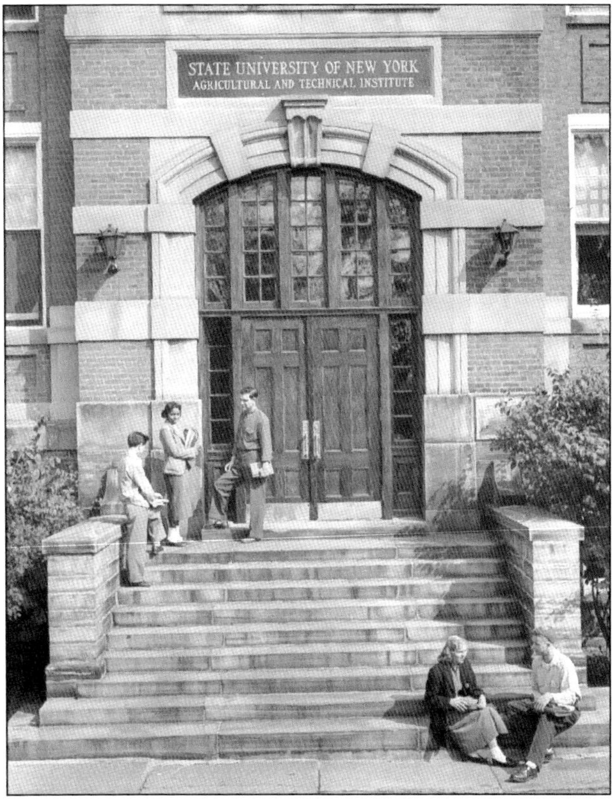

Two major events took place in 1948 that would shape the future of the college over the next two decades. The first was that the name of the college changed from the New York State Agricultural and Technical Institute to the State University of New York Agricultural and Technical Institute. This was the third name change since the school's founding in 1906. In this picture, an old, familiar building has taken on the new name.

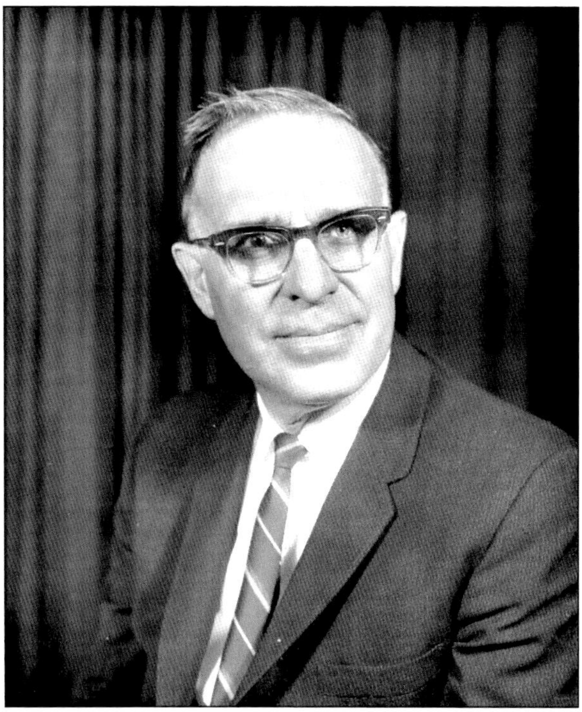

The other major change that occurred in 1948 was that Dr. Albert French became director of SUNY ATI. Like Director Whittemore, Dr. French would serve for about 24 years. During his tenure, there would be two major building projects, including a new location on the other side of the village of Canton.

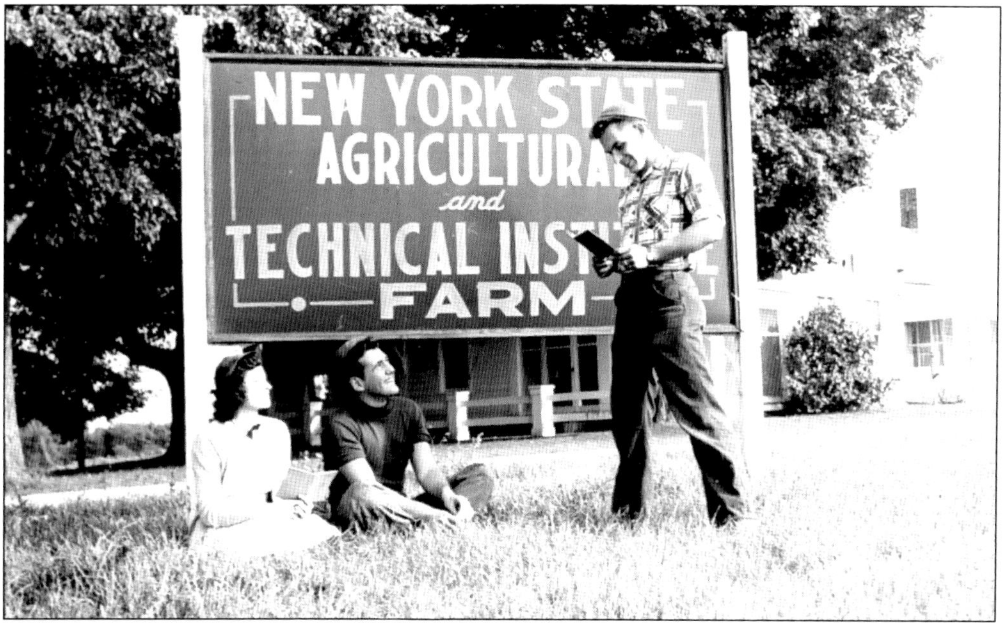

This close-up of the ATI farm on State Route 68 between Canton and Langdon Corners was taken in 1951. Over a half century later, the farmhouse looks very much the same.

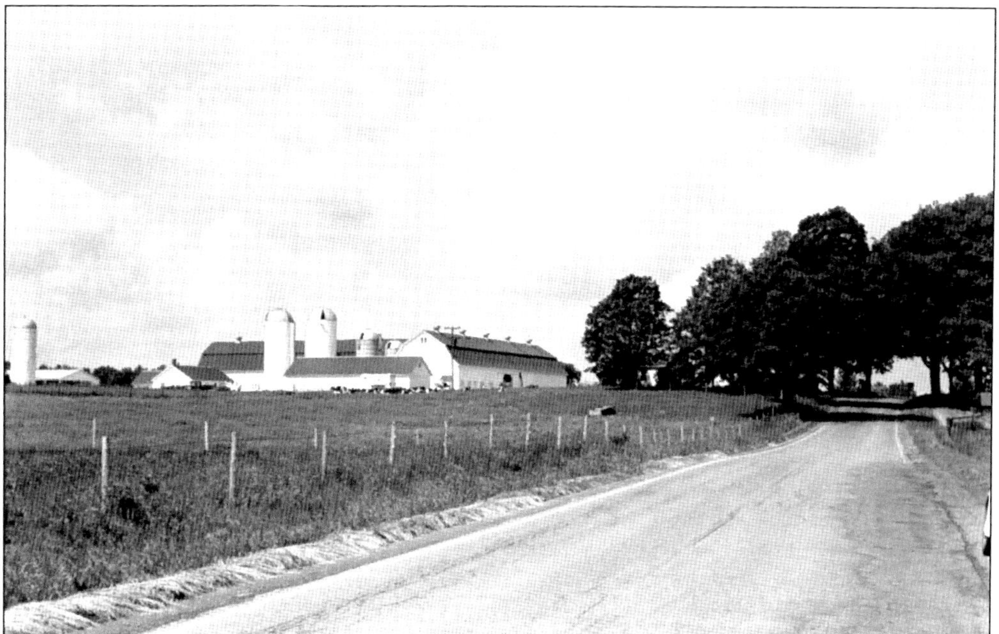

The SUNY ATI farm is shown in a picture taken from the east side. The house is mostly hidden in the maple trees near the road. The farm was a valuable laboratory of hands-on experience for agriculture students. The farm was typical of North Country farms and therefore provided students with a realistic idea of the challenges and opportunities they would face in northern New York agriculture.

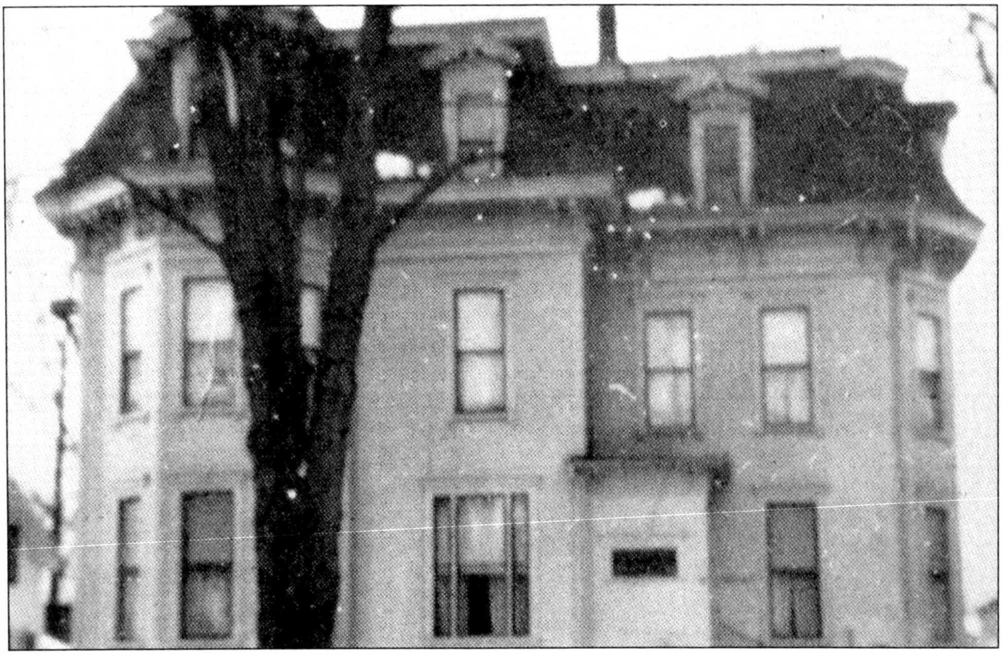

Mitchell Hall, a big, old house at 34 Park Street, was the freshman women's dorm. It was only a short walk down Park Street to the SUNY ATI campus or to Main Street in Canton. Mitchell Hall was also located next door to the Lantern at 36 Park Street, where many female students worked and learned coffeehouse management skills.

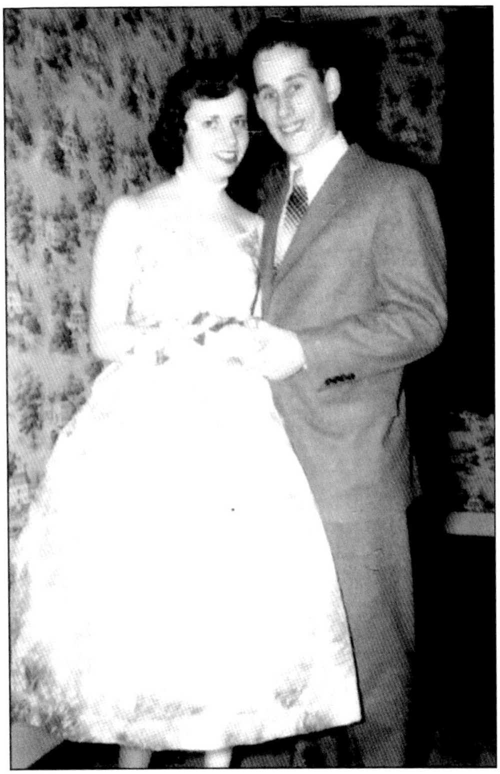

SUNY ATI students Lou Harmin and Evelyn Oberst are pictured in Mitchell Hall on the night of the Spring Formal in 1956. It was also Oberst's 18th birthday. (Courtesy of Lou Harmin.)

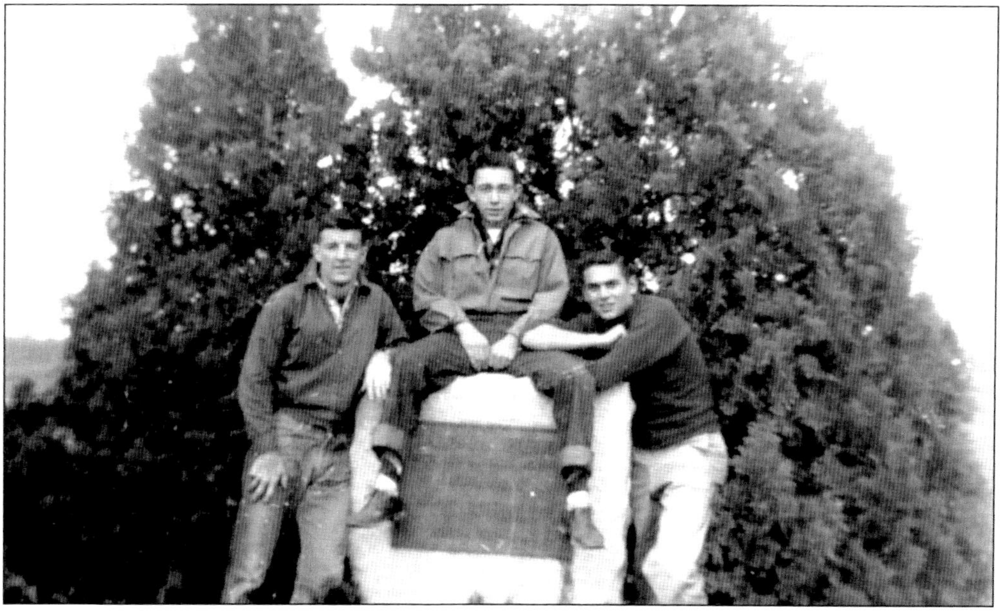

Three friends, from left to right, Don Frenia, Al Ciocca, and Tony Mastronicola, pose at Alumni Field in 1952. All three were students in the mechanical technology curriculum. This picture first appeared in the 1953 edition of *The Paysonian*. The Alumni Field plaque is housed in the college archives in the Merritt Wright Room of Southworth Library. (Courtesy of Don Frenia.)

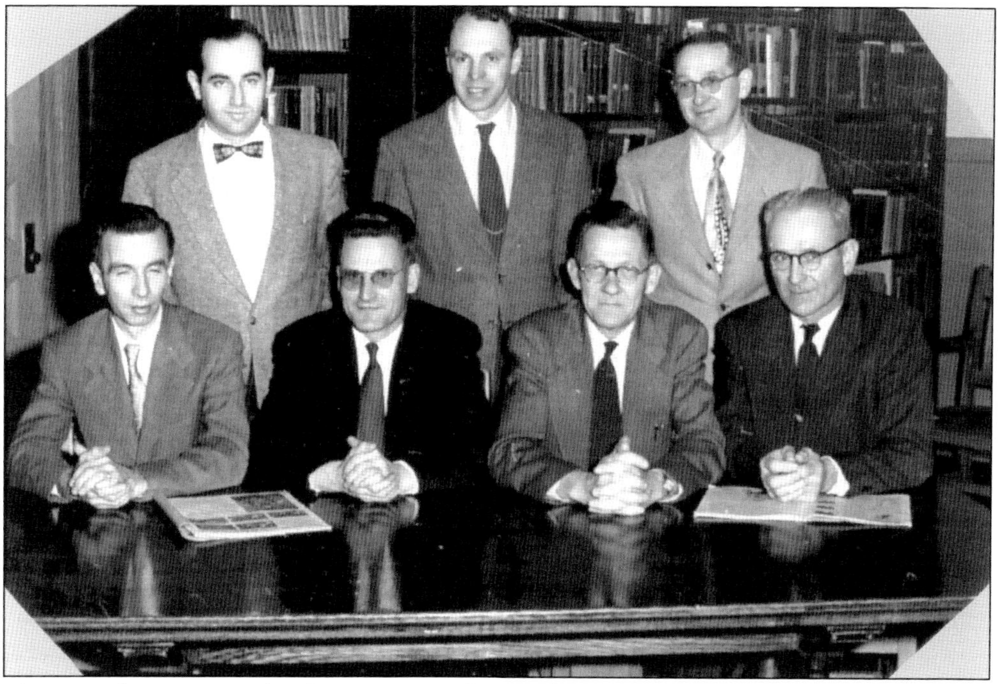

The agriculture science faculty appears in this 1954 photograph. They are, from left to right, as follows: (seated) Mr. Hicks, Mr. Dana, Mr. Hill, and Mr. Long; (standing) Mr. Clapp, Mr. Nearing, and Mr. Rawlins. The library was located on the third floor of Cook Hall.

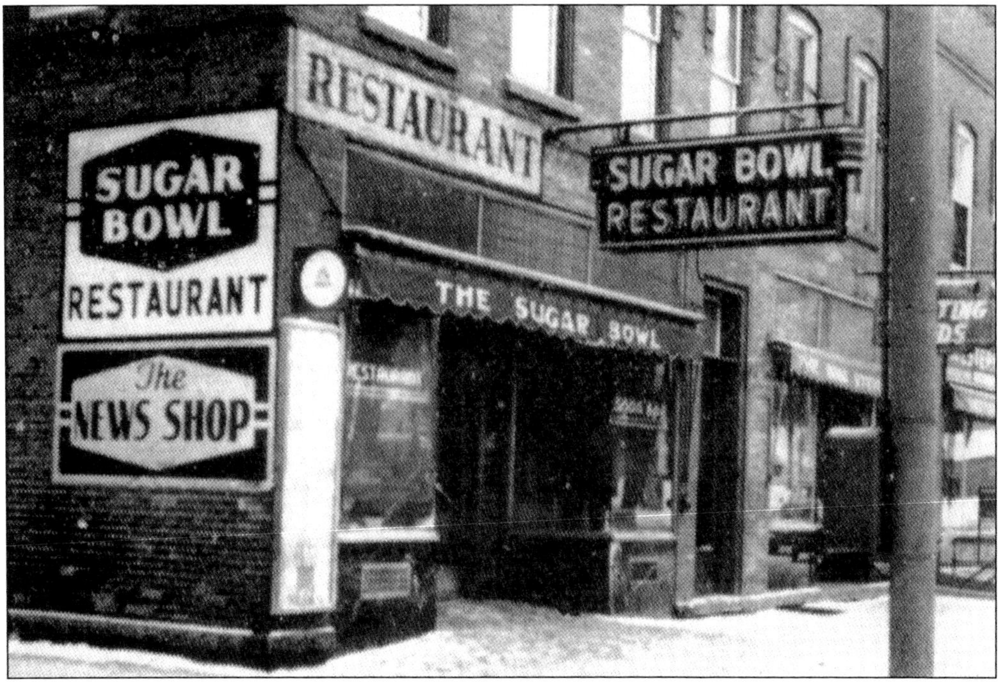

The Sugar Bowl Restaurant, located at Main Street and Court Street, was a Canton Village landmark for many years. Students who roomed in private homes often took their meals at local restaurants. The Sugar Bowl was often frequented by students for snacks.

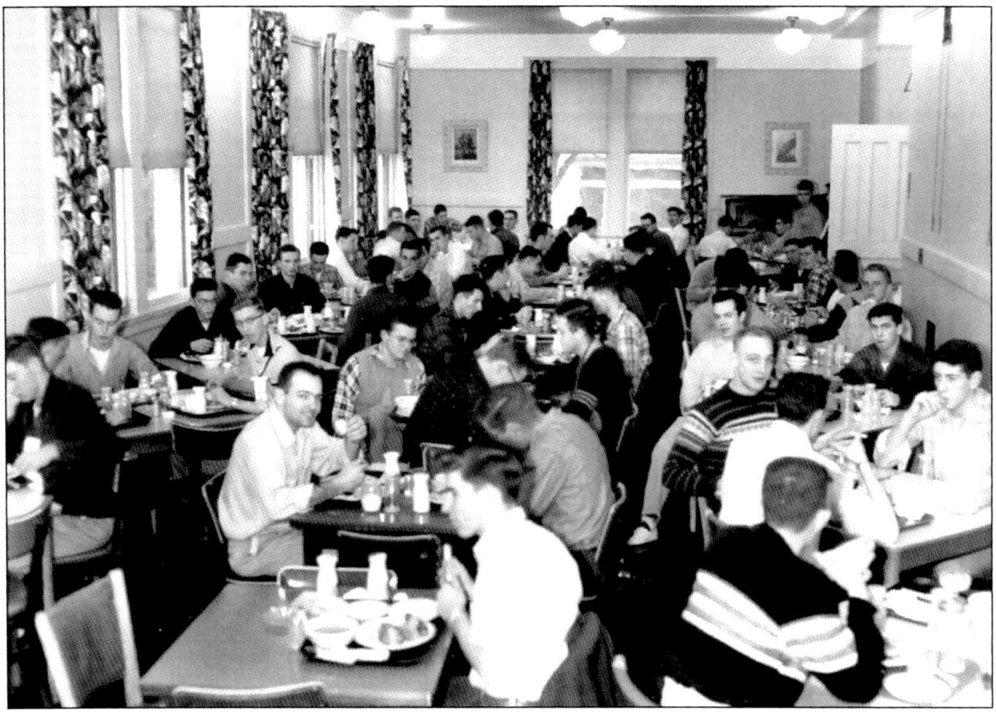

Before the construction of Alumni Hall with its dining room and student lounge, SUNY ATI students often ate in this small cafeteria on campus.

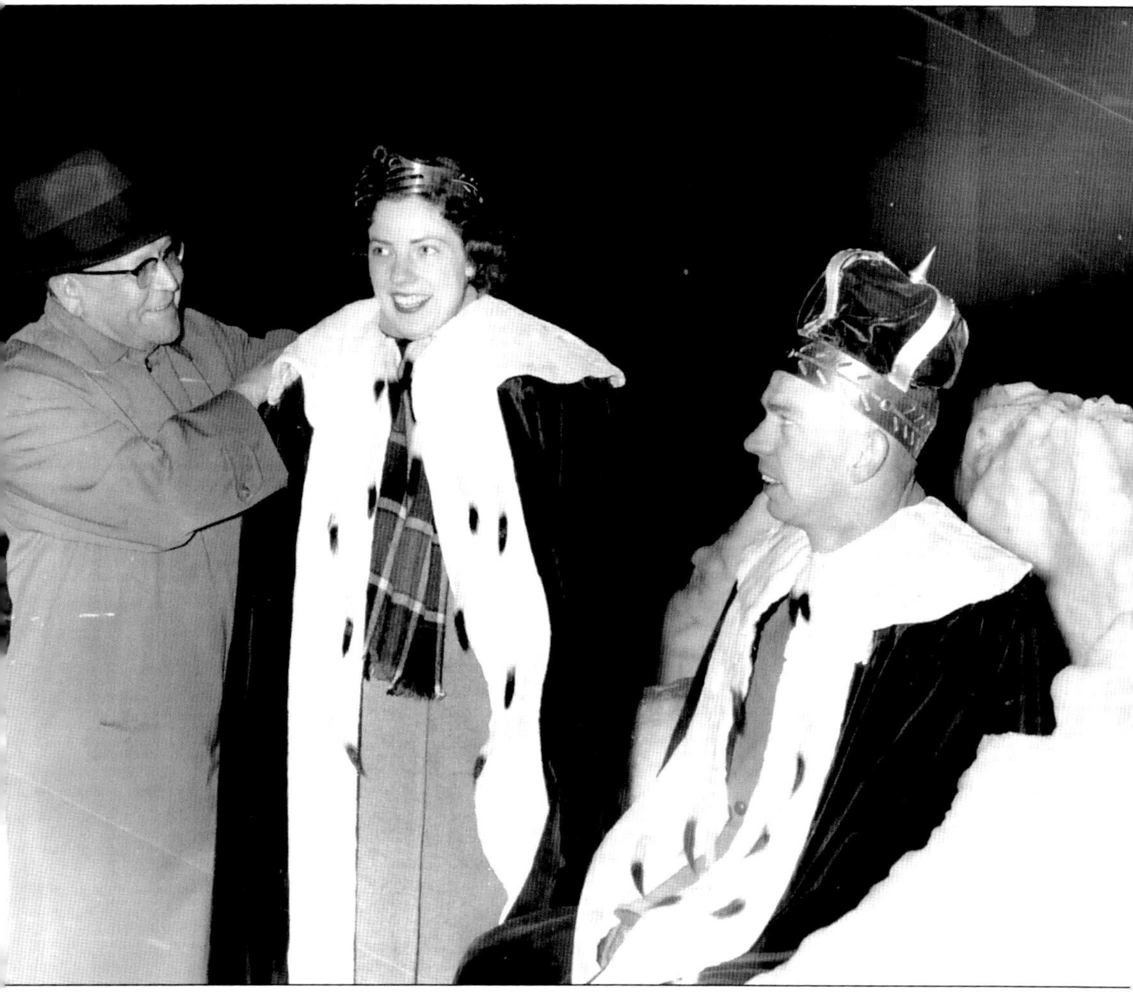

Winter Weekend events took place for many years and today hold many memories for alumni. Snow sculptures, a big dance, and the crowning of a king and queen were regular events. Here the king and queen of the 1958 Winter Weekend are shown shortly after being crowned.

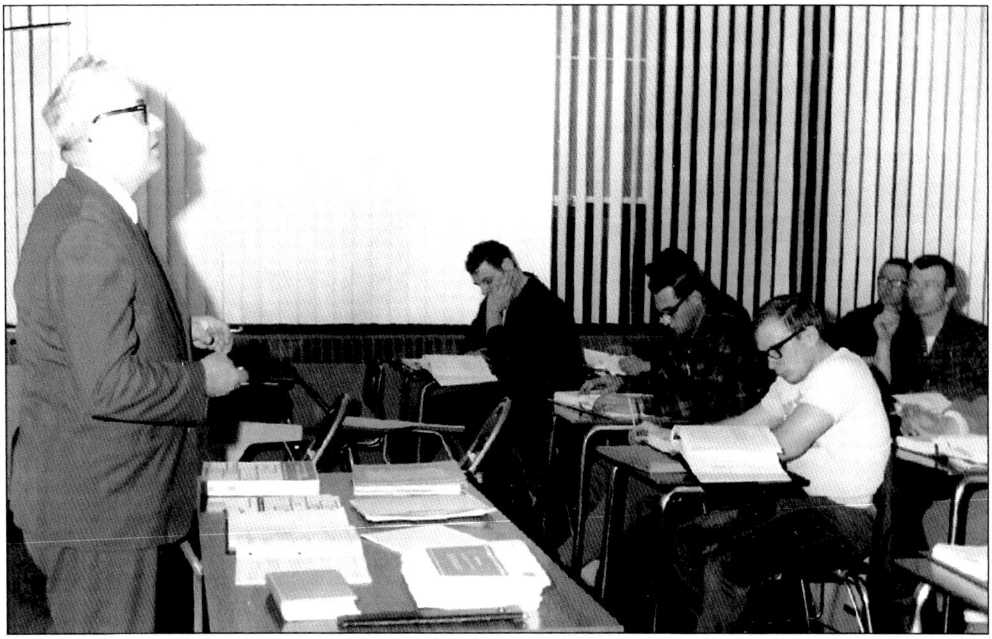

Professor Harry King, who taught air conditioning engineering technology, stands before a class of ATI students on the old campus. He taught at the college for 37 years.

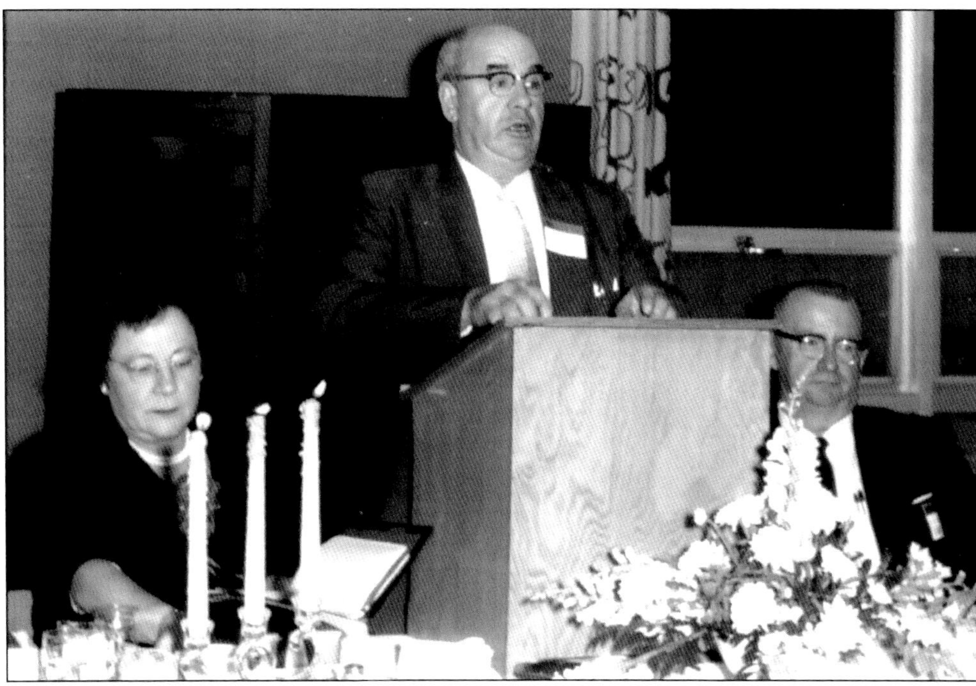

Canton ATI's Rollo Wicks speaks at the American Junior College Association of the Middle States. One of the main classroom buildings on the new campus, Wicks Hall, was named in his honor.

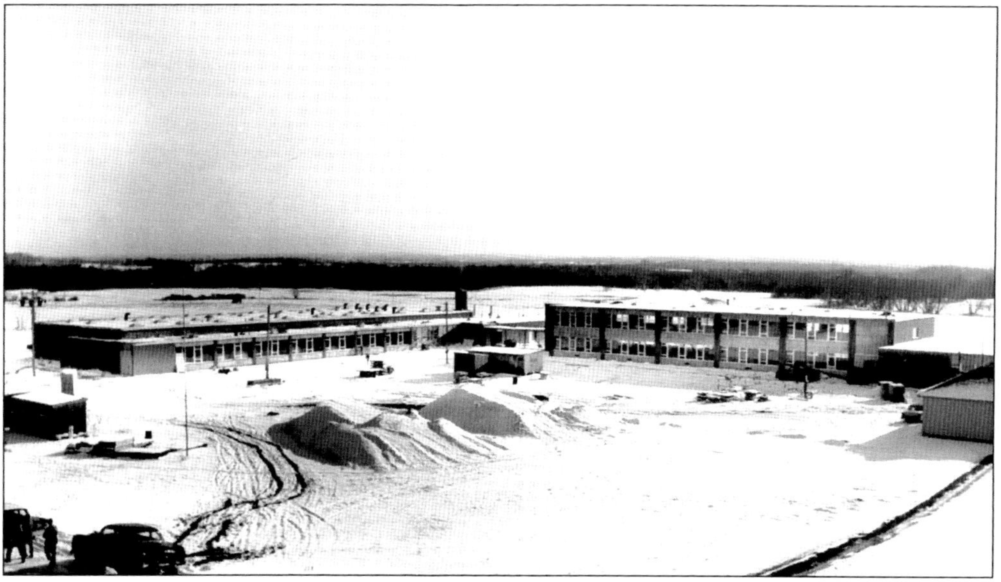

By the mid-1950s, educators were anticipating the arrival of the baby boomers, and another building initiative was planned for the SUNY ATI campus. Between 1958 and 1960, three more buildings were added. This photograph, taken late in the construction phase, shows the single-story technology lab building to the left and the two-story technology classroom building to the right. The low single-story building to the right of the classroom building is the new library.

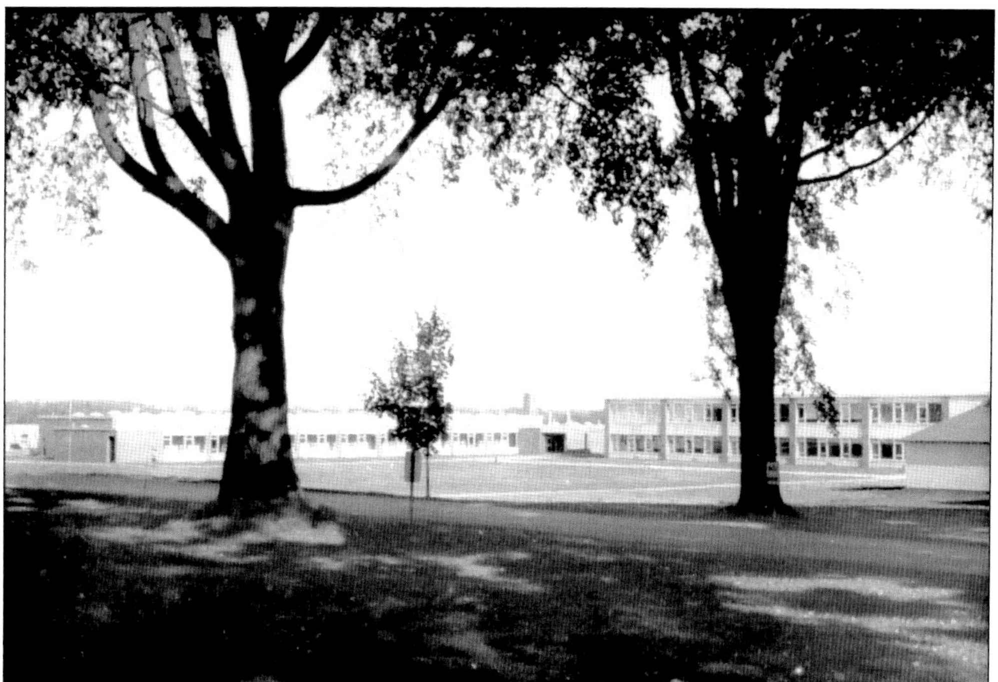

This picturesque view of the new industrial buildings at SUNY ATI was taken shortly before the open house celebrating their official opening.

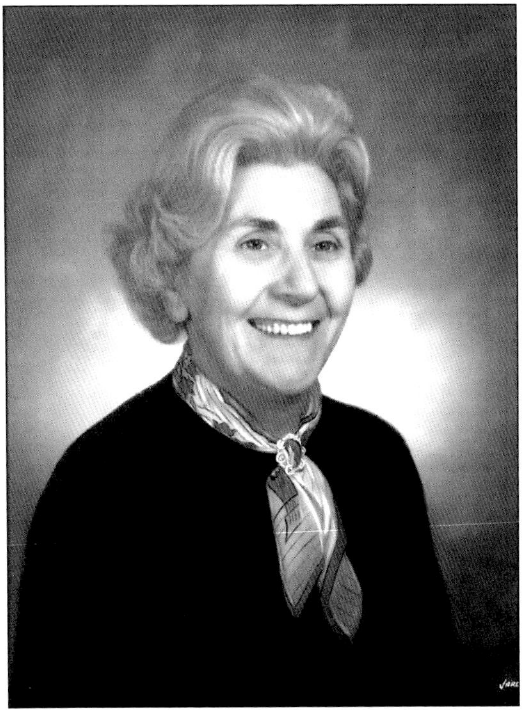

This portrait of Mary Overlease, then Mary G. Parker and later Mary Wurster, the ATI librarian from 1949–1970, hangs in the Southworth Library. During her tenure, the library was moved twice. The first time was on the old campus, when the industrial building opened. In the late 1960s, the library would move again to its current home.

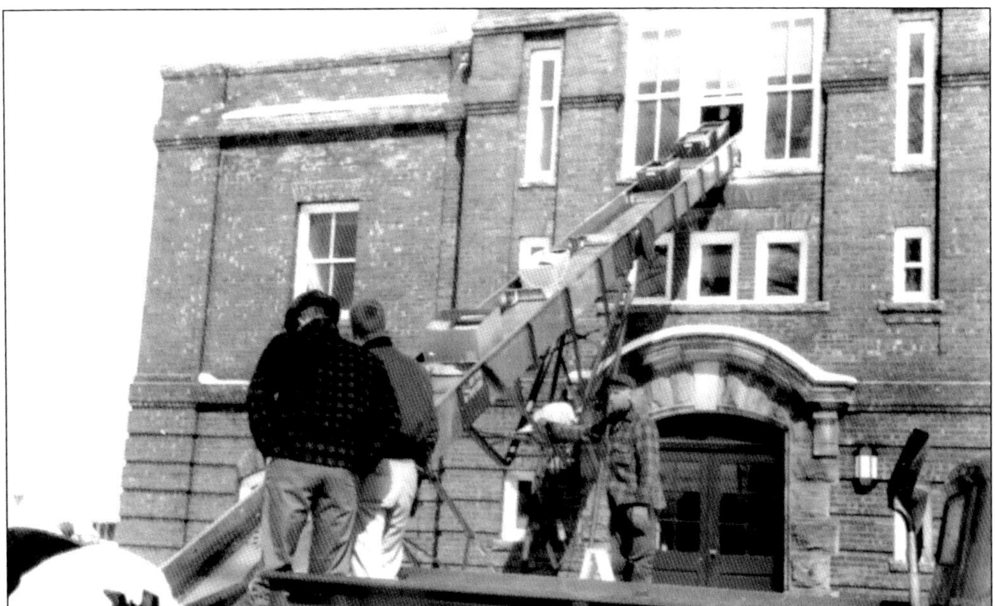

When it was time to move the library from the third floor of Cook Hall to new quarters in the industrial building, a hay elevator was used. Here books are being sent down the hay elevator and loaded on a pickup truck for moving.

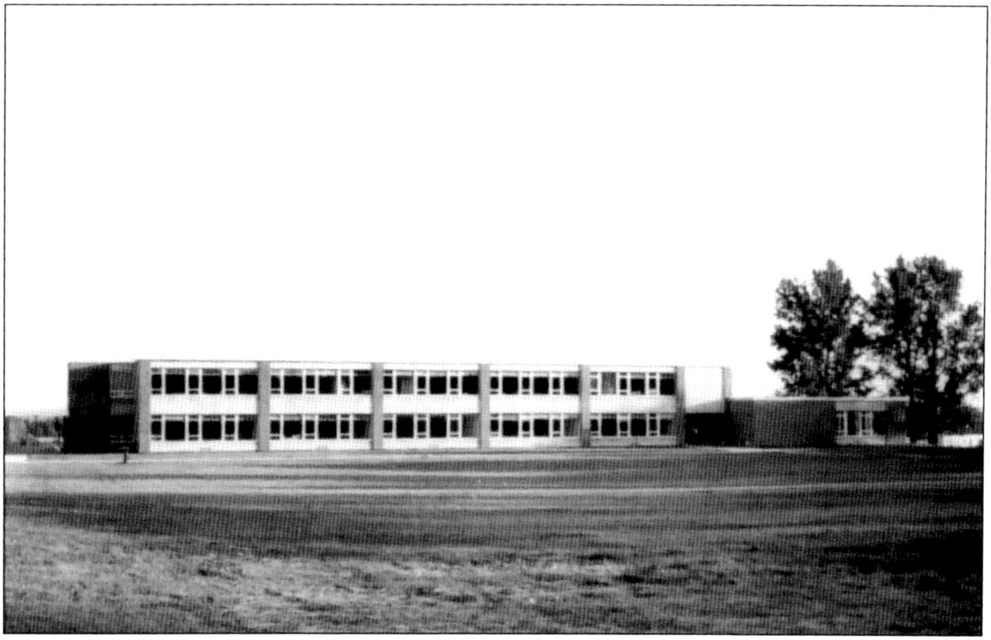

The new library is the low, single-story building to the right surrounded by trees.

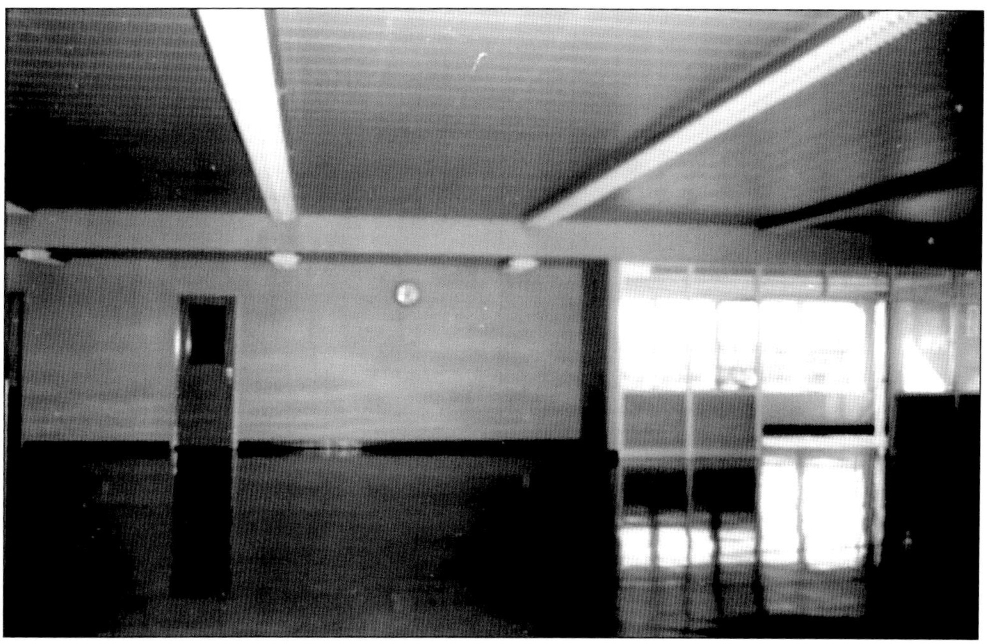

This is a rare photograph of the interior of the new library in the industrial building. In a few short years, the whole SUNY ATI campus was turned over to St. Lawrence University. This space became known as the Valentine Reading Room and housed the science library until the mid-1990s. The Launders Science Library now occupies the upper floor of Madill Hall.

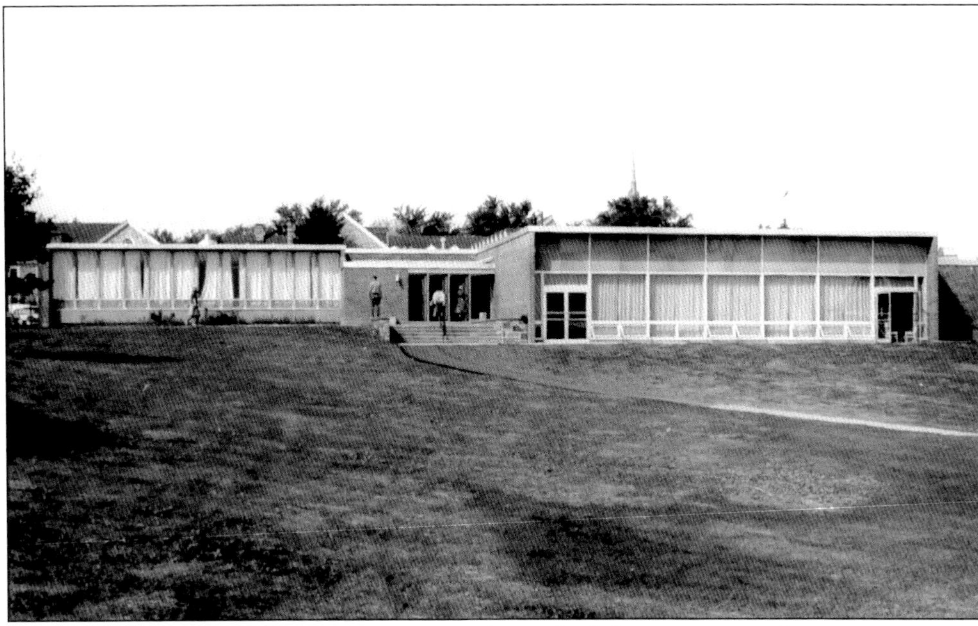

The other part of the building project at the end of the 1950s was the construction of Alumni Hall between Cook Hall and the farm shop. It housed the student lounge and cafeteria. Today the building that was once Alumni Hall now houses the health center and campus security for St. Lawrence University.

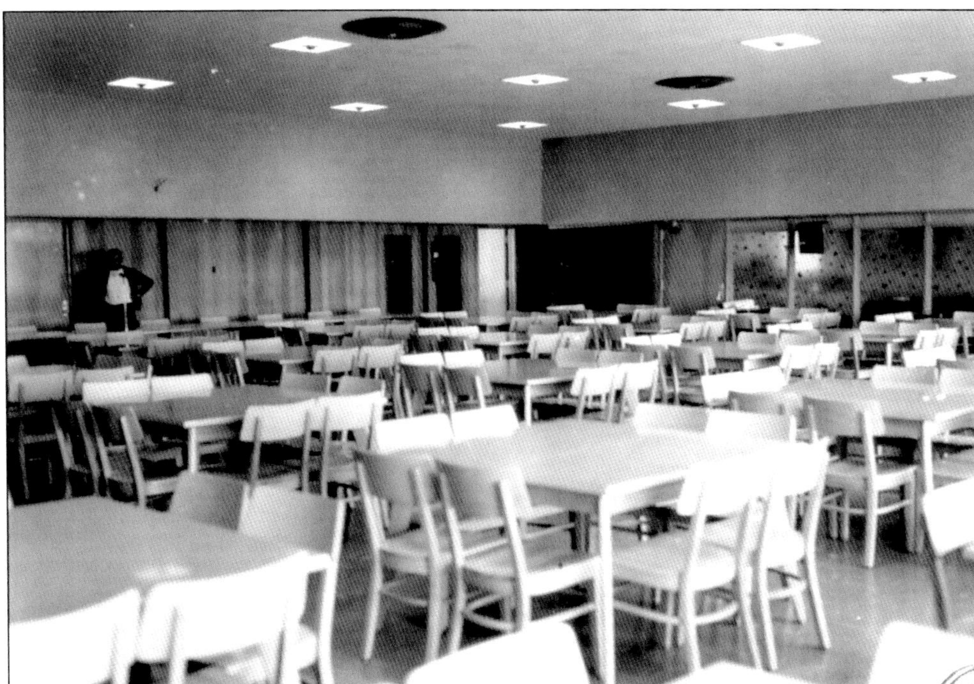

The new cafeteria in Alumni Hall was spacious compared to the small, narrow facility that had previously been used.

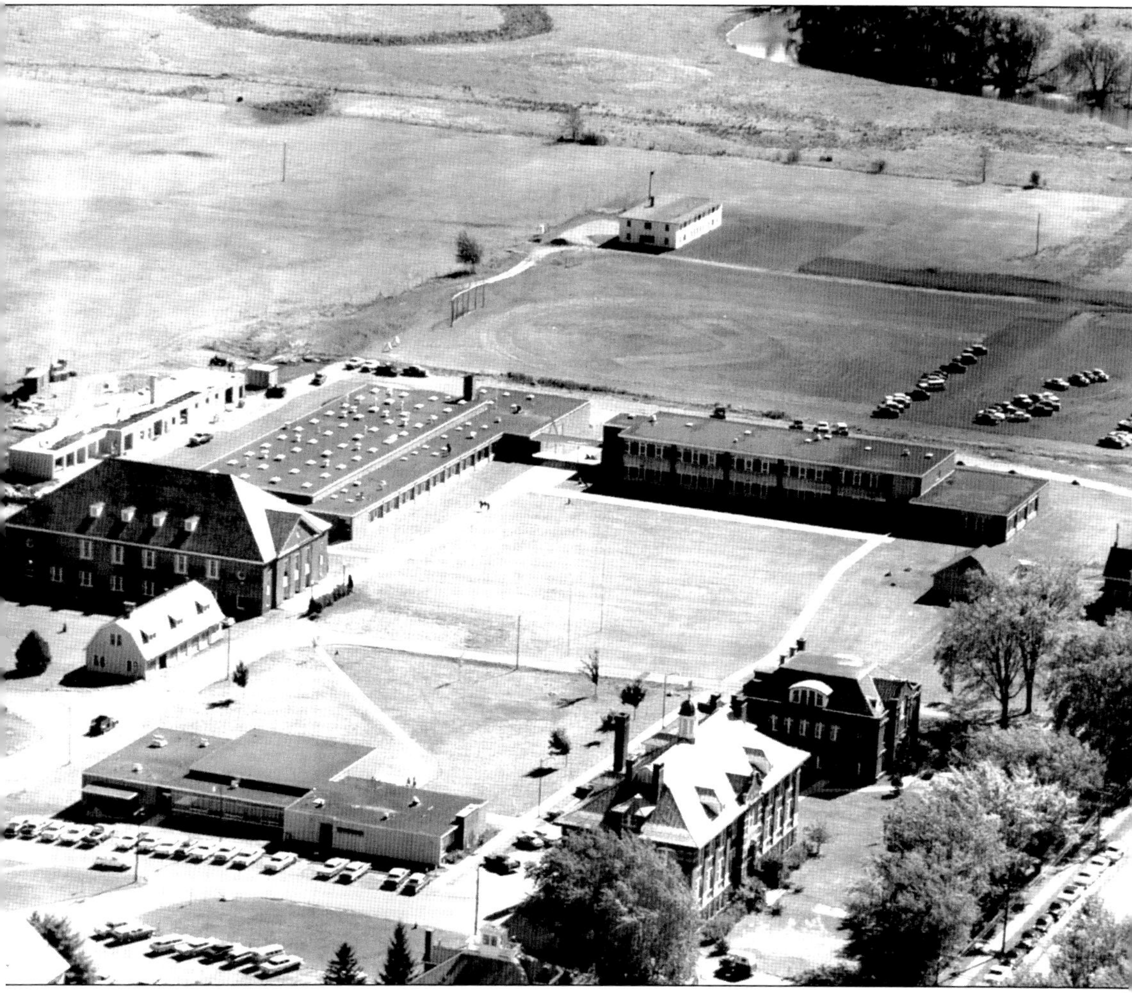

The SUNY ATI campus is shown as it was at the end of its final building phase at the old campus. Alumni Hall, the industrial building, and the library have been added. Note that the poultry building has been torn down to make room for the industrial laboratory building. No sooner than the construction projects were over, it was announced that SUNY ATI would leave its location on the St. Lawrence University campus. Suddenly the future and very existence of the institution were in question again. There was talk of moving the college out of Canton. A delegation to Albany received assurances that the SUNY ATI would stay in Canton. Canton businessman Edson Martin gave the State of New York farm property on the northwestern edge of Canton in order to ensure the college did not leave the community.

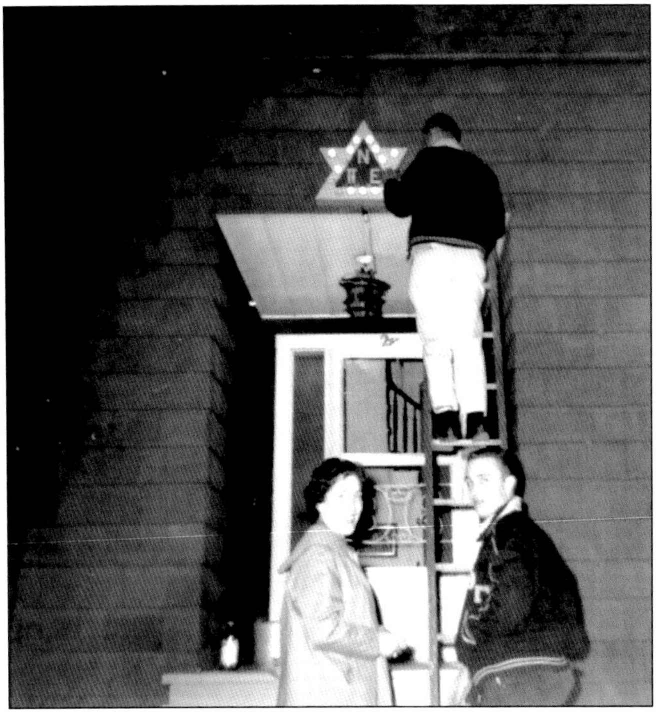

The Pi Nu Epsilon sorority was located on Hodskin Street. Two members of Alpha Theta Gamma fraternity, Andrew Widay (on the ladder) and Paul Bisaillon (standing), are cleaning the sign and replacing light bulbs. They were making amends for taking the bulbs as a prank. Pi Nu Epsilon president Phyllis Snyder Shimmel looks on. This photograph was taken in the fall of 1960. (Courtesy of Phyllis Snyder Shimmel.)

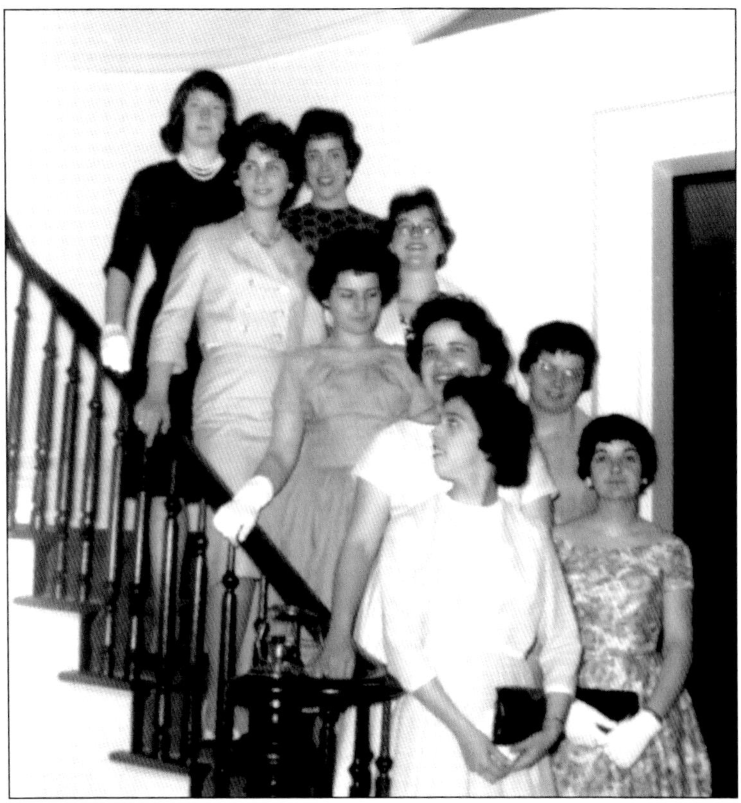

Senior members of the Pi Nu Epsilon sorority had their picture taken in June 1961 before heading off to the senior banquet. Standing next to the railing, from top to bottom, are Patricia Mooney, Virginia Tetro, Judy Felio, Norma Green, and Doris Peterson. In the other row, from top to bottom, are Phyllis Snyder, Madeline Martin, Sandra Hall, and Janice David. (Courtesy of Phyllis Snyder Shimmel.)

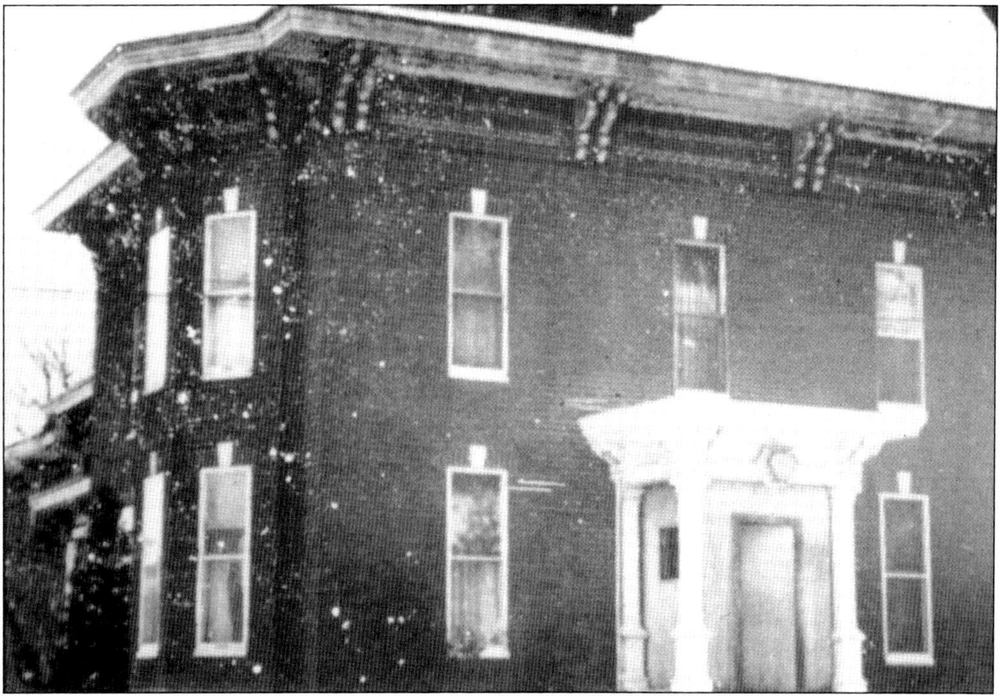

The Alpha Chi Omicron House was located at 19 Hodskin Street.

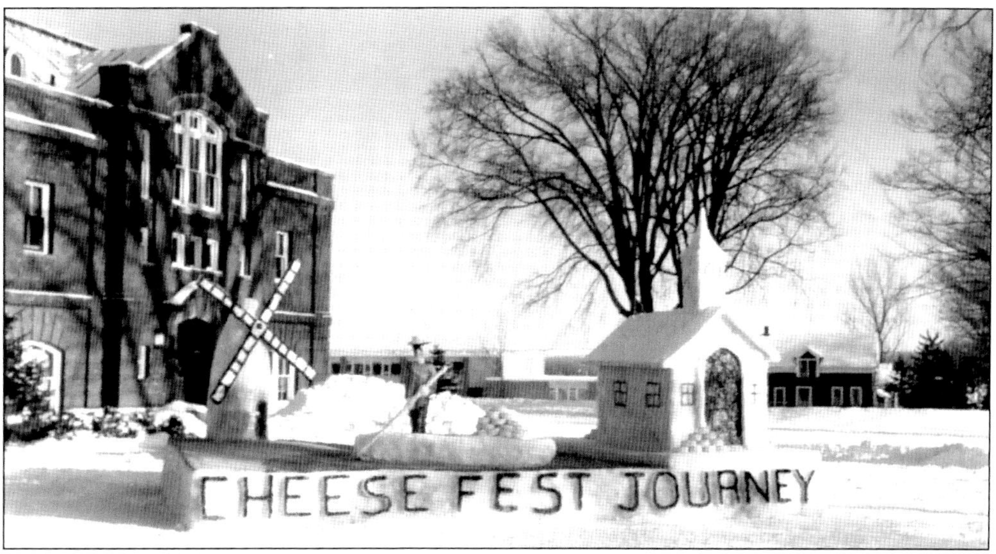

The Cheese Fest Journey snow sculpture was part of the Winter Weekend in February 1963. In the background is the dairy building, later known as Payson Hall.

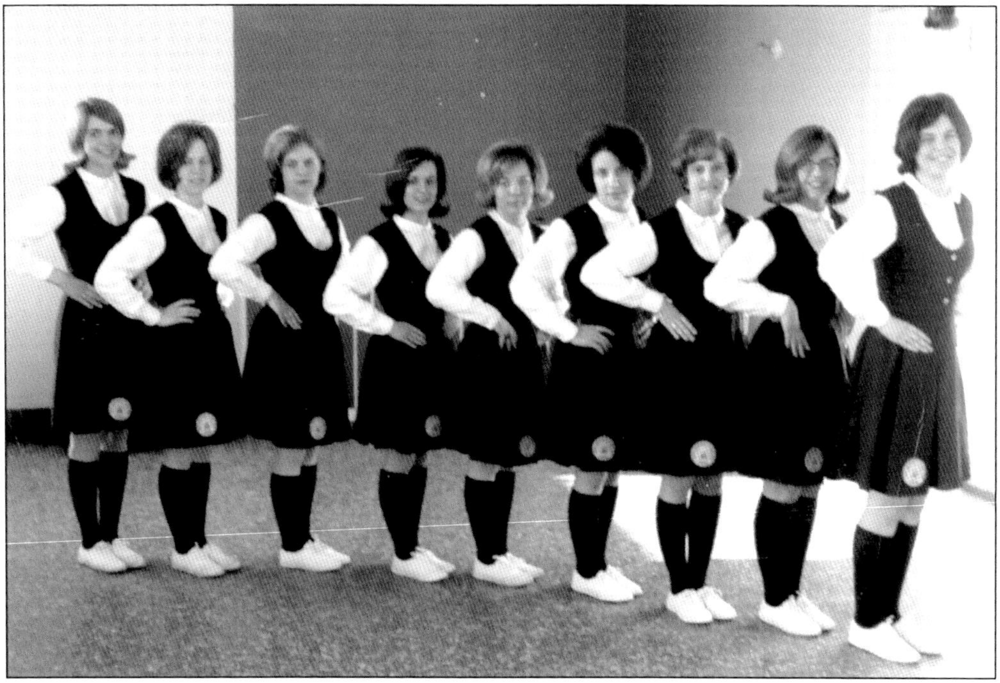

The 1964–1965 cheerleading squad had their yearbook picture taken. Pictured, from left to right, are Peggy Hopkins, Sandi De Wolfe, Sandy Coor, Noreen Brassard, Donna DuVall, Mary Ellen LaDuke, Jean Mascali, Shelia, and Nancy Kall.

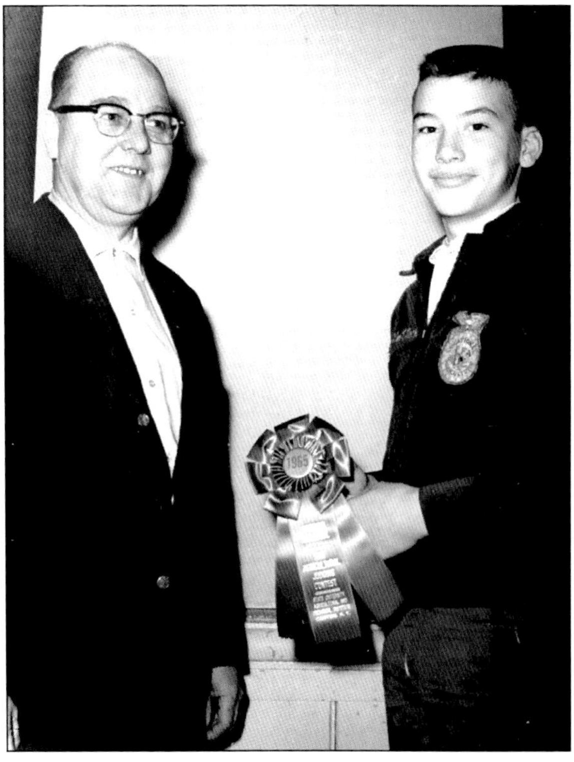

Even though most activities took place at the farm, agriculture still had an active role to play. In 1965, the dairy judging contest was held for the 51st time, and Robert Johnston (right) of Gouverneur received an award. That same year, the college's name changed for the fourth time in its 59-year history. Canton ATI became SUNY Agricultural and Technical College at Canton.

Concern about growing U.S. involvement in the Vietnam War was shared on campus as well as elsewhere around the nation. Petition drives such as this one, which was held on the old campus, were common.

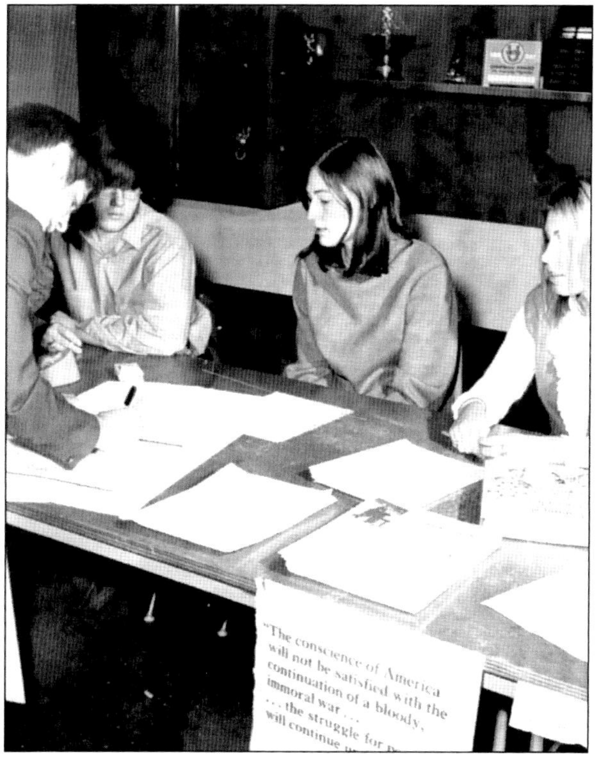

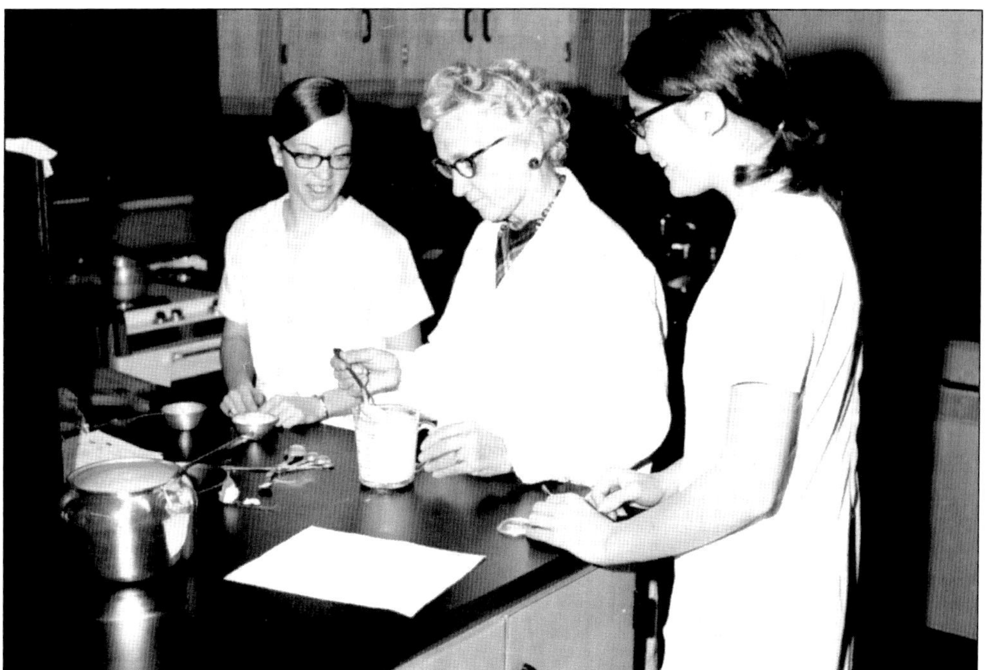

Alice Martin works with two unidentified students in the food lab in the mid- to late 1960s.

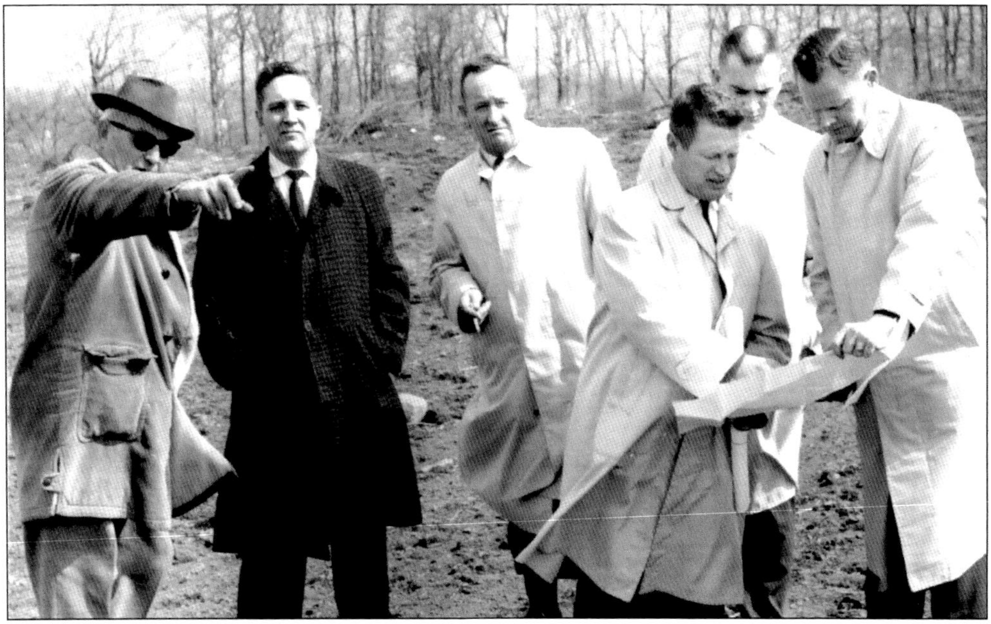

Construction on the new campus started in 1965. It was a huge undertaking that took three years to complete. The new campus was dedicated in 1968. The photograph shows, from left to right, Edson Martin, Glenn Wright, Hugh Quinn, and Bill Cooper, along with two unidentified state officials discussing construction plans and progress.

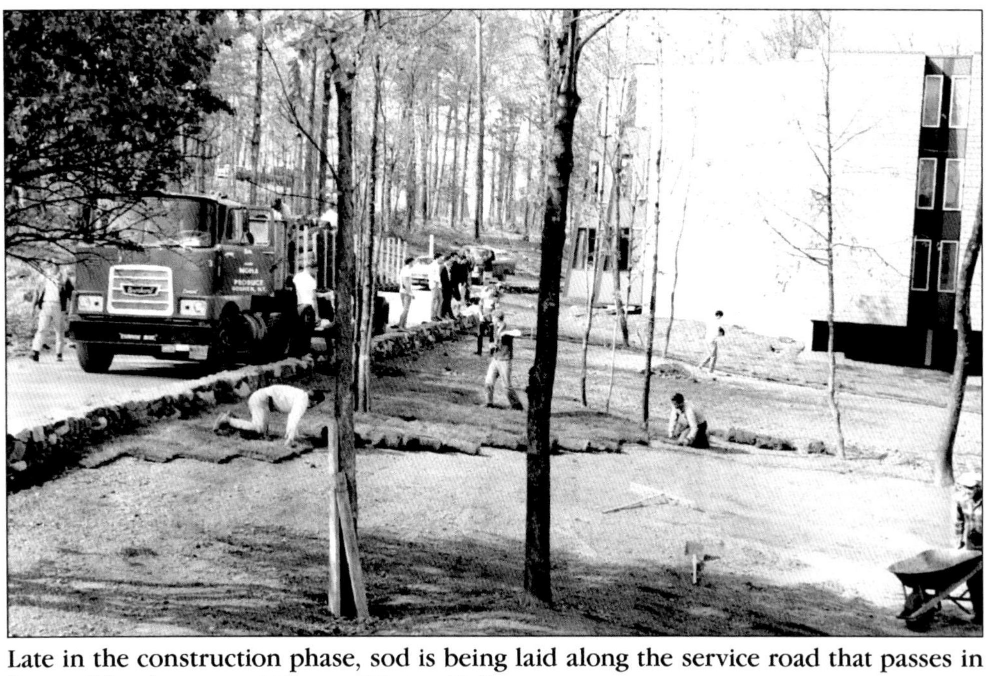

Late in the construction phase, sod is being laid along the service road that passes in front of the dorms and Chaney Dining Hall.

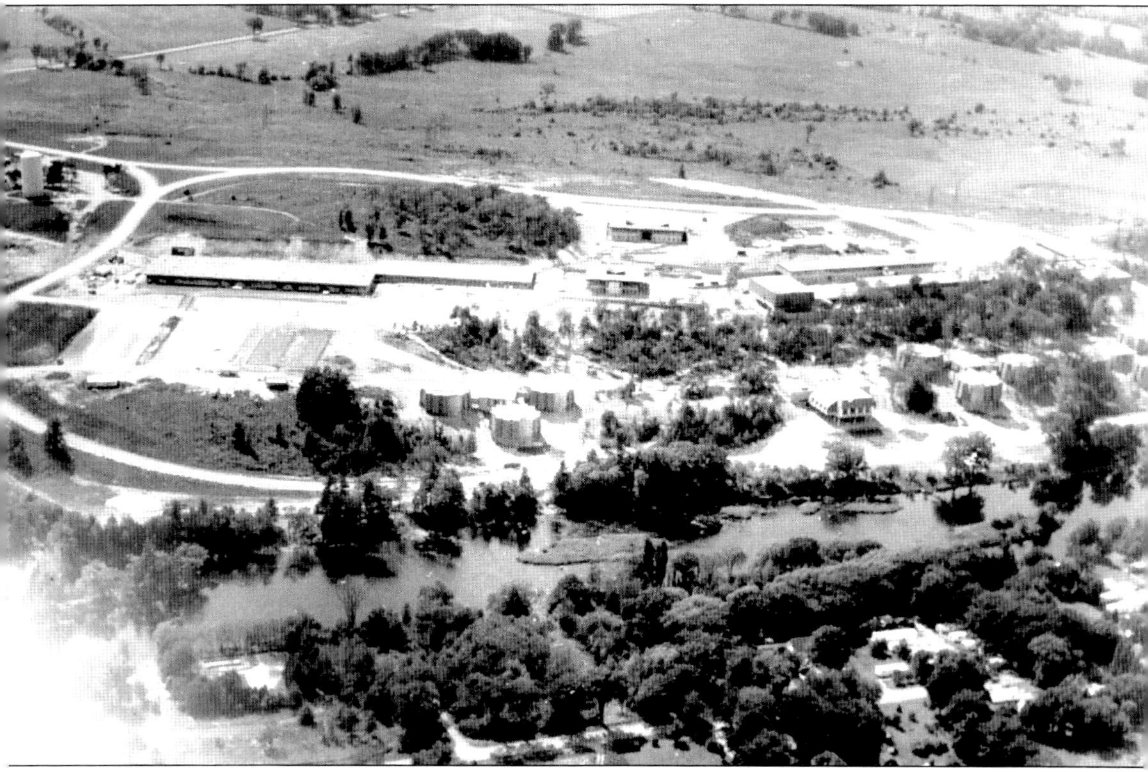

This aerial photograph shows the new campus as being very much a work in progress. Plenty of dirt is still visible. There is no service complex or faculty office building. Nonetheless, the main part of the campus is clearly discernible with the dorms and Chaney Dining Center along the river and the academic buildings, administration building, and the library further up the hill.

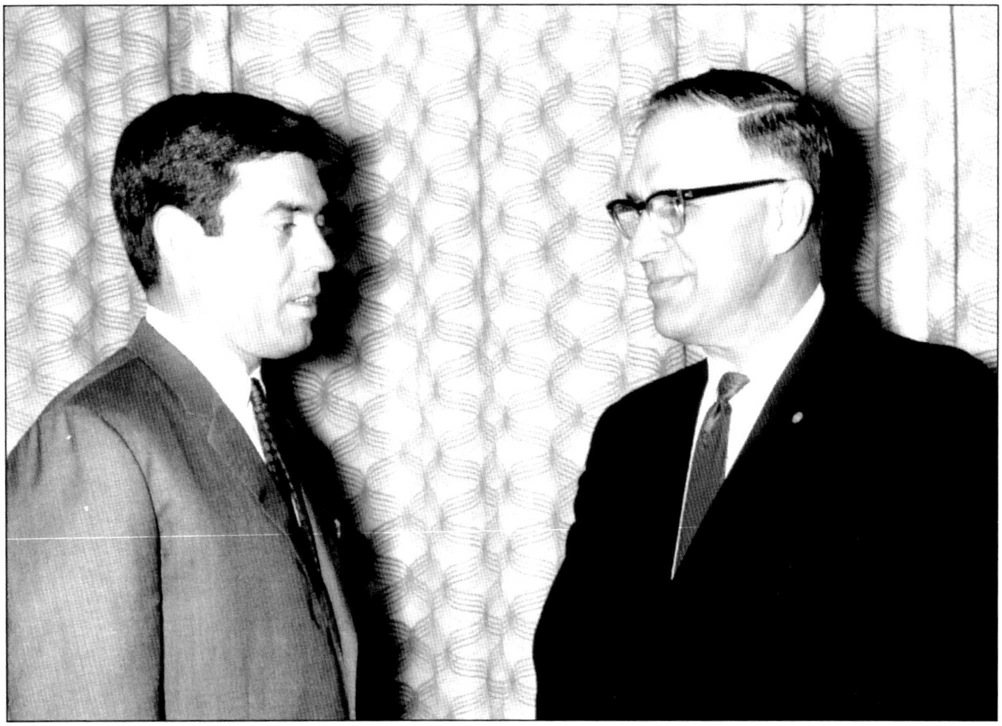

CBS newsman Dan Rather visited campus in 1967. Here he shares a word with college president Dr. Albert French.

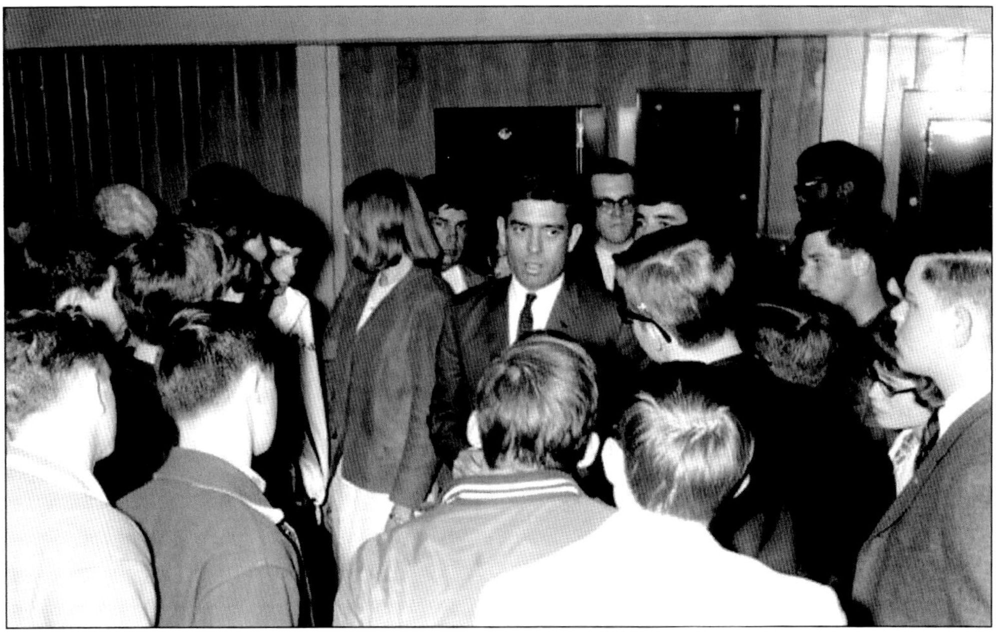

Dan Rather meets with SUNY Agricultural and Technical College (ATC) students during his campus visit. Visits from big name speakers to the college happened only occasionally. There was a great deal of interest in Rather's visit, and he was well received.

Five

The First Quarter Century on a Different Campus 1968–1992

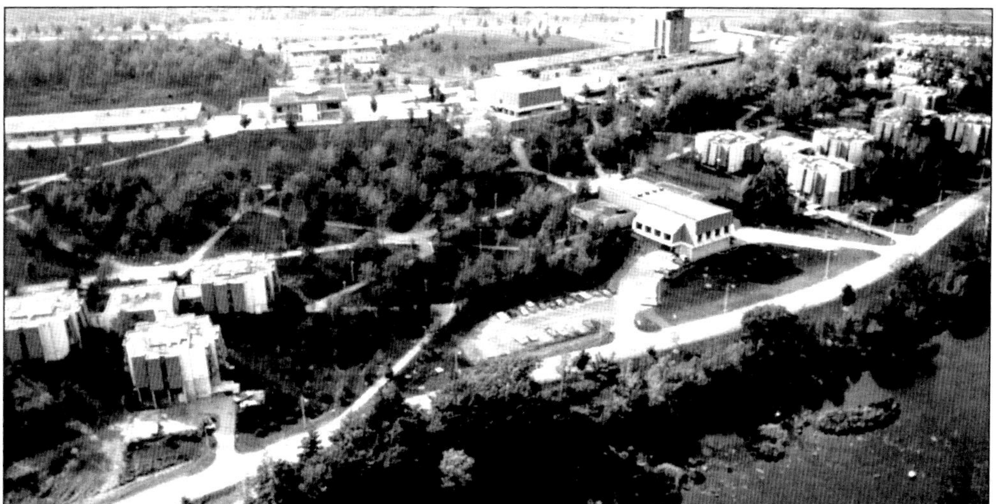

This aerial photograph captures the new campus as it looked for most of the two decades between 1968 and 1988. Note that the faculty office building appears in this picture for the first time. In the early 1970s, budget constraints led to empty faculty lines and delayed or cancelled some construction projects.

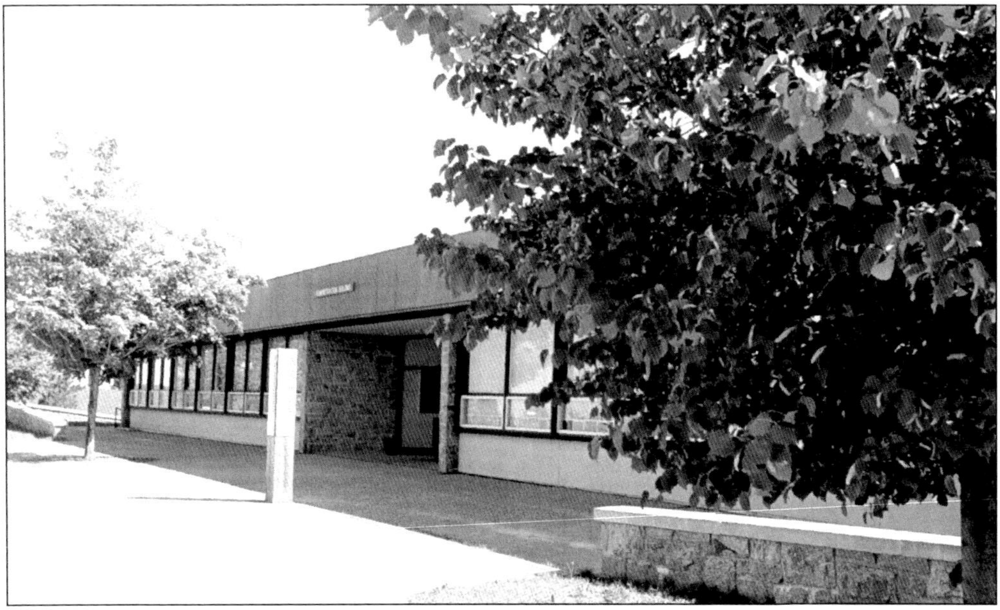

French Hall was the administration building during the years that Dr. French and Dr. MacArthur served as president of the college. The semicircular driveway and parking area were attractive features of the campus. Located at the top of the hill, the offices on the back side of French Hall overlooked the rest of the campus. In 1997, campus administration offices moved to the sixth floor of the faculty office building.

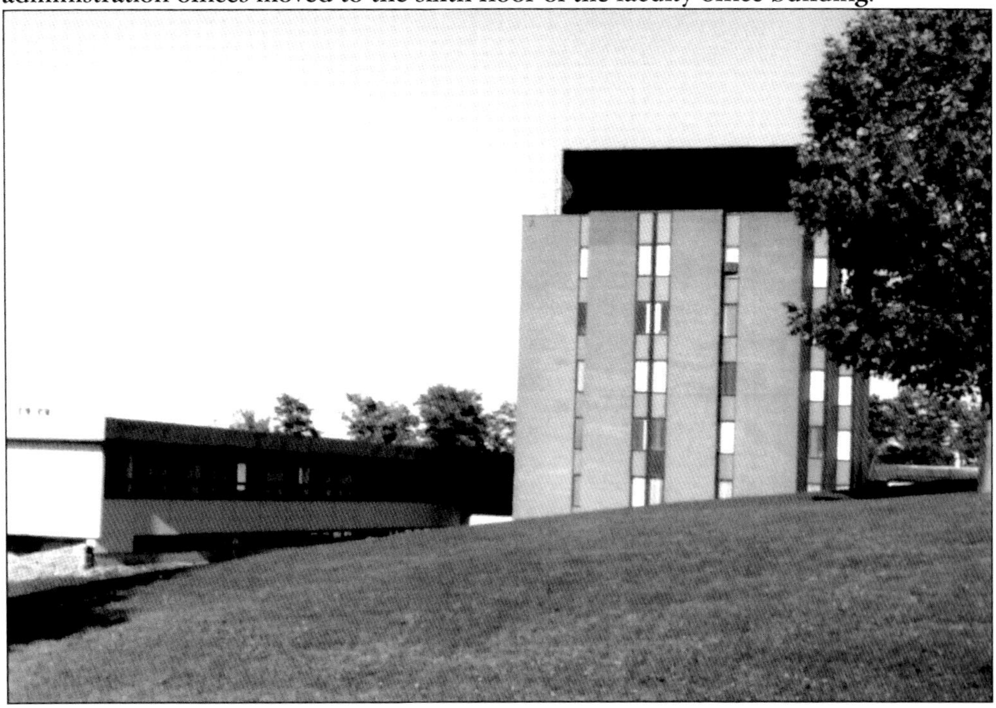

Wicks Hall is on the left, and the faculty office building is on the right. The two buildings are attached. Wicks Hall was named after Rollo Wicks, who led general education for many years.

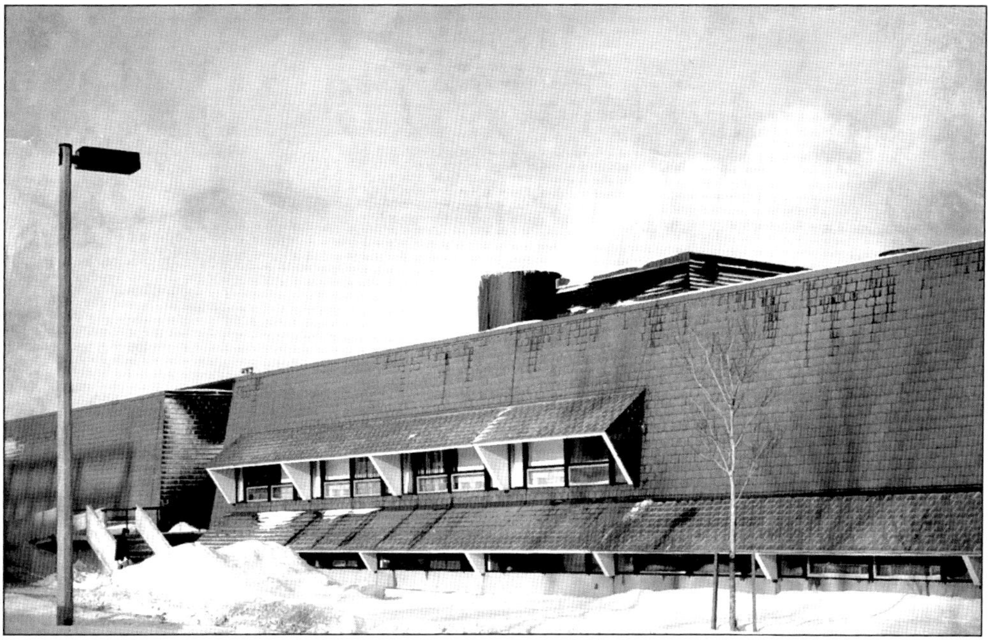

Dana Hall houses the gym, pool, and other athletic facilities. Various sporting events are held in the building, which is at the far end of the campus from State Route 68. The college's commencement exercises are held in Dana Hall. Canton High School also uses the facility for their graduation.

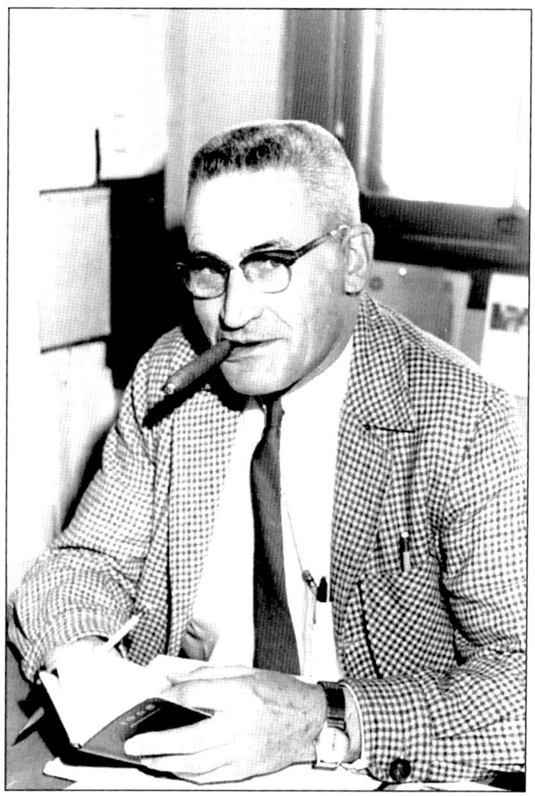

Dana Hall is named after Evan Dana, who was affiliated with the college for 40 years. He taught agriculture and chaired the department.

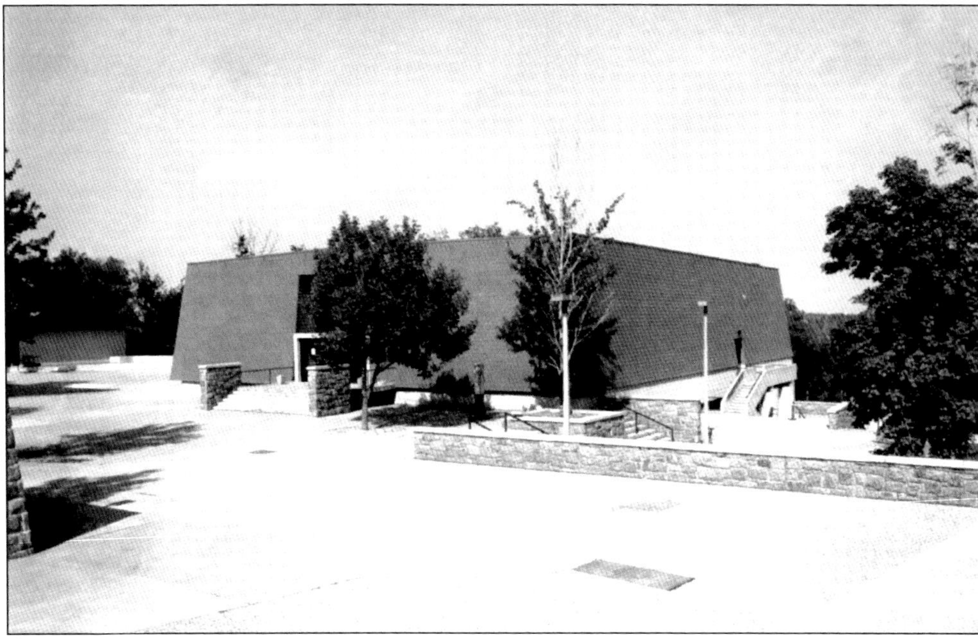

Kingston Theater was located on the plaza between Southworth Library to the south and Cook and Payson Halls to the north. It burned in July 1997 while the first campus center was under construction. Faculty meetings were often held in the theater, as were numerous group events, such as plays.

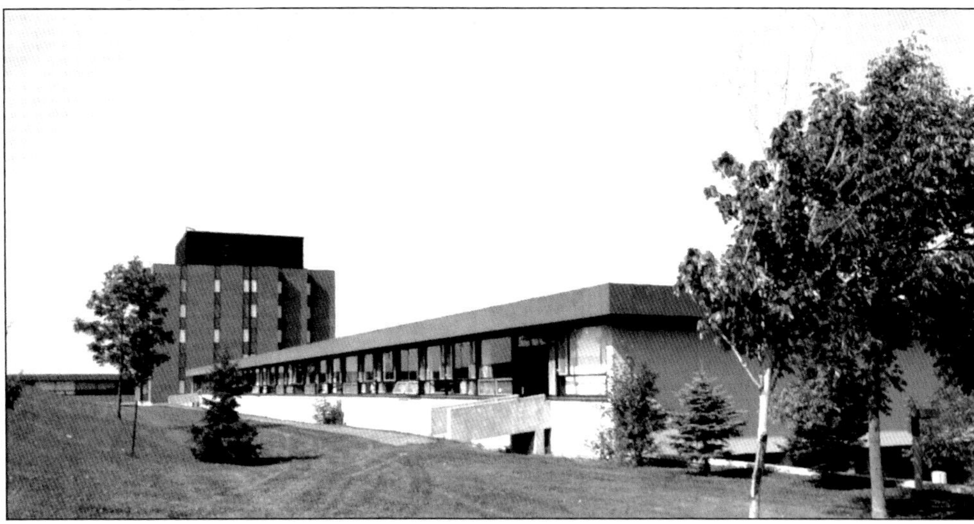

Since much of campus is built into a hillside, many of the buildings have two elevations. Pictured here is the upper elevation of Cook Hall, with the faculty office building in the background. The first floors of the two buildings are connected to one another. The lower level of Cook Hall opens on the plaza and is adjacent to Payson Hall. Cook Hall was named after Dr. Herbert Cook, who was director of the School of Agriculture from 1908–1917. The first building erected on the old campus was named after him. Until the 1990s, there were Cook Halls on both the SUNY Canton and St. Lawrence University campuses. On the latter campus, Cook Hall has been renamed to honor another president, Dr. Frank Piskor.

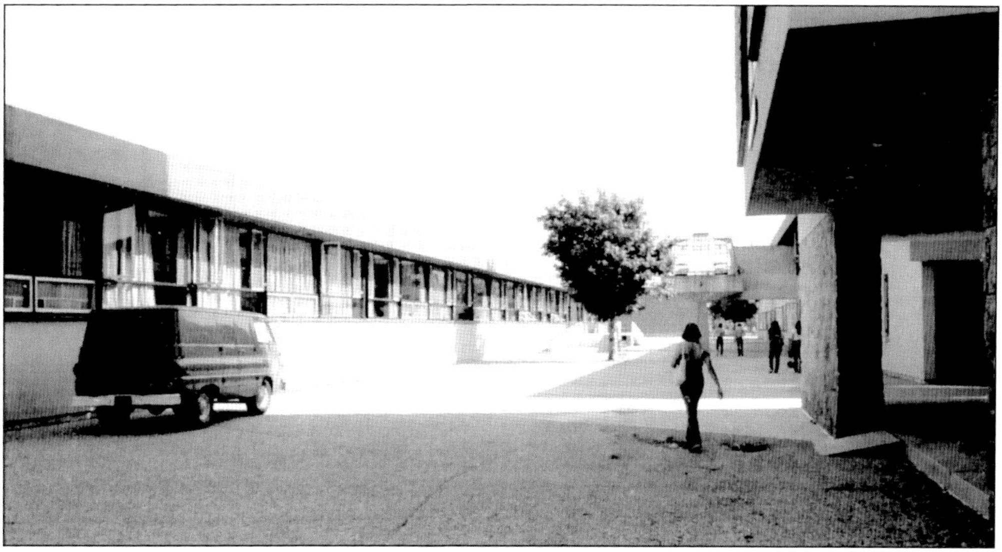

Payson Hall was named in honor of Dr. James Payson, who worked at the School of Agriculture for 22 years. There still remains a Payson Hall on the St. Lawrence University campus today. SUNY Canton's Payson Hall can be seen here on the left. It too has a lower elevation. To the right, the corner of the overhang for the faculty office building can be seen. The tower greenhouse can be seen in the distance, to the right of the tree on the plaza, its glass sides reflected in the sunlight. The greenhouse was removed during the renovation of the plaza between Cook and Payson Halls in the summer of 2000.

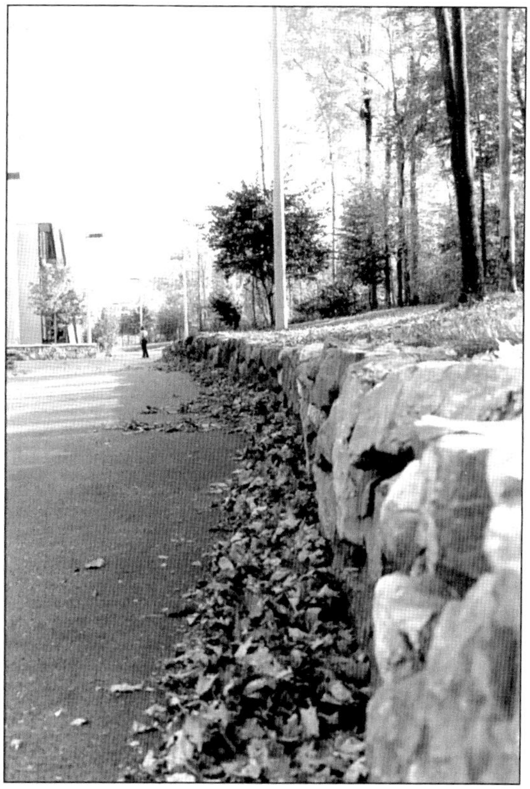

This fall scene was taken on the new SUNY Canton campus near the dorms, along the lower service road that also doubles as a walkway.

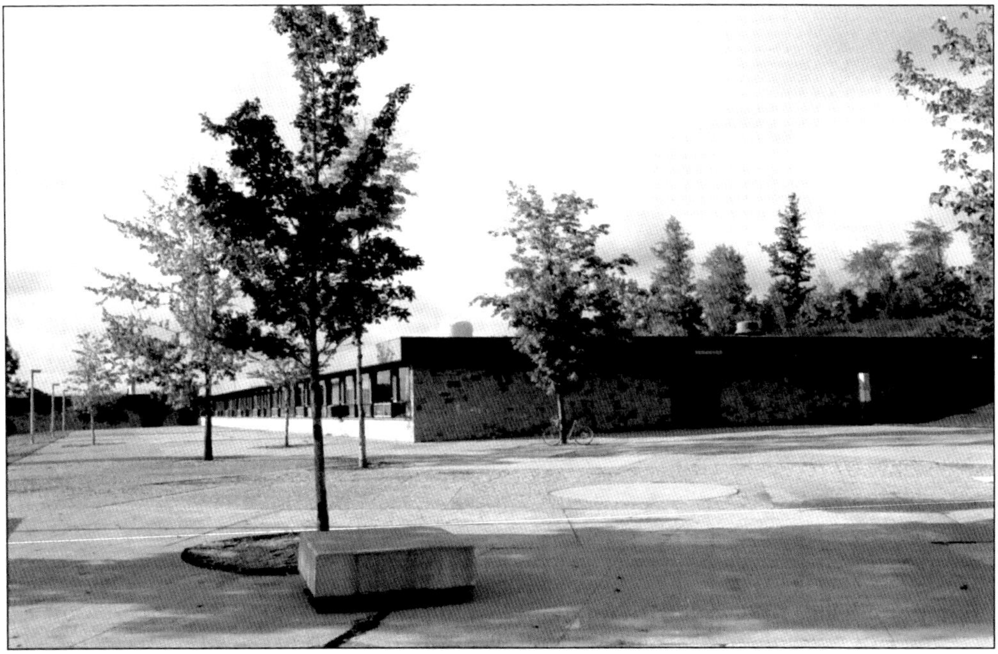

Nevaldine North Hall, as viewed from the plaza near Southworth Library, is pictured here. The north end of Nevaldine South can be seen in the background. The new technology and engineering buildings were named after Peter Nevaldine, who did much to shape the development of the college between his arrival in 1937 and his retirement in 1973.

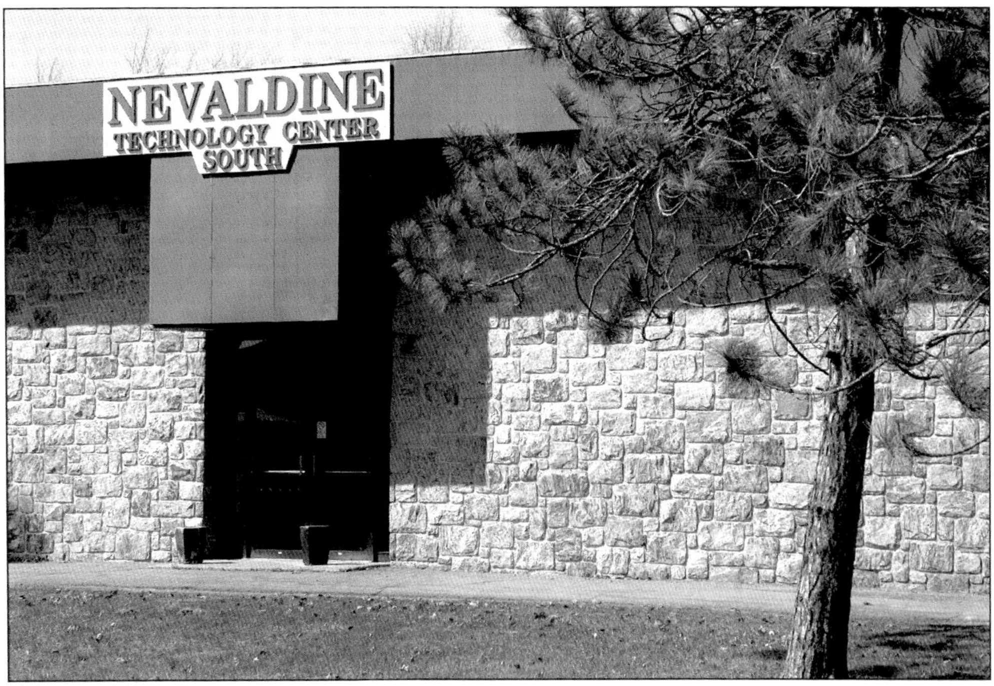

This recent picture shows the south end of Nevaldine South, which houses the automotive, motorsports, building trades, heating and plumbing, and air conditioning programs. Nevaldine North houses the engineering-related programs.

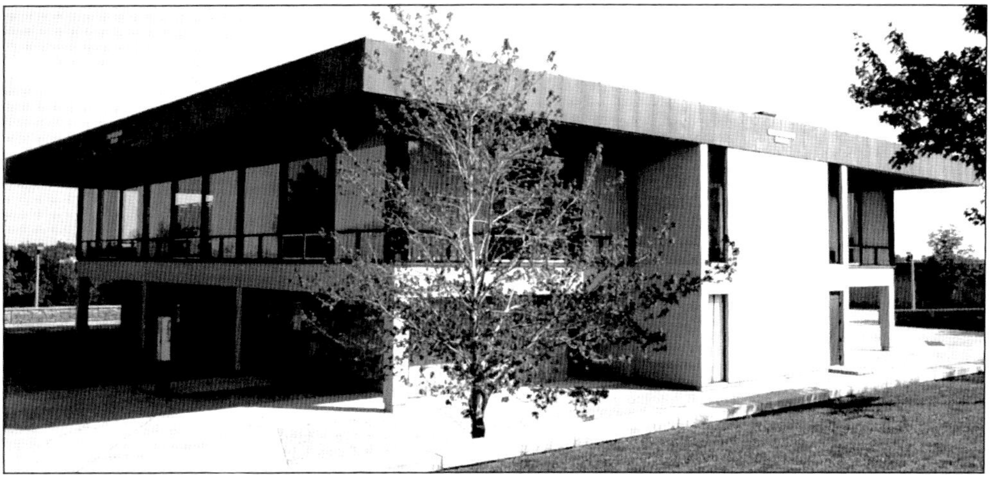

Southworth Library was named after Lottie Southworth, one of the important women in the early history of the college. She was a student at the School of Agriculture in 1918, after graduating from St. Lawrence University in 1914. She later returned to teach at the School of Agriculture in 1924, retiring in 1945. This is an early picture of the library.

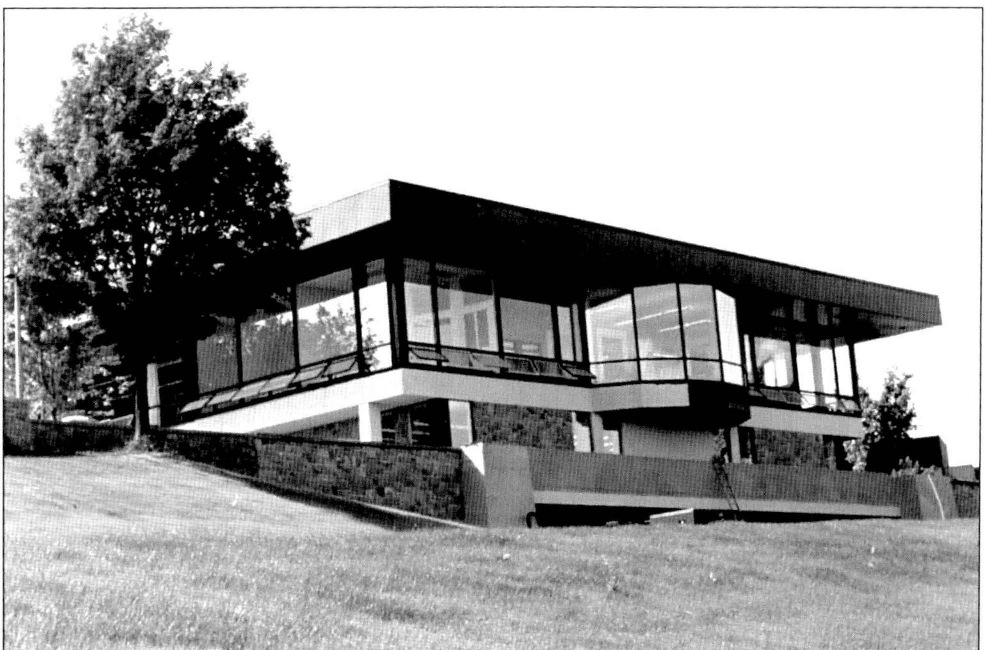

This later photograph of the library shows an addition of several thousand square feet, including a huge bay window, in the late 1980s. From the window seating area, there is a striking view of the village of Canton across the river. The steeples of St. Mary's Church, the county courthouse, Gunnison Chapel, and Waterman Hill, a northern foothill of the Adirondacks, are all visible.

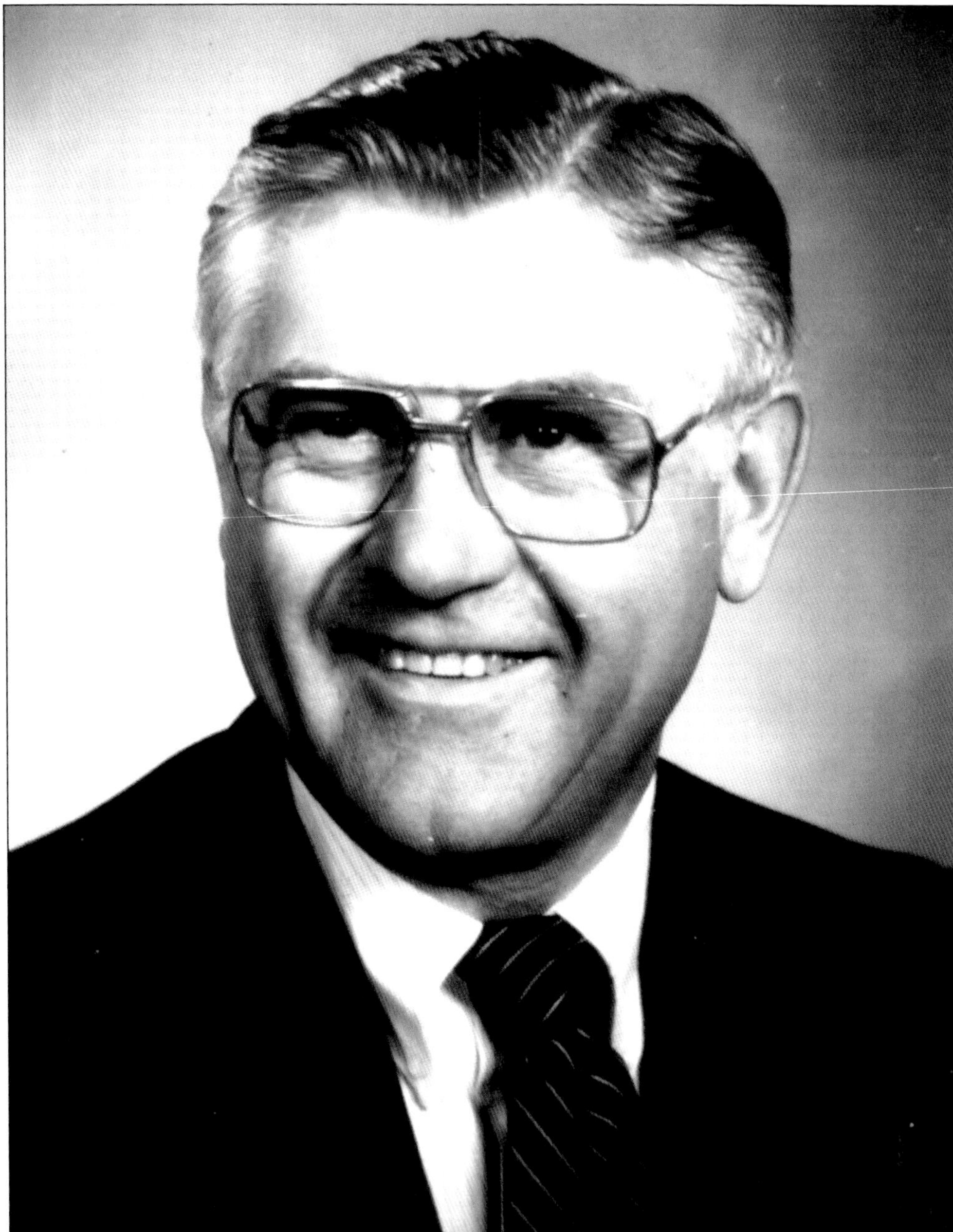

Dr. Earl MacArthur became president of SUNY ATC at Canton in 1972 and served until 1992. He had previously directed the continuing education program at Delhi. In 1971, enrollment had been 2077, and by 1975, enrollment reached 2833. With the winding down of the baby boom generation, maintaining enrollment numbers became increasingly difficult. Despite these challenges, Dr. MacArthur had many accomplishments, including founding the Canton College Foundation and the Office of Sponsored Research. He was also an advocate for the Educational Opportunity Program and computer literacy. His years of service and accomplishment were honored with the college's Distinguished Citizen Award in May 2005.

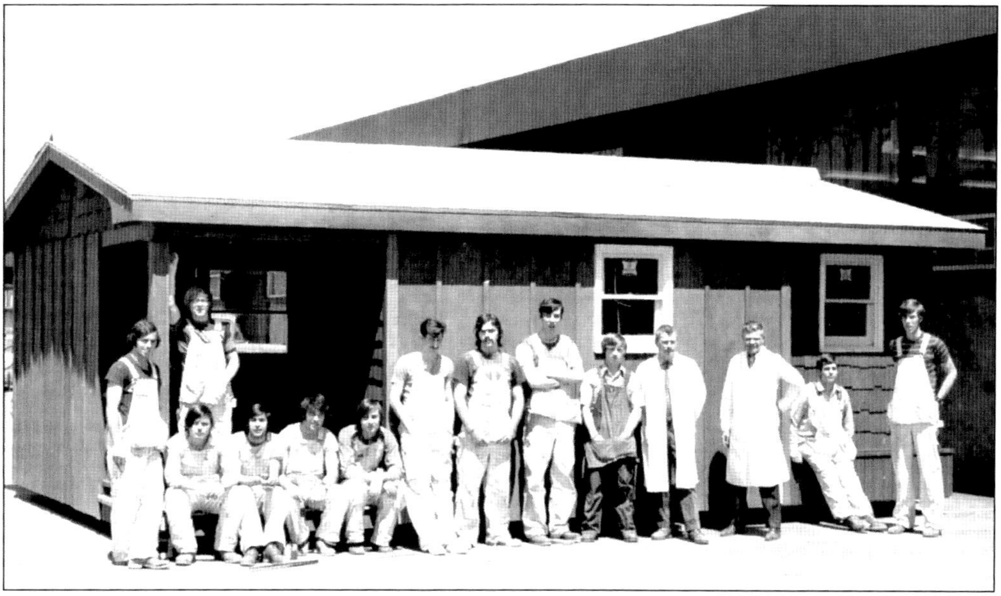

Again, the practical aspects of the college's programs are shown in this photograph of the one-year construction certificate program. Instructor Art Hibbard and technical assistant Bob Belyea, along with their class, stand in front of a building built by students. Projects such as this continue to this day.

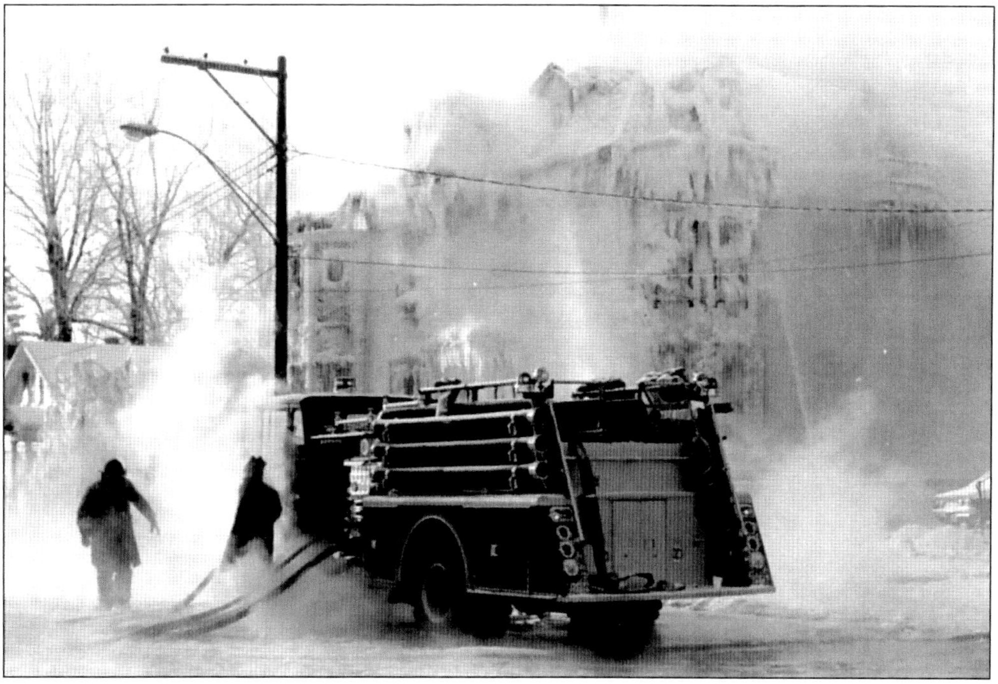

The former Mitchell Hall, which was the Zeta Alpha Phi fraternity house at the time, located at 34 Park Street, burned on a frigid January morning in the early to mid-1970s, turning it into an ice palace. Pictured here are firefighters hosing down the building. Today a newer building housing a local real estate business is located on this site. Note that the Old Lantern building next door remained unscathed.

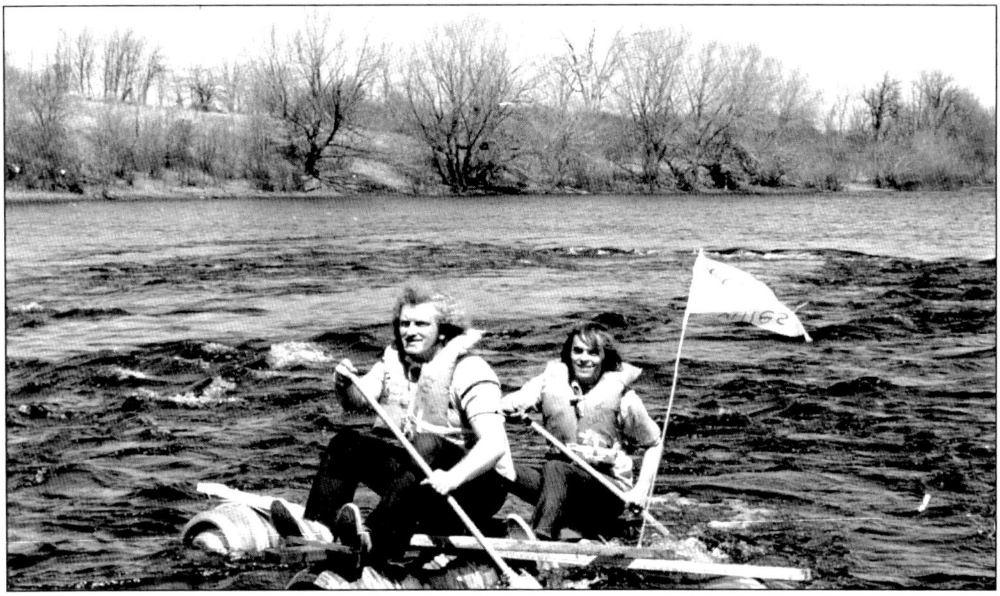

Raft races were popular for many years. Either too much water or too little water sometimes created logistical problems. Here the water is high. Ingenuity and improvisation have always been a part of college life. This raft was made of beer kegs and two by fours. The student in the front is using a broom as a paddle.

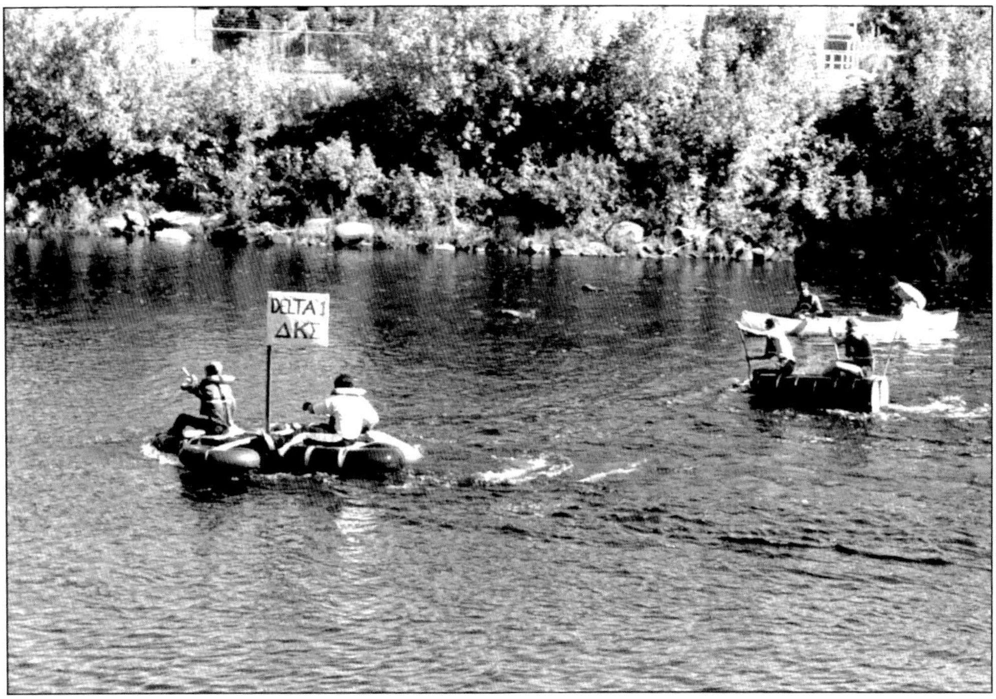

Low water sometimes led to the cancellation of raft races, but not when this picture was taken. One raft was made out of inner tubes, and the other was constructed of 55-gallon drums. In the back, someone even used a canoe.

Jean M. Parker became the first woman vice president at SUNY Canton in 1976, when she was appointed vice president for student affairs. She retired in 1984, having served the college for 15 years. At the end of the 20th century and the beginning of the 21st century, both Dr. Dale Bower and Sue Rummel would serve as vice president for academic affairs.

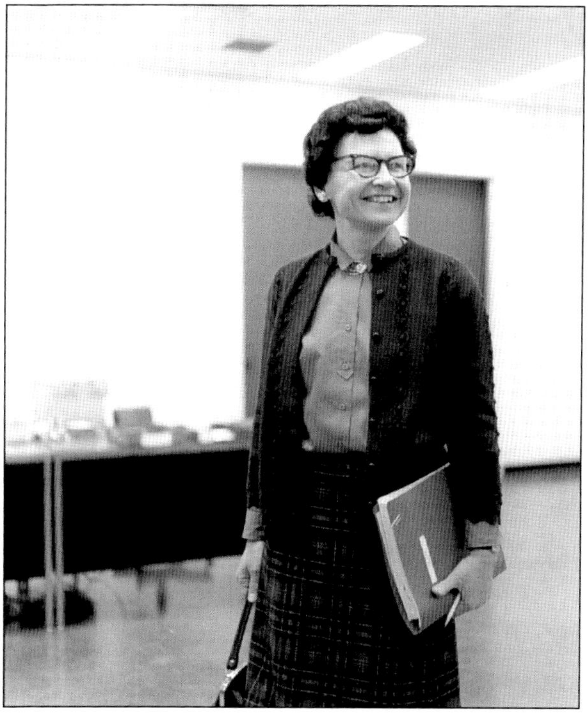

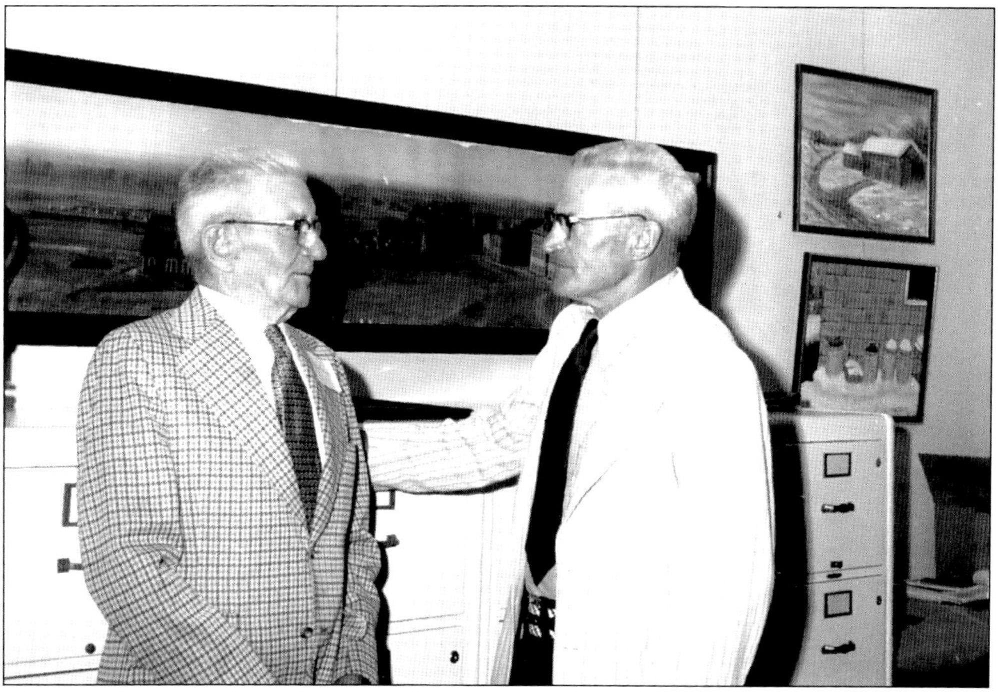

Clement Flanagan, class of 1909, and Evan Dana, class of 1931, talk on Alumni Weekend at SUNY Canton in 1976. It was both the college's 70th anniversary and the nation's bicentennial year.

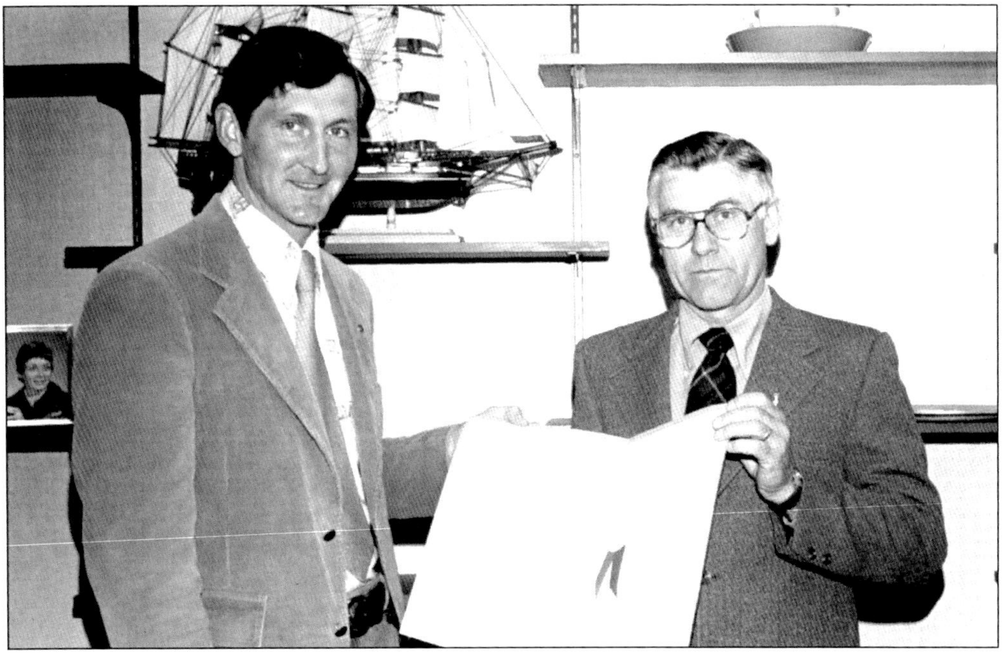

In 1981, assemblyman David Martin and college president Dr. Earl MacArthur display a legislative resolution honoring the 75th anniversary of the founding of SUNY Canton.

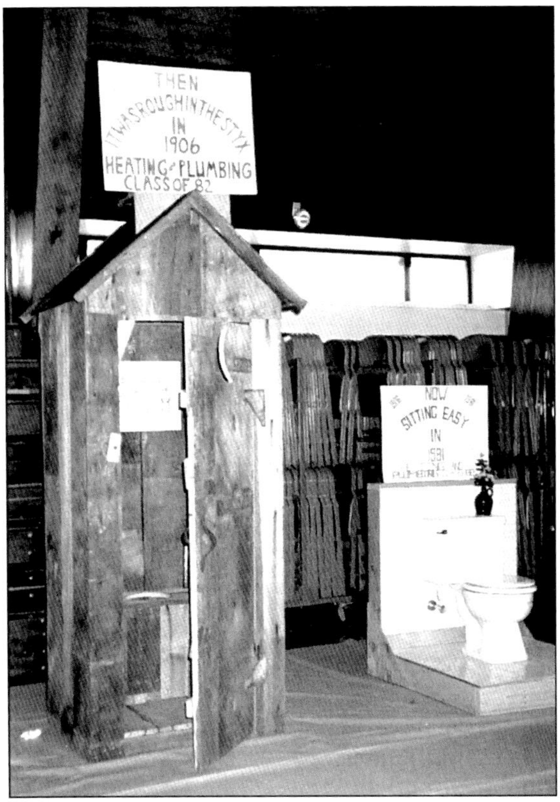

The heating and plumbing class of 1982 had a less decorous, but more humorous, take on the college's diamond anniversary with their display. Historically speaking, it is not exactly true. The early construction of the School of Agriculture between 1907 and 1913 included a sewage treatment plant.

SUNY Canton basketball star Tony Jackson is all smiles as he passed the 1000-point mark on January 25, 1983. Jackson, the college's all-time leading basketball scorer, was not done yet. He finished his college career with 1,257 points. Jackson later served as an admissions counselor for SUNY Canton.

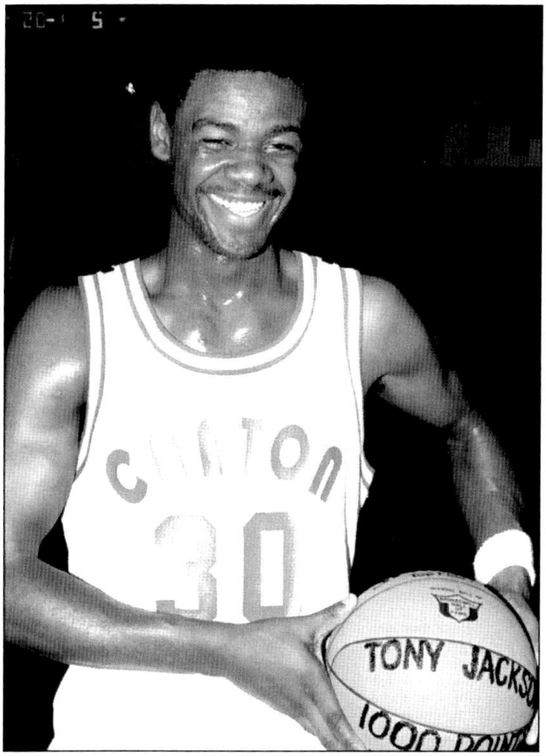

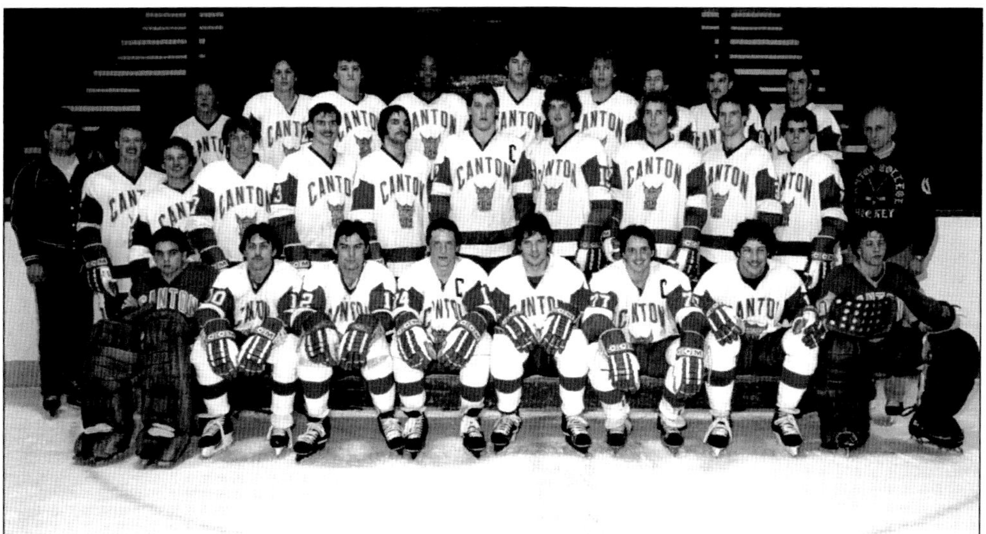

The hockey team had one of its many hockey championships during the 1983 season. Men's hockey arrived at the college relatively late, starting in the 1959–1960 academic year. Pictured here are, from left to right, the following: (first row) Dan Perillo, John Bourbannais, Jim Ward, Gary Matura, Steve McTiernan, Mart Taylor, Ed Lanyi, and Gerry Hourihan; (second row) assistant coach Bill Coakley, Ted Dancy, Terry Gray, Bob Flaro, Jerry Inebnit, Mark Kemp, Guy Hoffbert, Dean McIntosh, Michael Jones, Joe Meager, Tim Trombley, and coach Terry Martin; (third row) Jeff Hunt, Mike Albano, Steve Whyte, Brett Stewart, Ed McCaffrey, Todd Bliss, Bob Stemmler, Jeff Proulx, and Scott Clements.

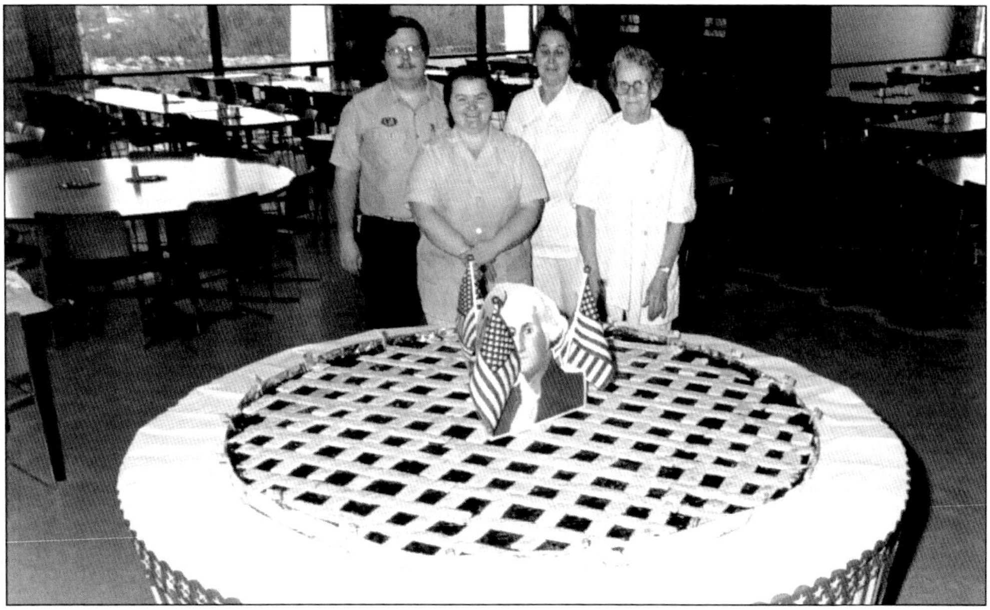

In 1984, Chaney Dining Center workers put together a giant cherry pie for Washington's Birthday at Canton ATC. Pictured, from left to right, are Eric Westcott, Debra VanBrocklin, Mary Ames, and Avis Todd.

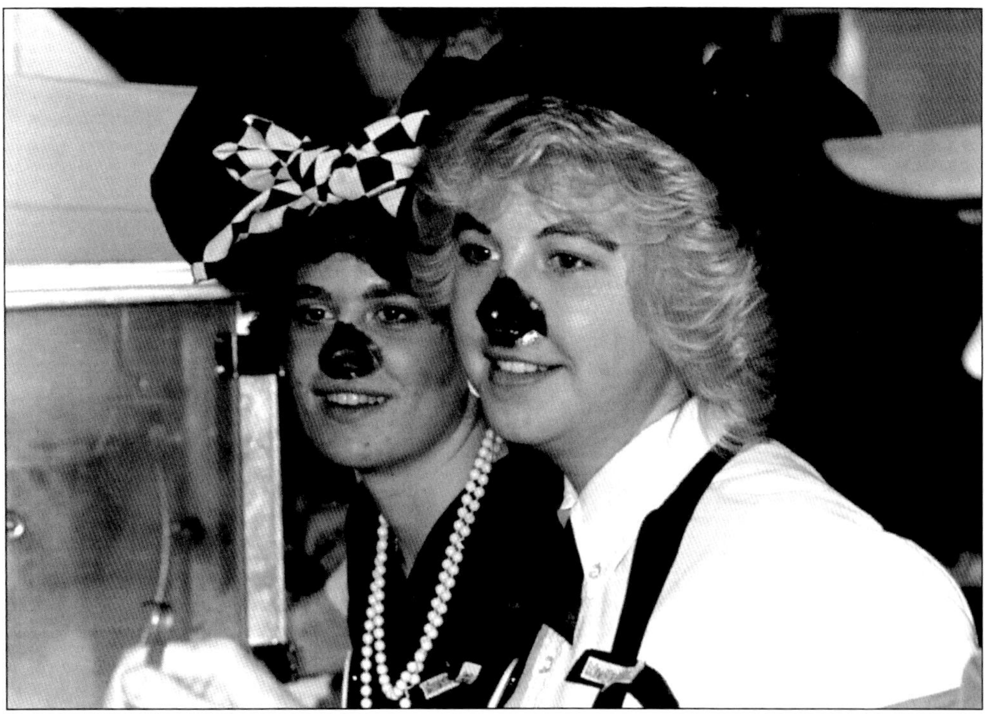

Two unidentified Mardi Gras participants are shown here in 1986. Mardi Gras was a mid-winter celebration usually held in February, often on Tuesday evenings. It was attended by faculty and students alike.

Cold, snow, and the occasional ice storm are all part of a typical North Country winter. During the 1991 ice storm, the campus was buried under a layer of ice. Seven years later, the campus was closed by state officials for a week during the historic 1998 ice storm that essentially took out the power infrastructure in northern New York.

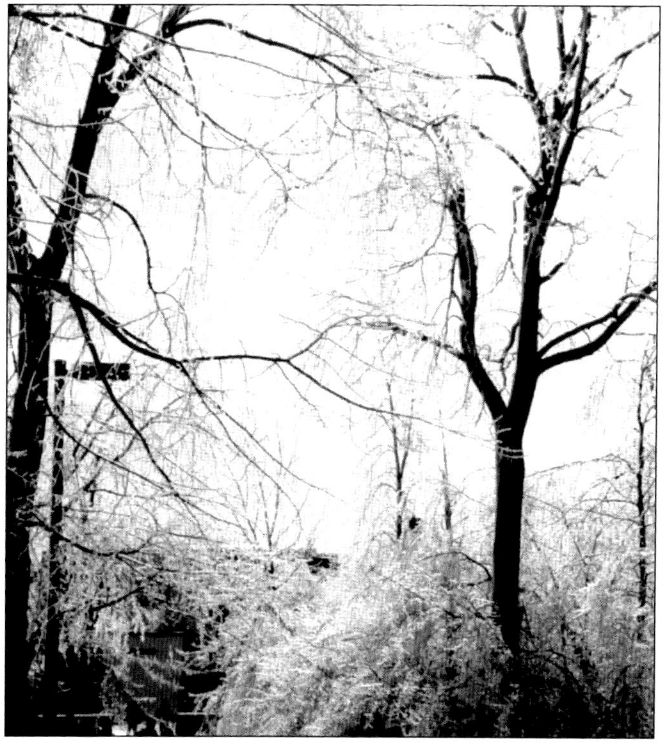

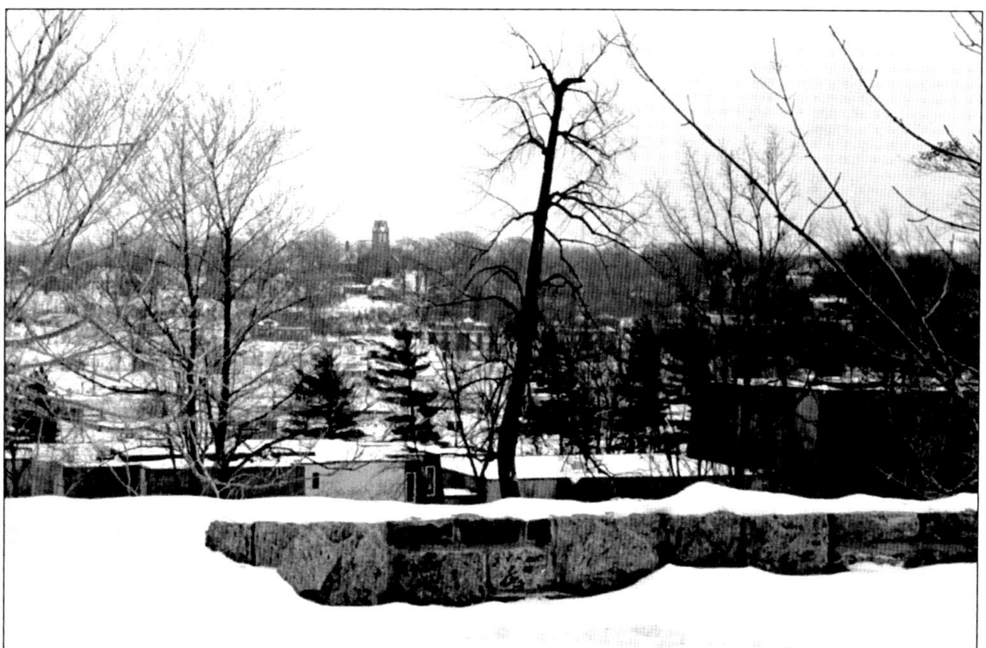

The view from SUNY Canton's hillside campus is lovely any time of year. This shot, taken in winter, shows a residential section of town with St. Mary's steeple in the background.

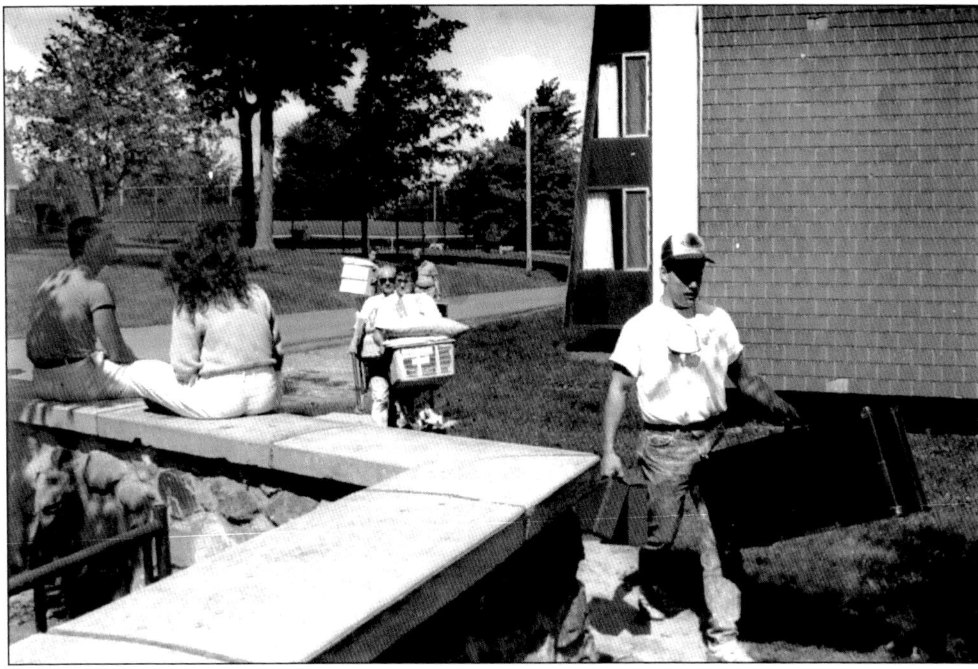

One of the rituals of campus life is arriving on campus for the start of the academic year. Moving In Day 1988 was sunny. As always, many hands make light work.

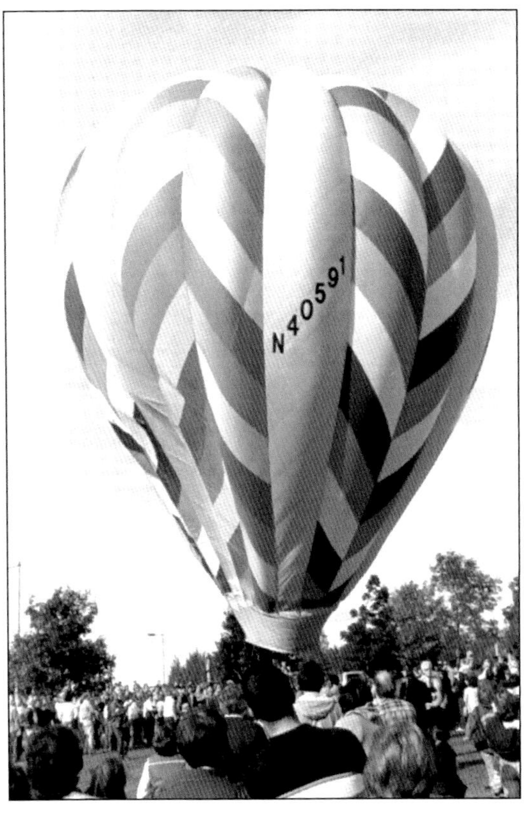

For many years, the balloon festival was a big part of SUNY Canton's Parents' Weekend. The balloons were large and colorful—and visible from miles away as they floated high above Canton.

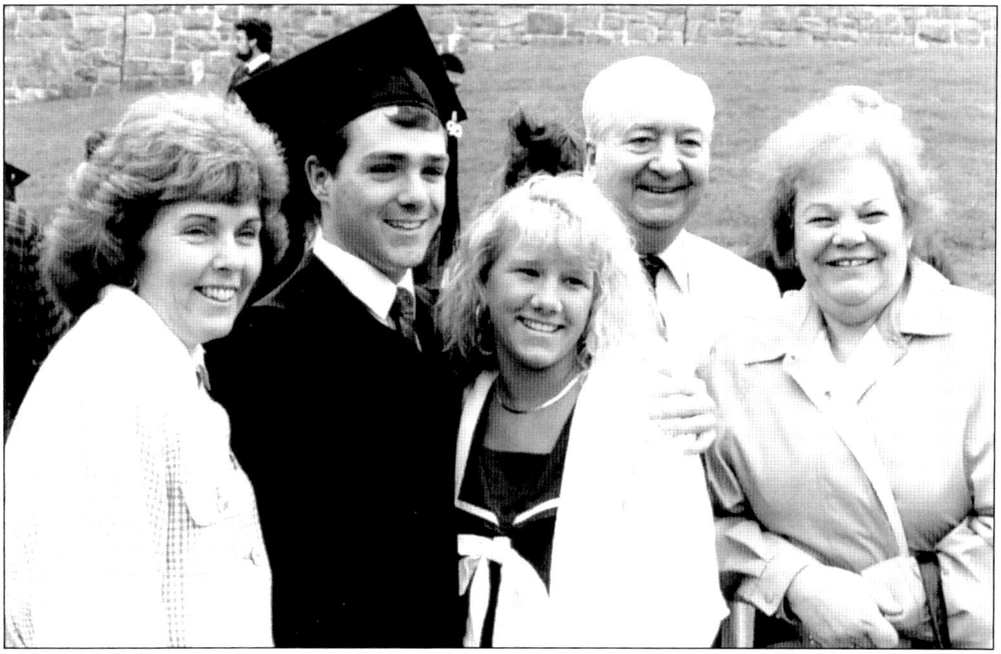

The culmination of the academic year is commencement. Here an unidentified student and his family are all smiles. College is full of hard work and stress for students and, in many cases, means sacrifice for the family. On Graduation Day, it all seems worthwhile.

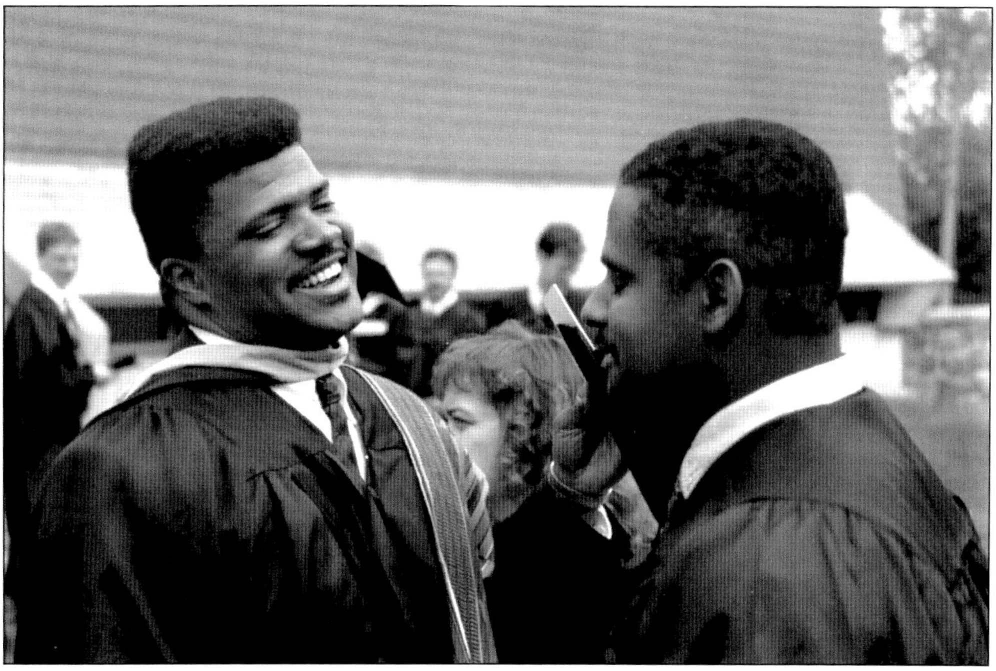

Commencement is a special time for the college's faculty and staff as well. After months of hard work, they can look back on a year of accomplishment and ahead to next year. College staffers Kahan Sablo and Ron Mason are all smiles and conversation following commencement exercises.

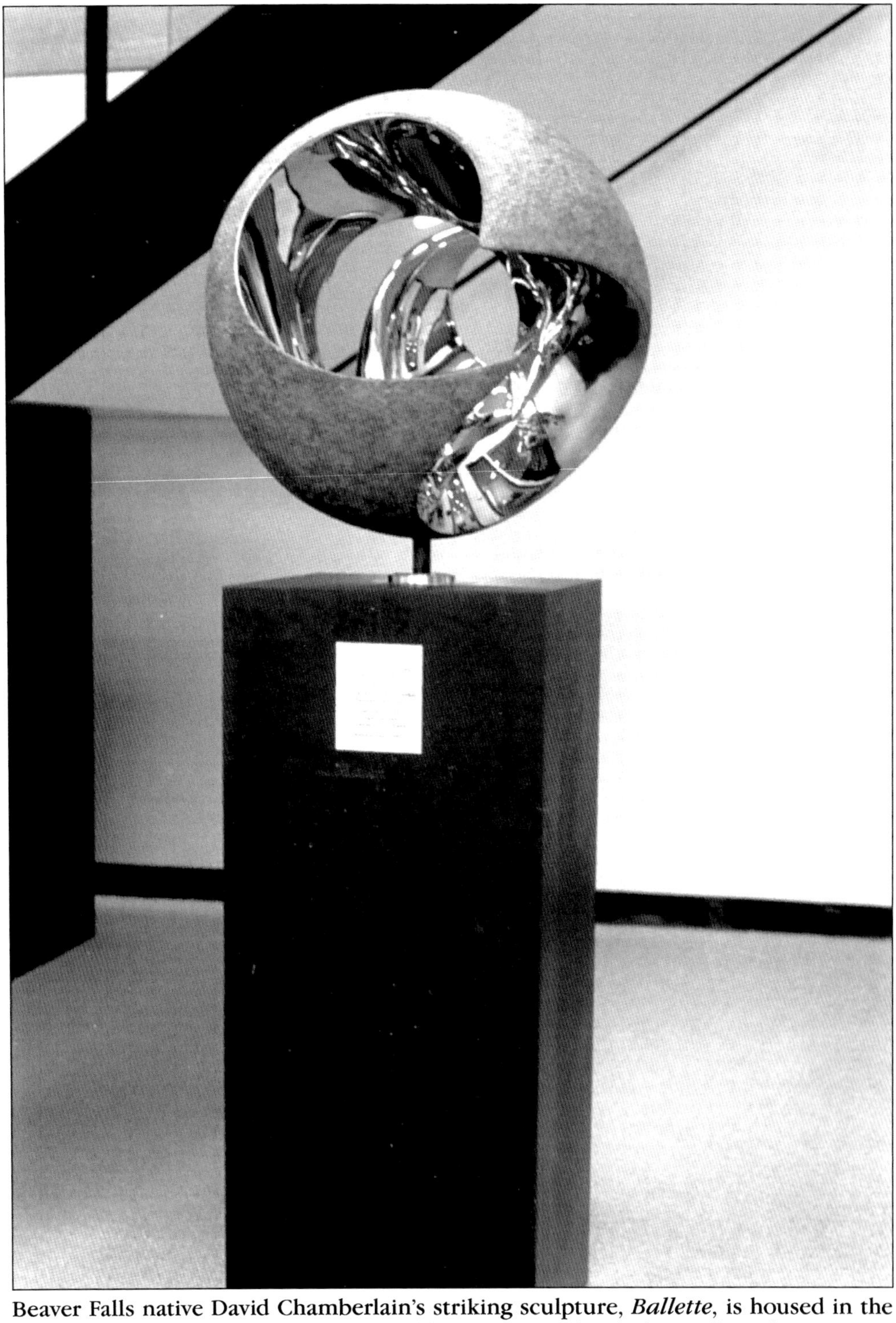

Beaver Falls native David Chamberlain's striking sculpture, *Ballette*, is housed in the Southworth Library. It was commissioned by T. Urling and Mabel B. Walker of Watertown, New York, who gave the sculpture to SUNY Canton. It was dedicated on May 2, 1992.

Six

Growth, Innovation, and a New Century 1993–Present

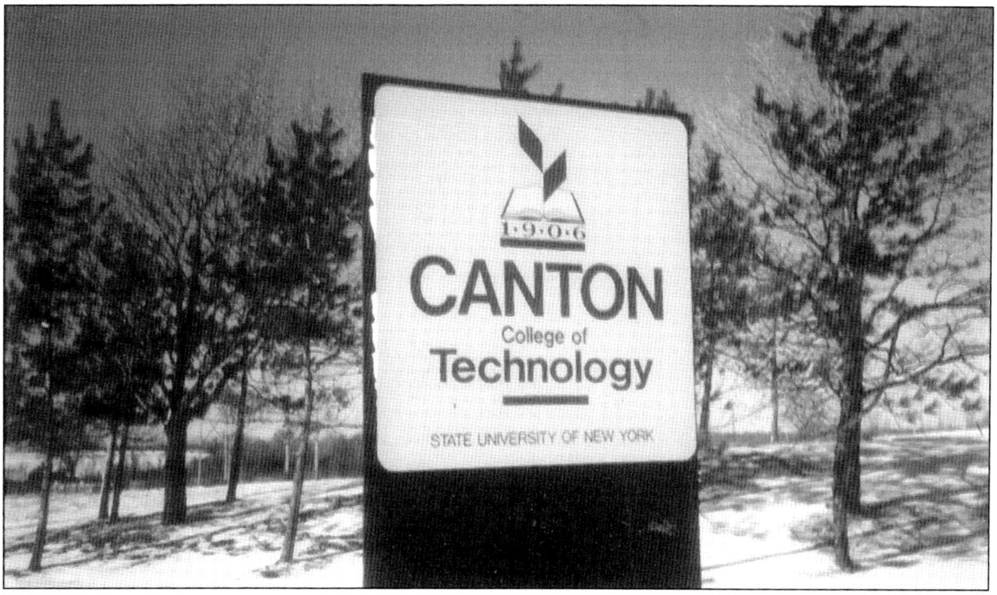

The campus sign at the intersection of Cornell Drive and State Highway 68 is a familiar landmark to the larger North Country community as well as to the academic community. Between 1965 and 1987, the college was known as the Agricultural and Technical College at Canton, or ATC. In 1987, the name was changed again to the College of Technology at Canton, reflecting the declining role of agriculture in the curriculum. In 1993, SUNY Canton became an acceptable shortened name and is now commonly used.

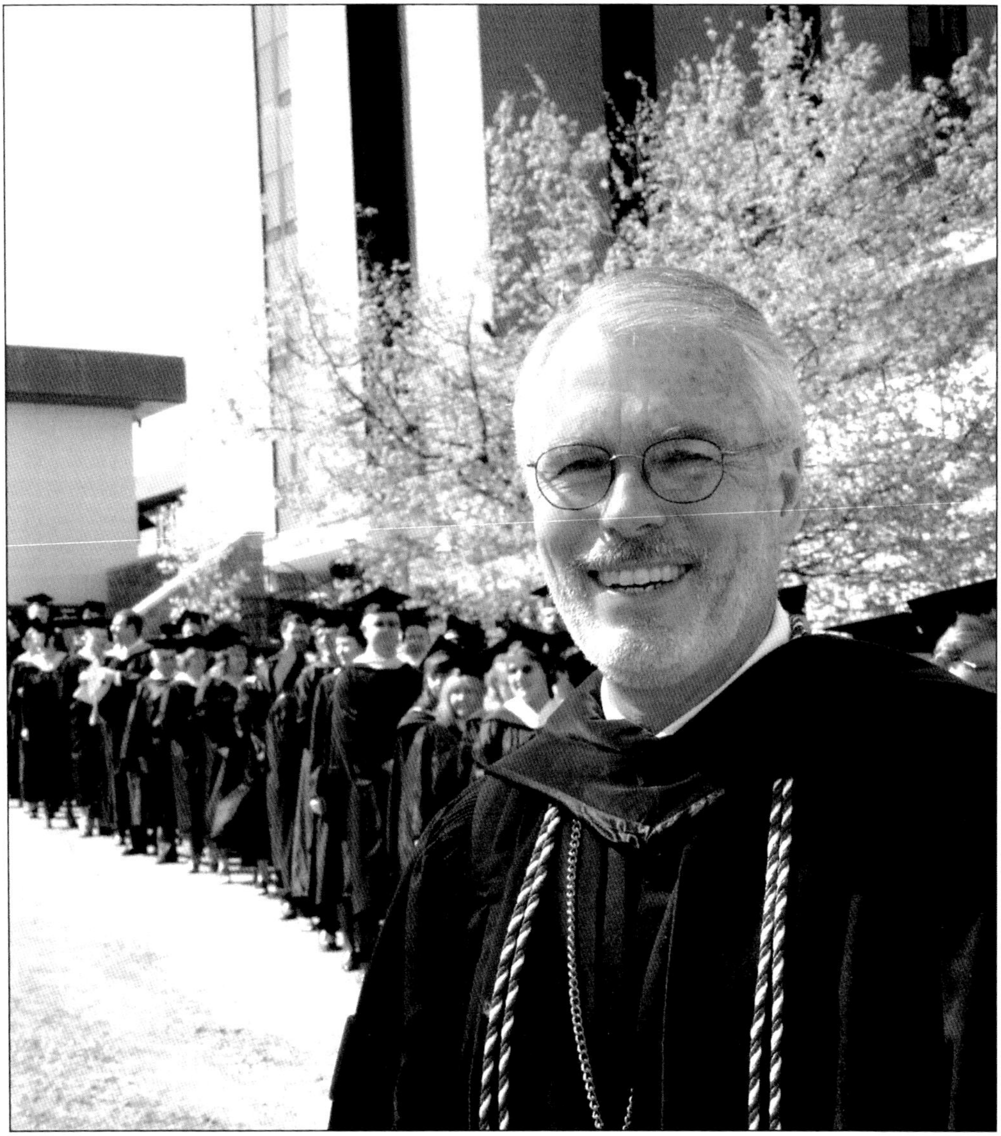

Dr. Joseph Kennedy started as college president on July 1, 1993, and was formally inaugurated on December 3, 1993. His tenure marked the beginning of another era of innovation in the curriculum and changes in the physical plant. New buildings include the first campus center as well as the Richard W. Miller Campus Center and the Newell Veterinary Technology building. The Roselle Academic Plaza has been renovated as well. Numerous new programs have been added. SUNY Canton added a mall location in Massena in 1999, a dramatic project that captures a spirit of innovation and entrepreneurship. The college has begun the transition to a baccalaureate-granting institution. The first such degree to be approved was the bachelor of technology in public safety in 1998, and the first bachelor degrees were awarded in December 1998. Since then, several other bachelor degree programs have been added, and more are planned. Other projects include the Small Business Development Center, North Country Emergency Medical Services, the David Sullivan/St. Lawrence County Law Enforcement Academy, and the Emergency Management Training Center of Northern New York.

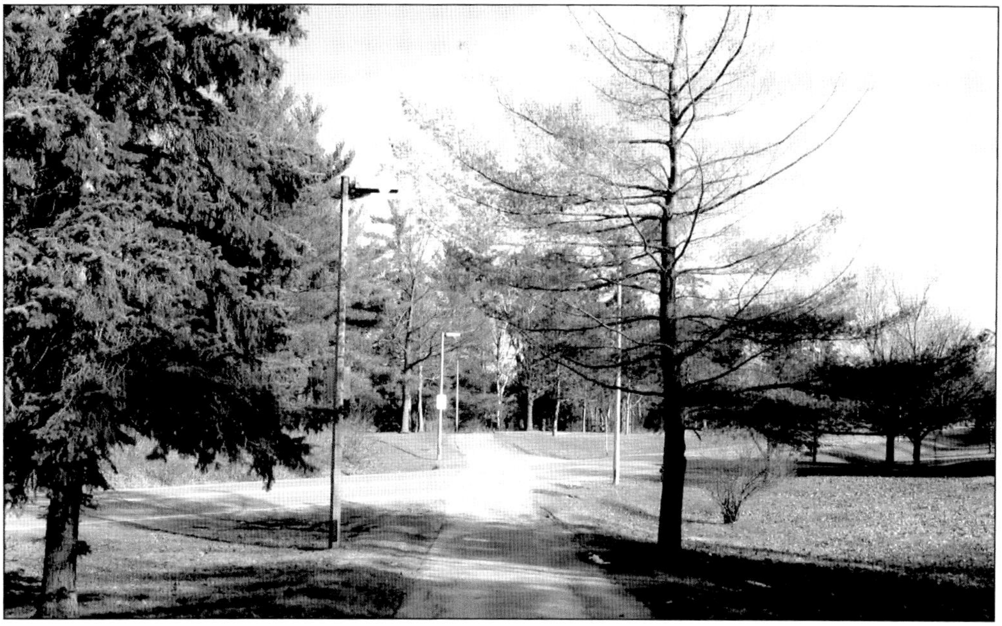

One of the strengths of the campus is its physical beauty. Here a walkway near the lower service road is pictured. The construction scars of a generation earlier have healed, and the trees have matured, adding to the appeal of the surroundings.

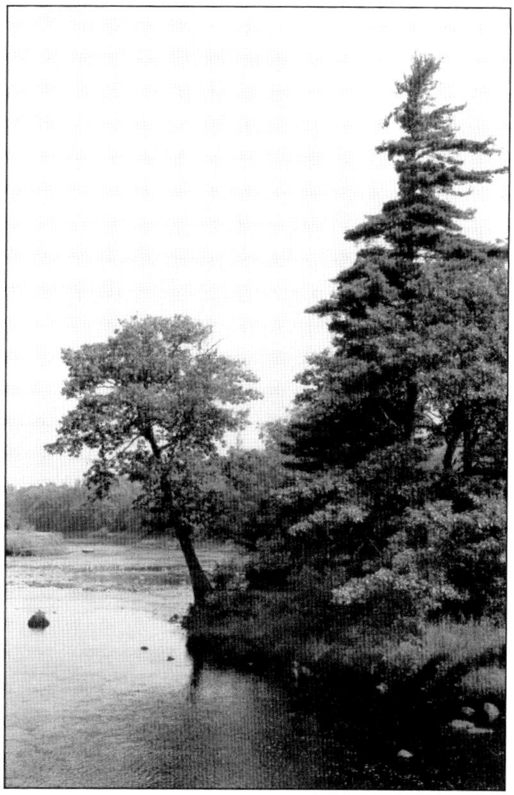

The power and appeal of the Grasse River cannot be underestimated. The footpath entrance to the campus on Riverside Drive crosses the river twice, and there are walking trails along its banks. In recent years, *The Paysonian*, the college yearbook, contained an ode to the river.

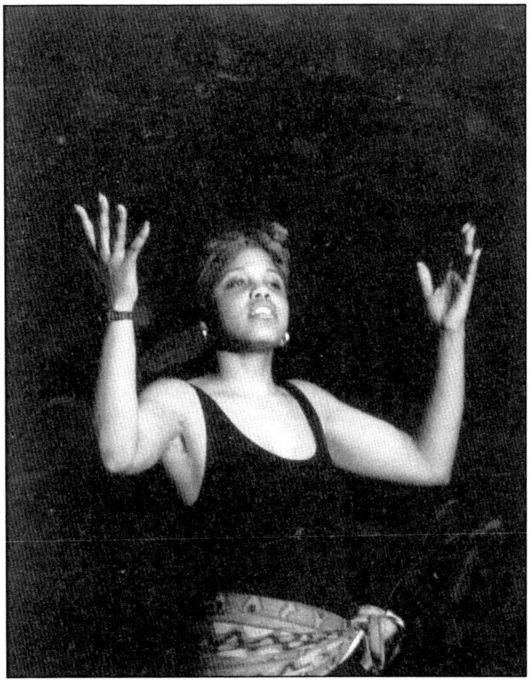

Tiah Rodriguez and Mike Katargi perform during the Afro-Latin Society poetry reading held in 1993.

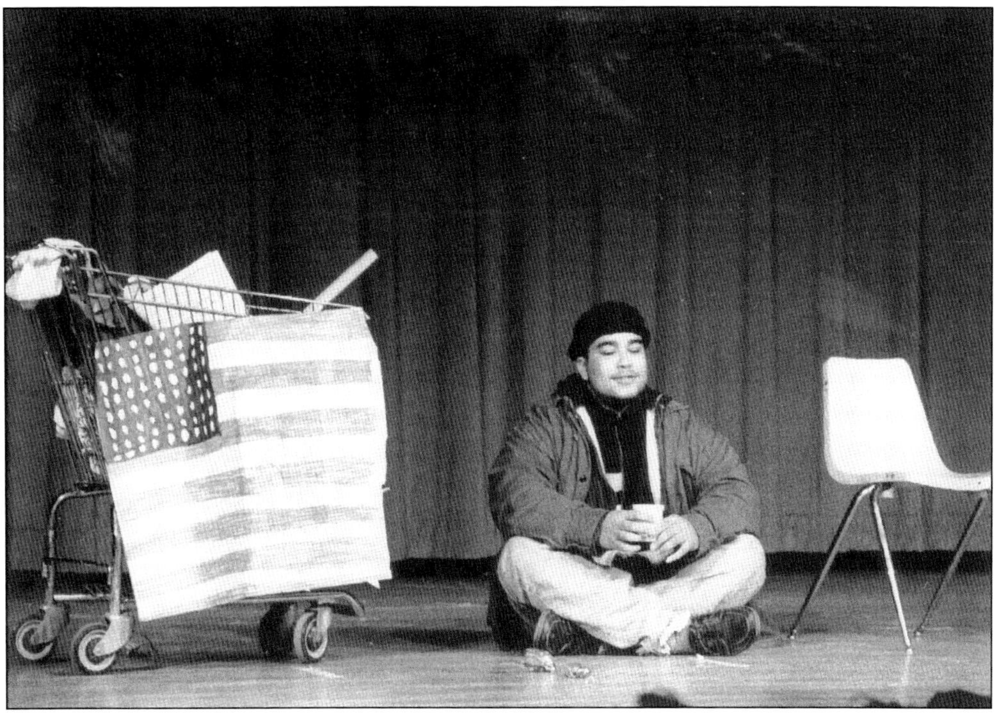

Football returned to SUNY Canton from 1995 to 2003. Former professional football coach Lou Saban, pictured here, gave the program instant credibility in its early years. He coached the team for six seasons.

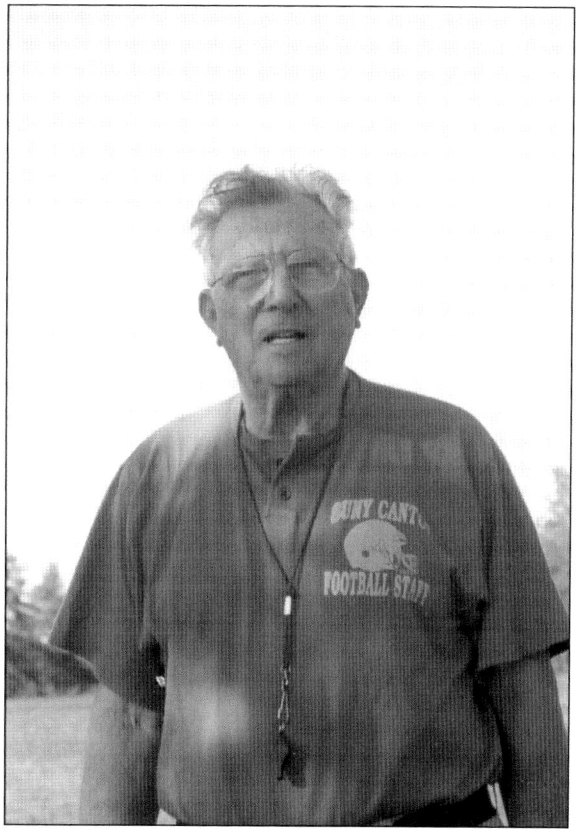

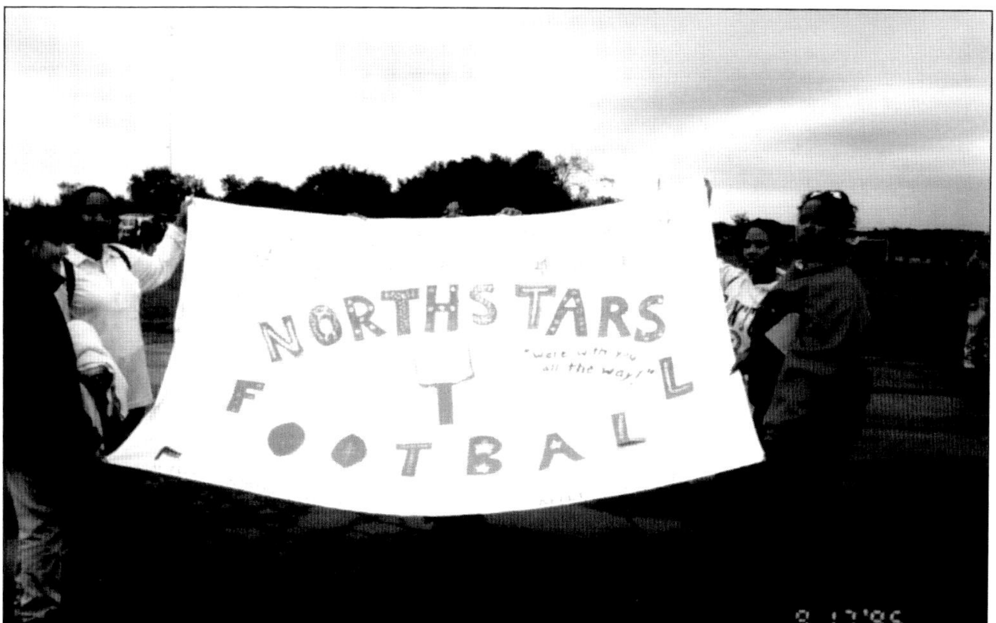

In addition to helping enrollment, the football program created excitement for both players and supporters, as shown here early in the inaugural season in September 1995.

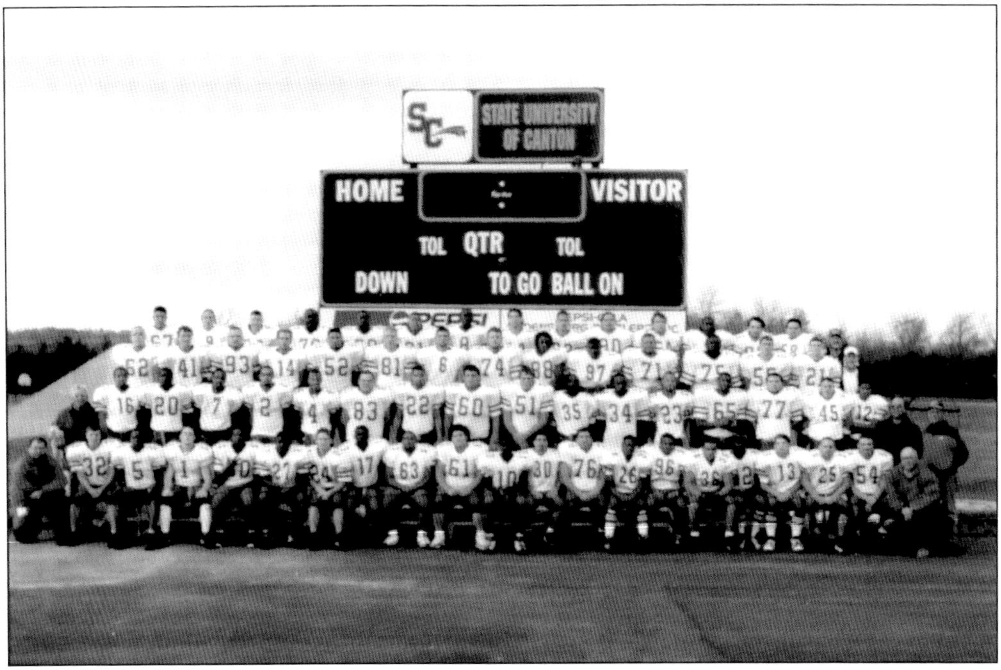

In this undated team photograph, coach Lou Saban is pictured on the far left in the second row. Assistant coach Jerry Sawyer is pictured in the first row on the far right. Improvements were made to the field, and later it was named Lou Saban Stadium..

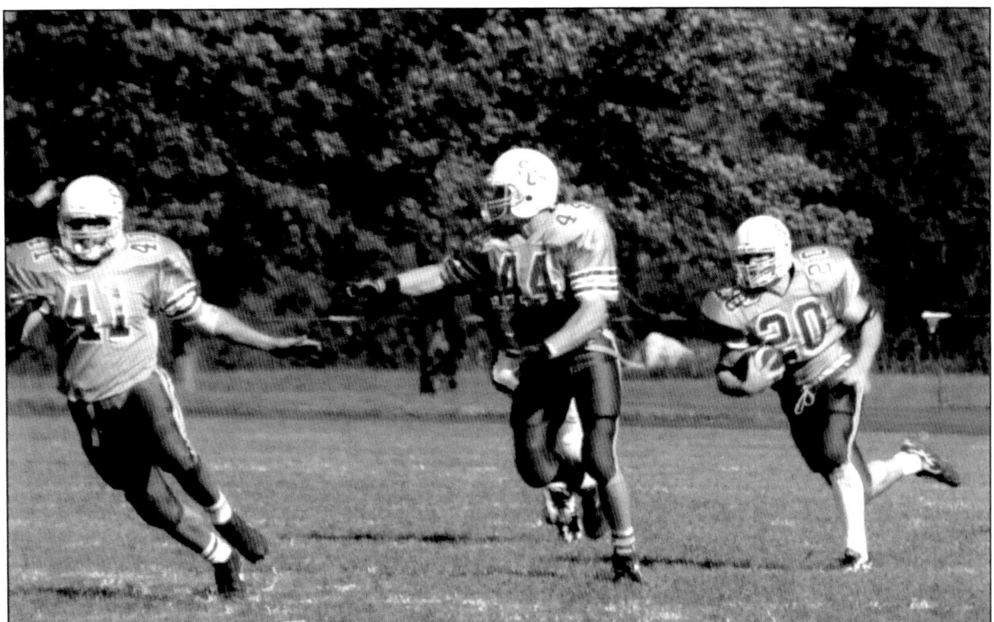

A SUNY Canton running back heads up the field with two blockers in front during a game against the Hamilton College junior varsity team in October 1996.

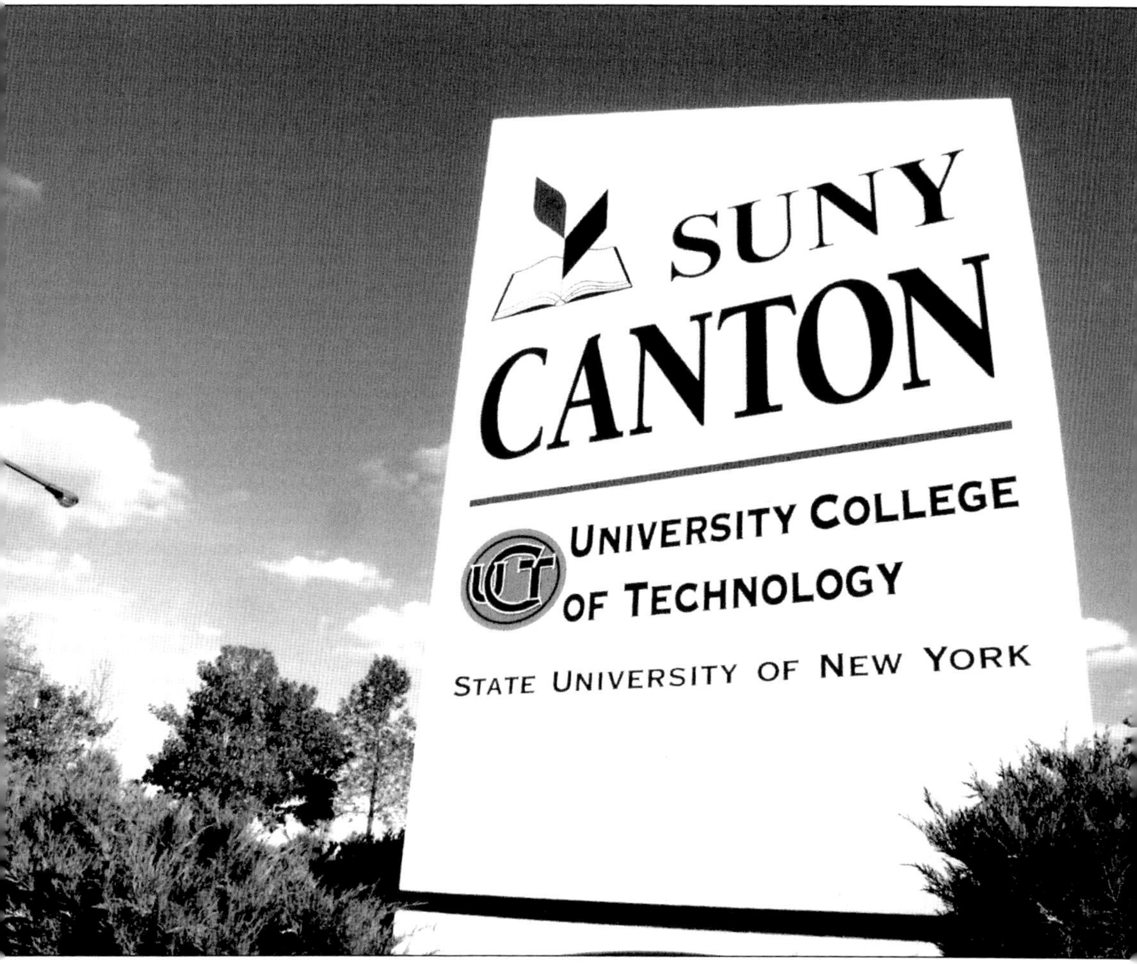

In 1996, the University College of Technology (UCT) was begun as an effort to integrate some of the activities of the technology colleges at Delhi, Cobleskill, Morrisville, Alfred, and Canton. While most activities, including the academic calendar, are no longer coordinated, this sign at the campus entrance reflects the five colleges' shared emphasis on technology-related curriculum.

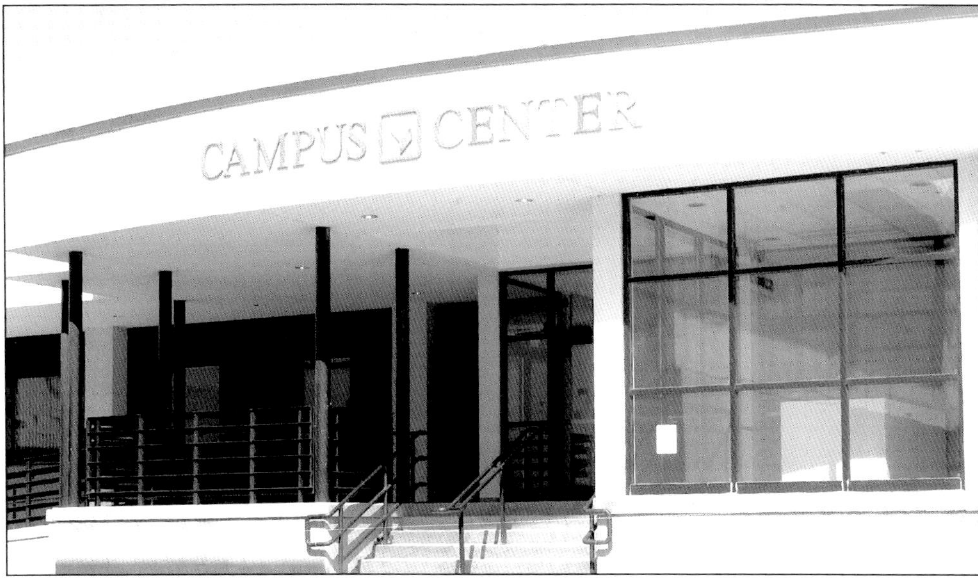

The campus center, or what turned out to be its initial phase, was built in 1997. It added much needed space for offices. It also housed the snack bar and campus store.

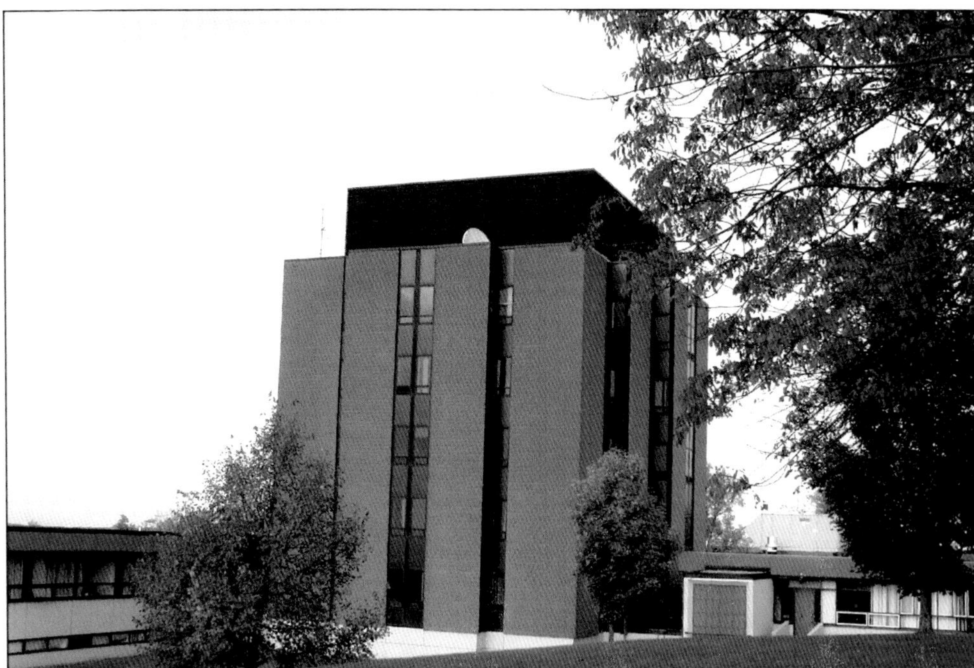

For almost 30 years, SUNY Canton administrative offices were located in French Hall. Since February 1997, the offices of the president, provost, and vice president have been located on the sixth floor of the faculty office building, which is pictured here.

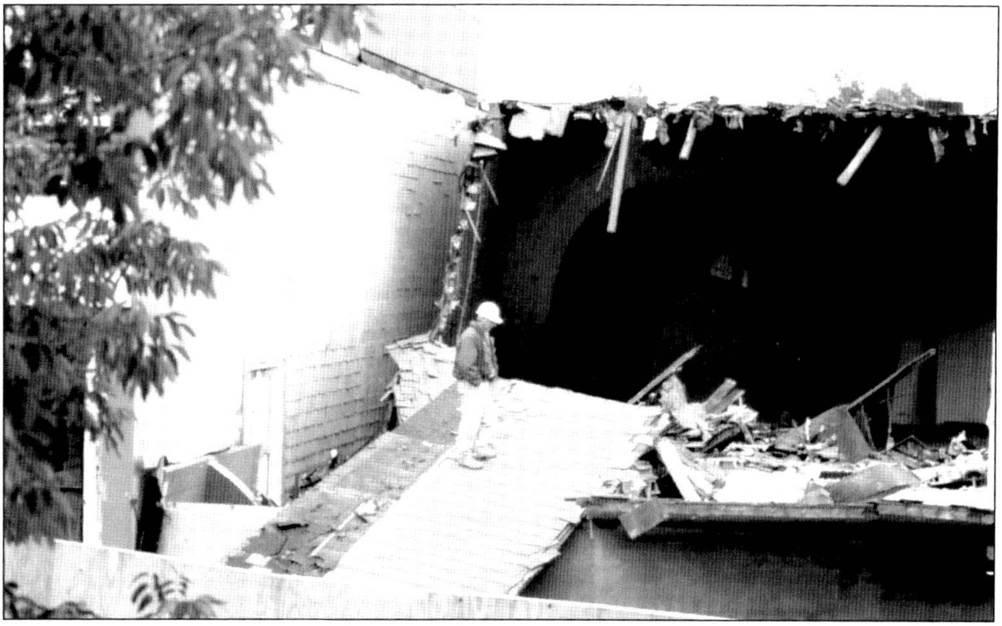

During the summer of 1997, Kingston Theater burned. The fire was caused by a contractor who had left solvent-soaked rags in a trash can. It was determined the building was damaged beyond repair and would have to be torn down, which was a major loss to the campus. Fortunately, the fire did not spread to the campus center or Payson Hall.

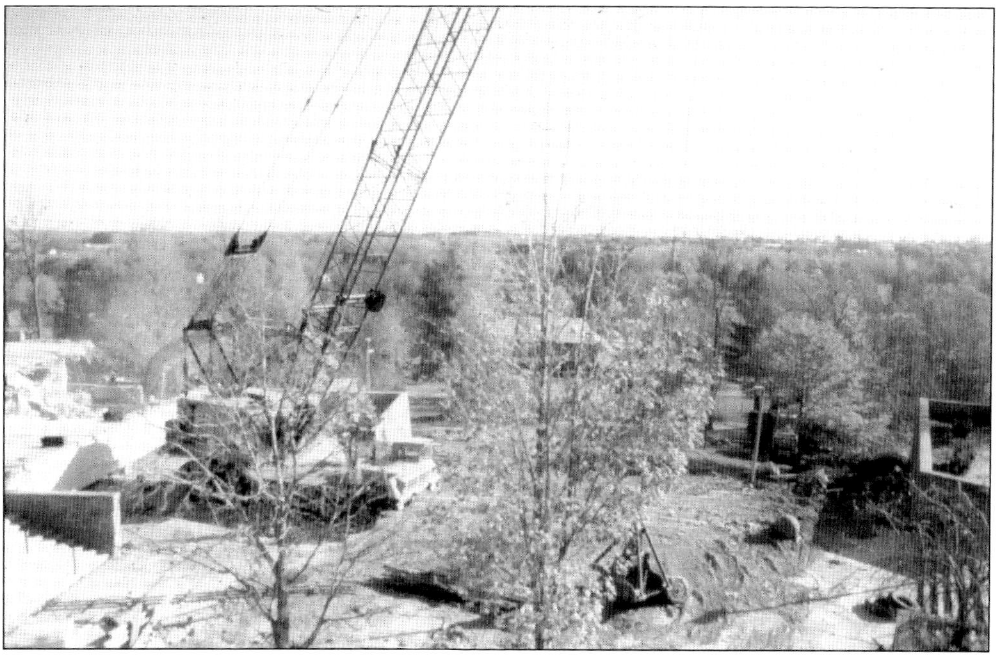

Clearing the debris of Kingston Theater was a major effort. Thousands of tons of concrete and steel had to be removed before the rebuilding process could begin. In this photograph, a crane works on the site of the former theater.

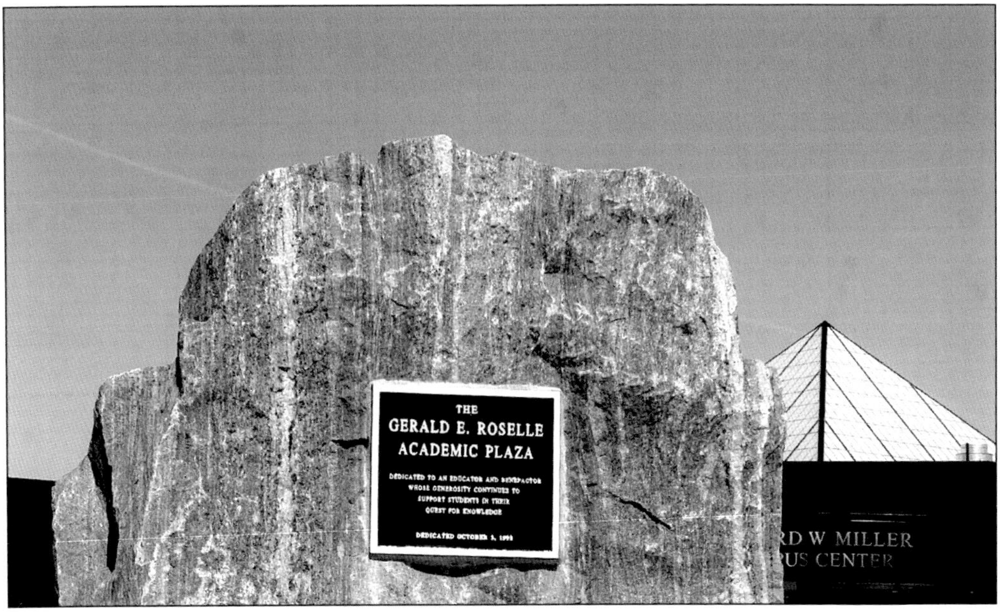

The plaza amidst the campus center, Cook Hall, and Southworth Library was named after former faculty member Gerald Roselle and dedicated in October 1998. The plaque honoring this event is mounted on the rock in the center of the plaza. In 2000, the whole plaza area from Nevaldine to Wicks Hall had been renovated with new pavers and landscaping. The tower greenhouse was also removed.

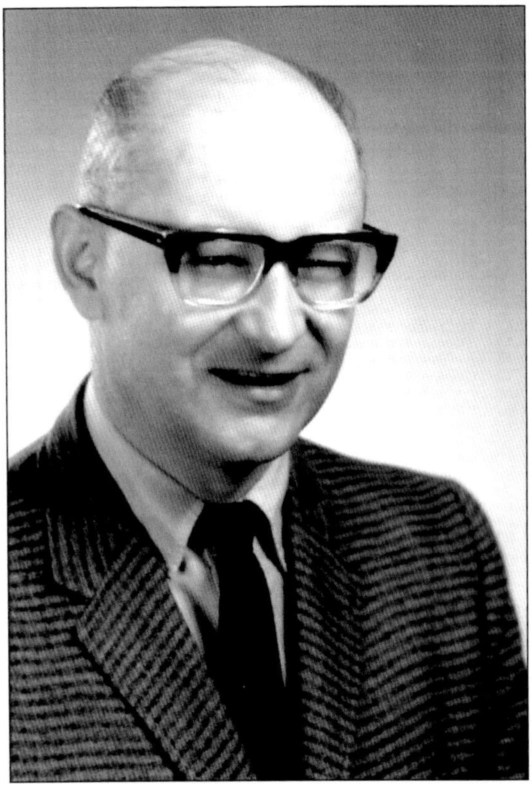

Gerald Roselle was a member of the English department and also served as chair from 1977 until 1982. He worked at SUNY Canton for 24 years. He was a dedicated educator and a benefactor of the college. In 1991, he established a scholarship that is made annually to a freshman humanities student.

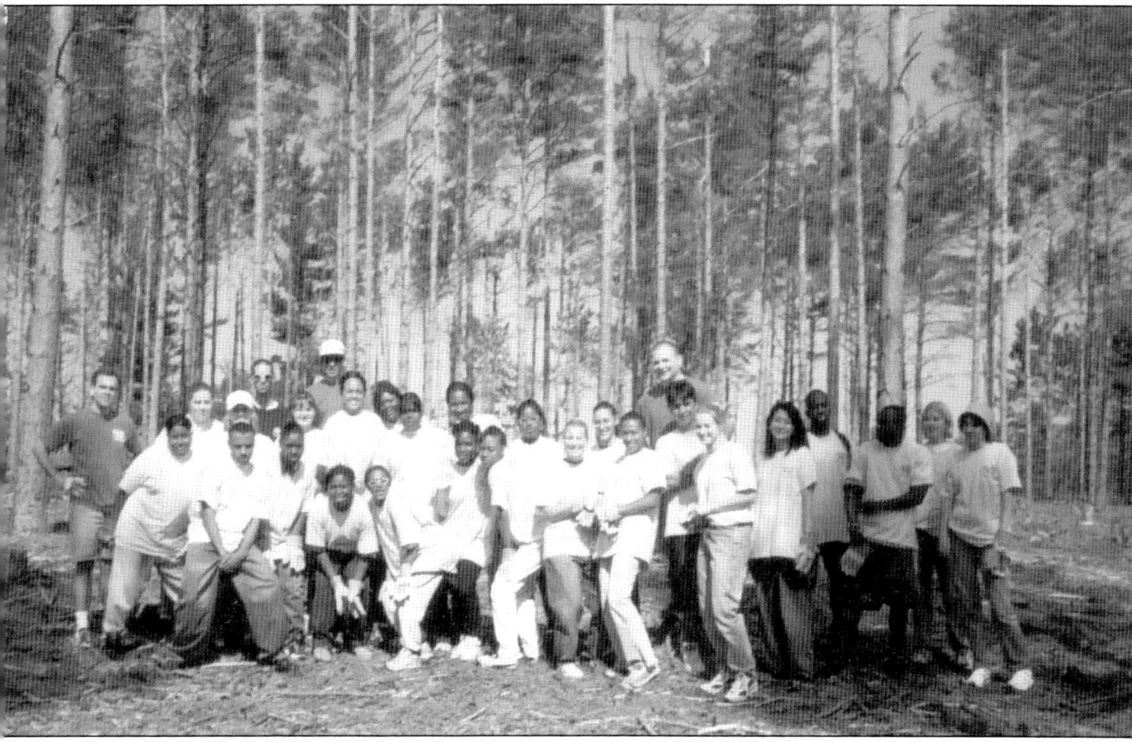

This group photograph shows some members of the faculty, staff, and student body who spent a beautiful day at Higley Flow State Park. Participants pulled trees and branches from the woods and took them to the road, where regular park employees fed the materials into huge chippers. College participants were bussed to the site by the campus and the College Association provided a picnic lunch afterward.

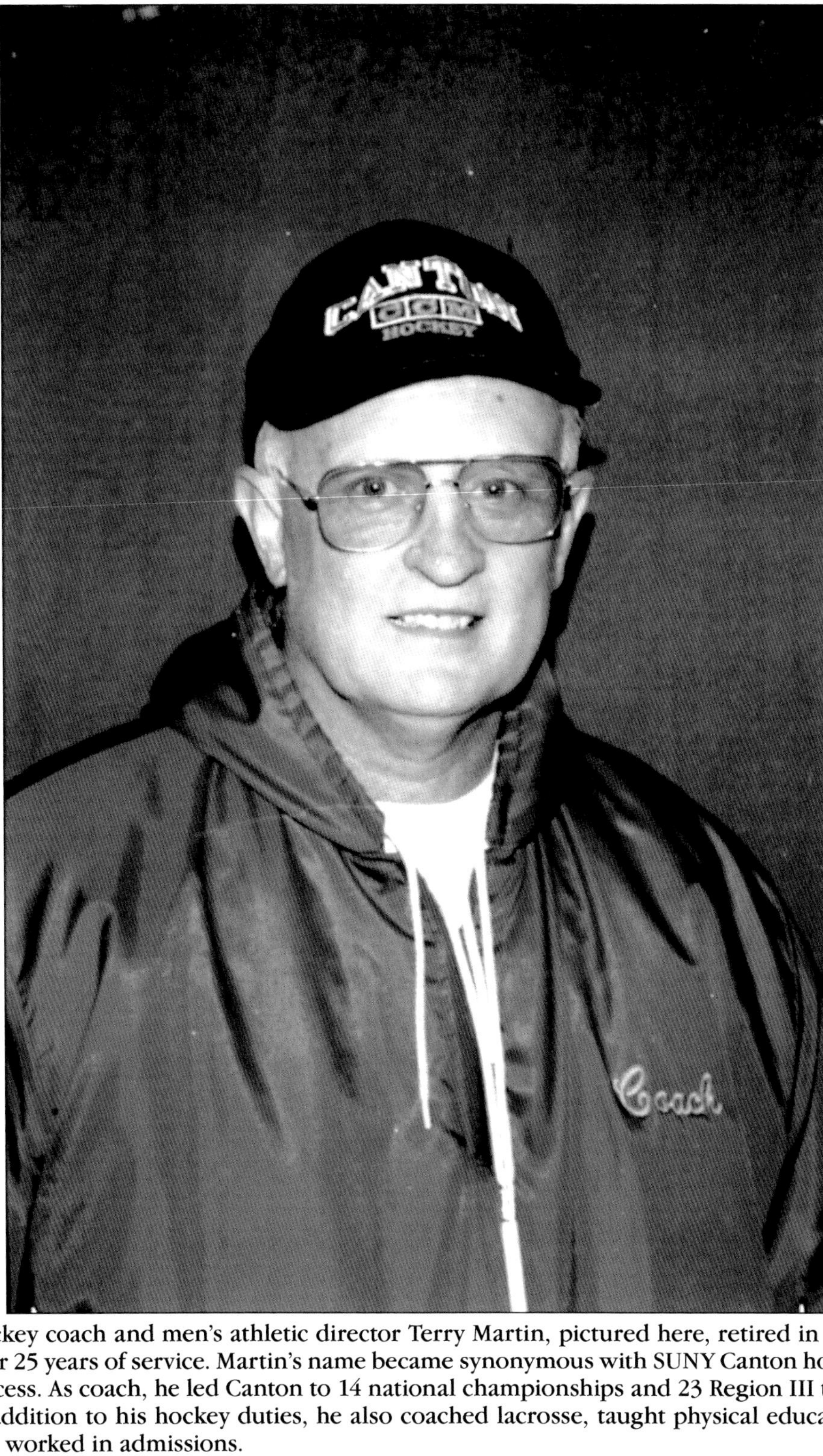

Hockey coach and men's athletic director Terry Martin, pictured here, retired in 1999 after 25 years of service. Martin's name became synonymous with SUNY Canton hockey success. As coach, he led Canton to 14 national championships and 23 Region III titles. In addition to his hockey duties, he also coached lacrosse, taught physical education, and worked in admissions.

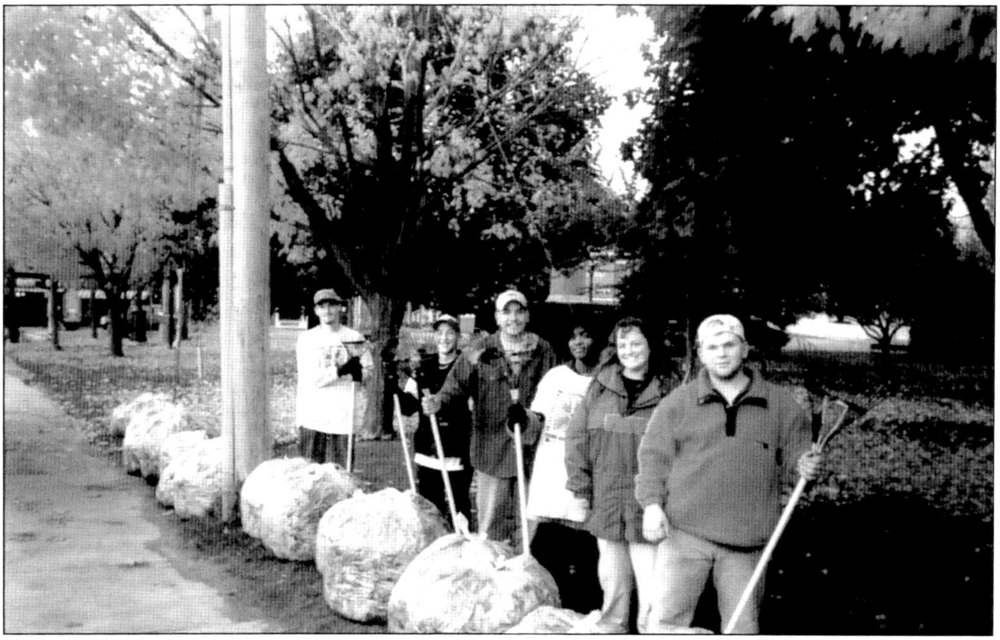

Another community service project was leaf raking. Here an unidentified group of SUNY Canton students works with Melinda Miller, a college counselor, in the Canton Village Park.

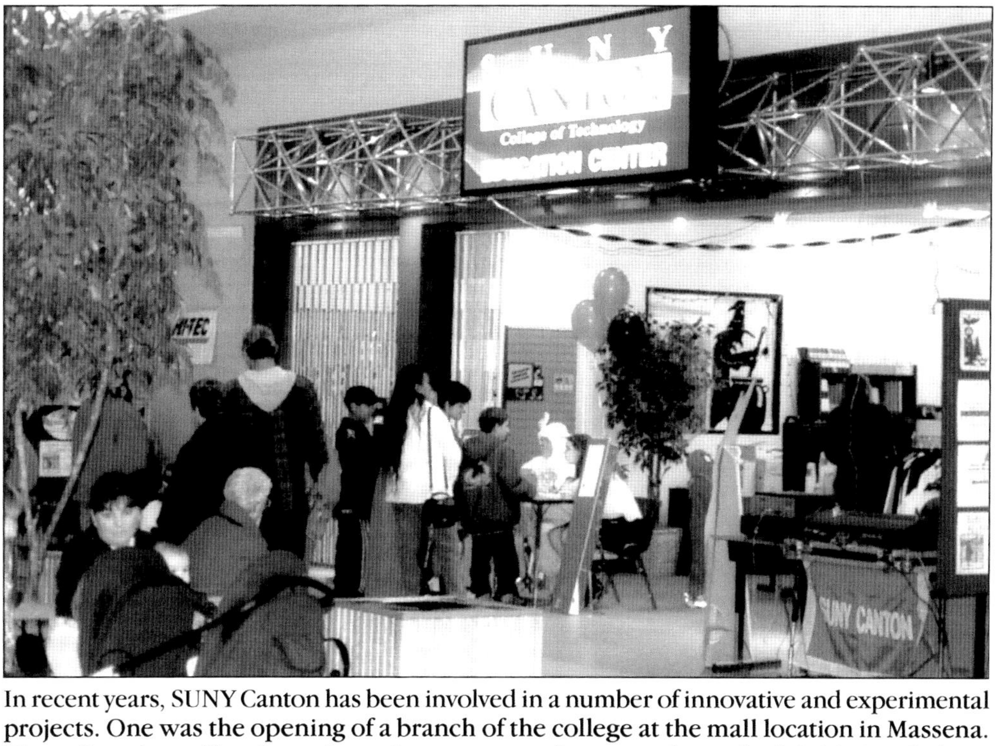

In recent years, SUNY Canton has been involved in a number of innovative and experimental projects. One was the opening of a branch of the college at the mall location in Massena. The college has offered a variety of programs and courses there. Such initiatives help to create more public awareness of the college and its mission.

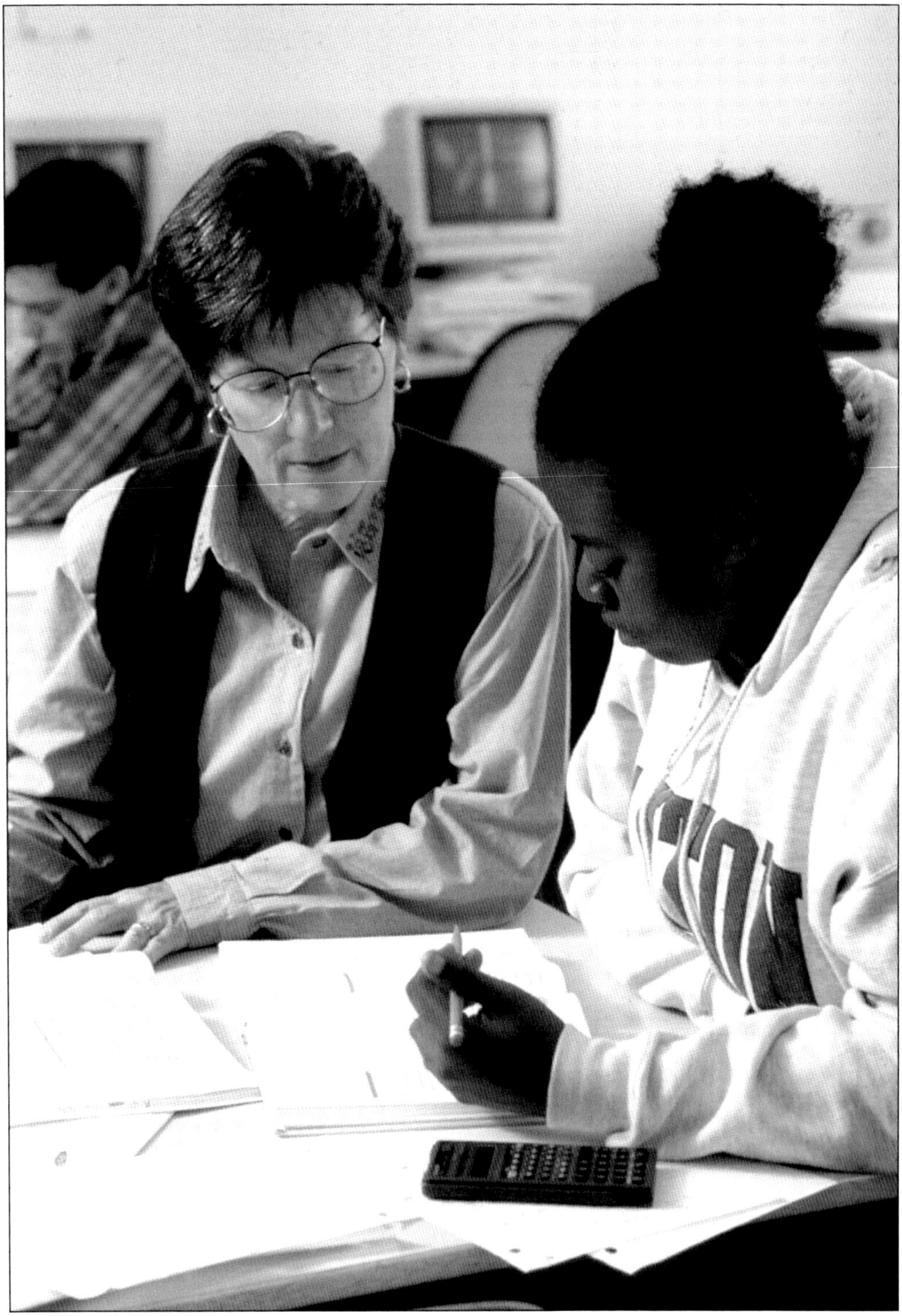

Whether faculty members, counselors, librarians, or writing or math lab instructors, the SUNY Canton faculty and staff members are there to help students succeed. Here Pat Cassara is shown working with an unidentified student.

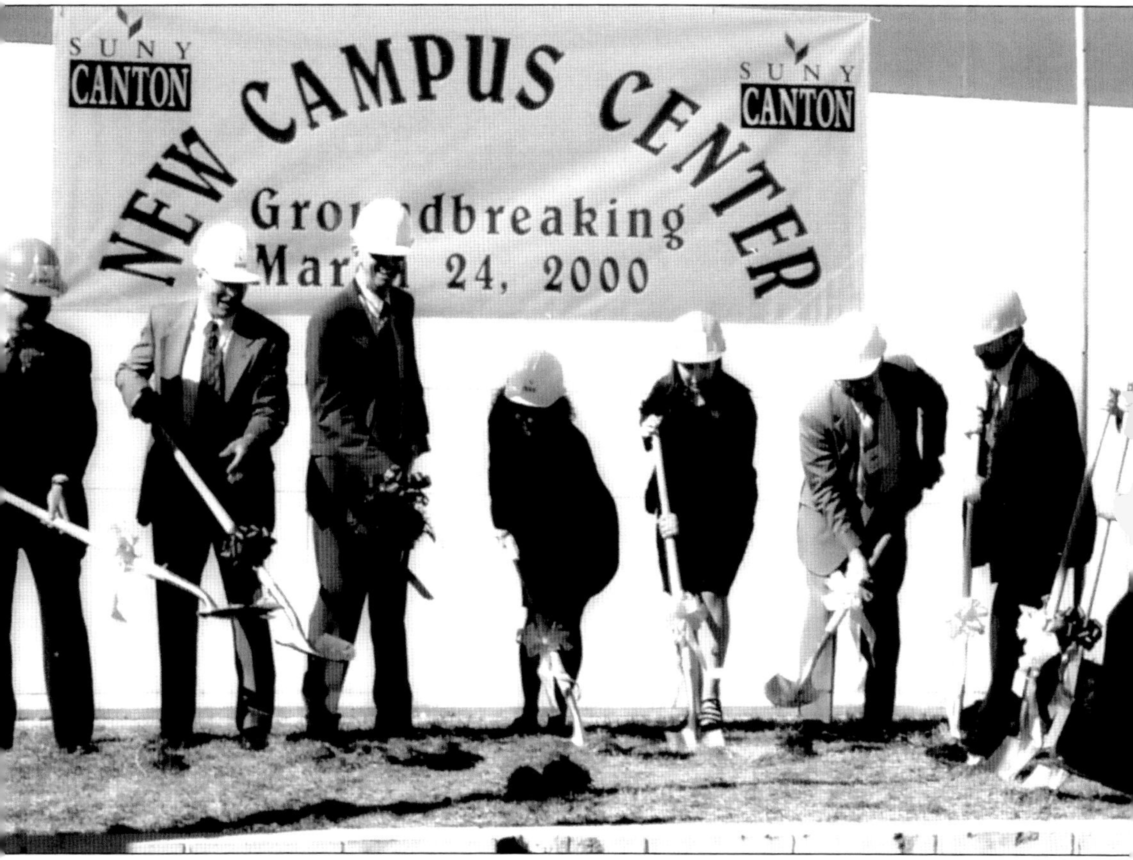

Almost three years after the Kingston Theater fire, the ground breaking for the new campus center took place on sunny March 24, 2000. It would be another two years before the center was open. The total cost of the project was approximately $12 million.

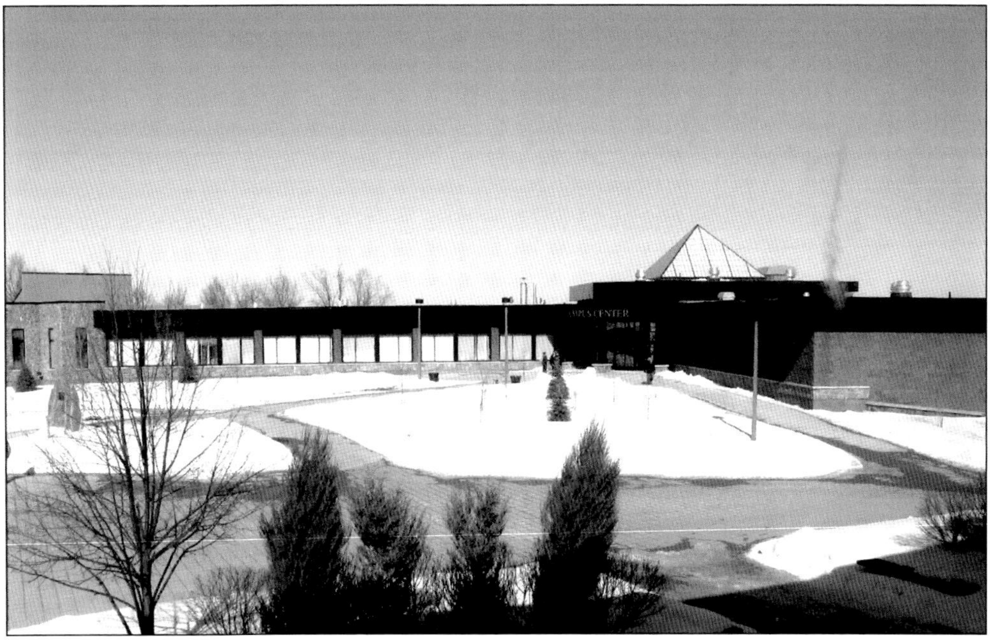

The completed campus center is pictured here. The left wing of the ground level contains various student activity offices and multipurpose meeting spaces. The right side contains lounge space, a staircase and atrium, and a conference room that also overlooks Kingston Theater.

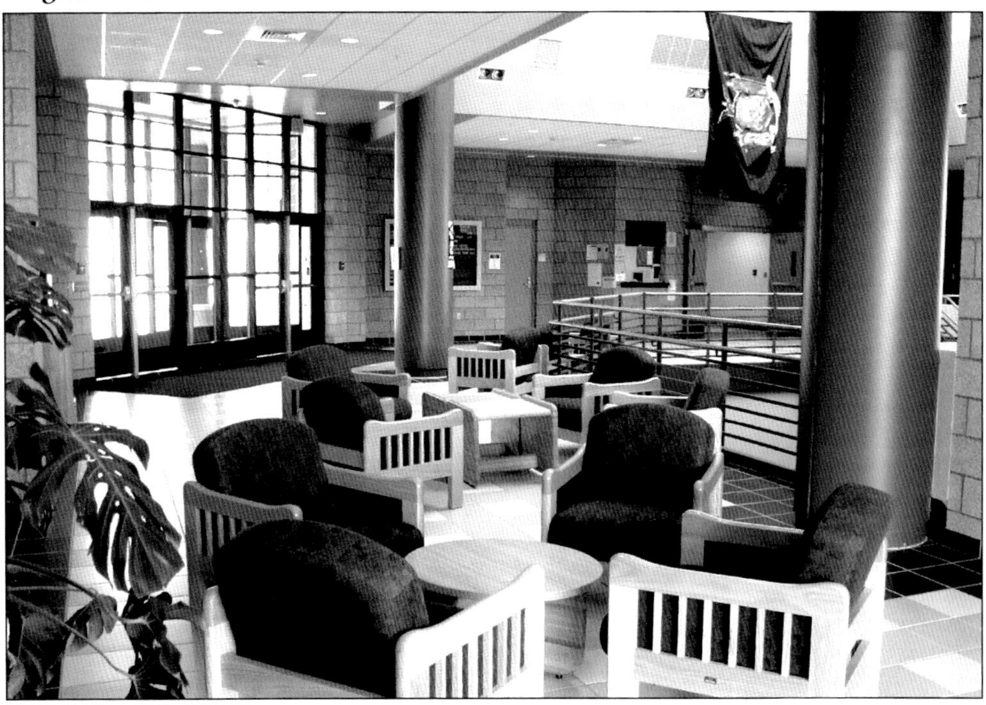

Lounge spaces such as this one are located on both the upper and lower levels of the building. The new campus center also contains the new Kingston Theater, the campus store, mailroom, health center, and intramural gym.

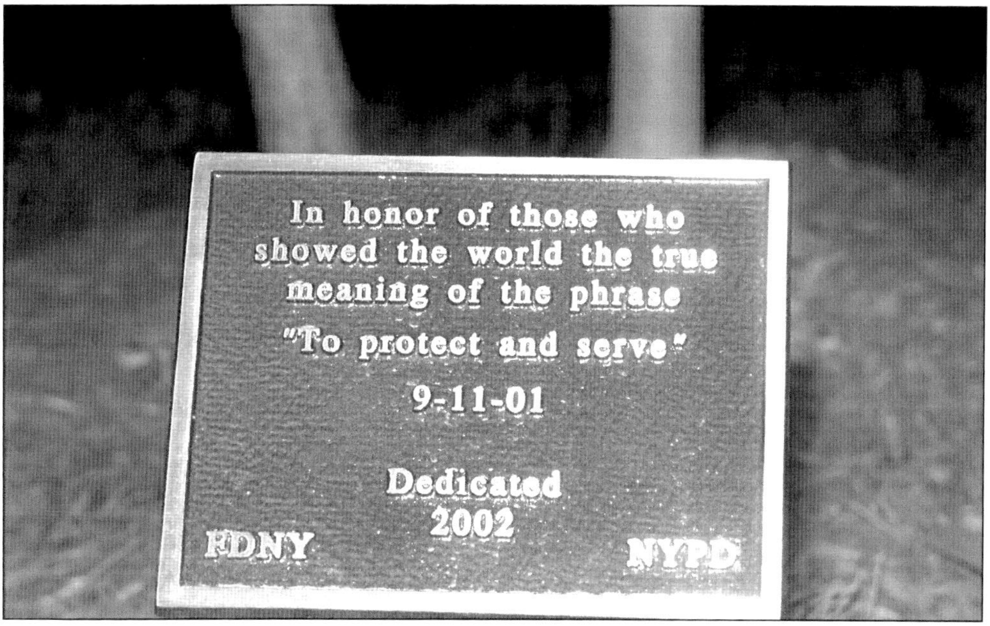

Like the rest of the nation, the events of September 11, 2001, deeply affected the campus community. A year later, a remembrance ceremony was held to honor the victims of the tragedy, and especially those police and firefighters who died in the line of duty. The plaque shown in this photograph was dedicated at this event.

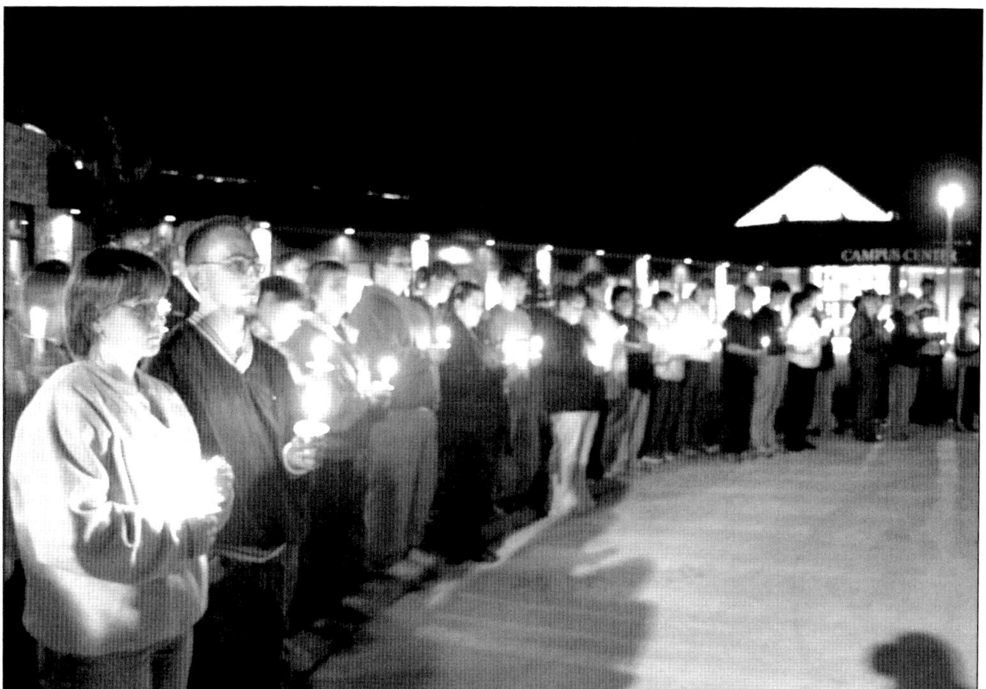
The Roselle Academic Plaza was filled with candlelight from a vigil that was part of the remembrance ceremony. Here part of the large crowd of students and staff can be seen.

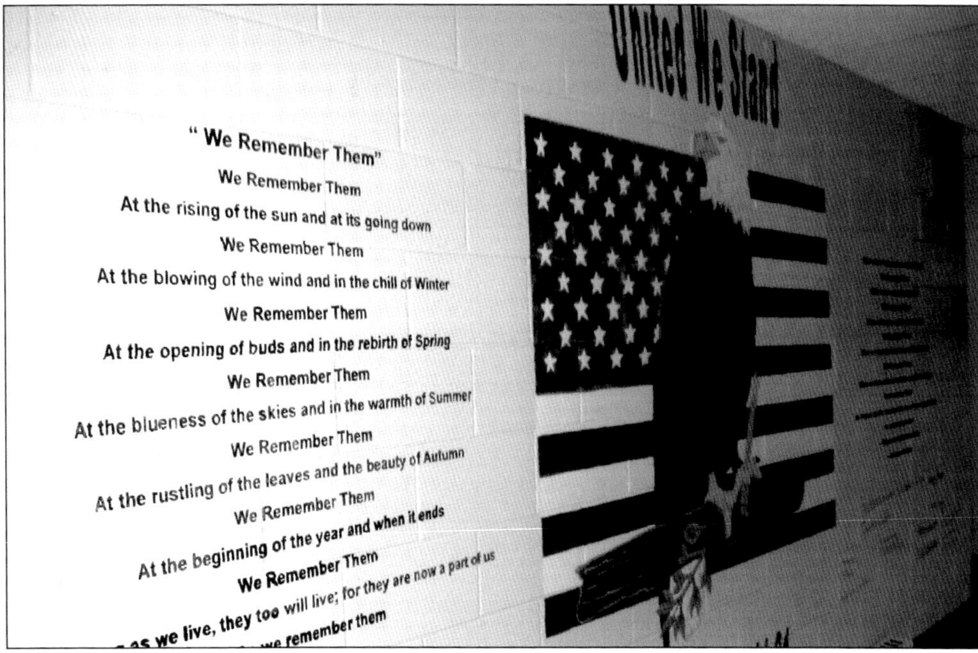

Another way that grief and shock over the events of September 11th found expression was in student artwork. The *United We Stand* mural was painted on a wall in Rushton Hall North with its own heartfelt tribute.

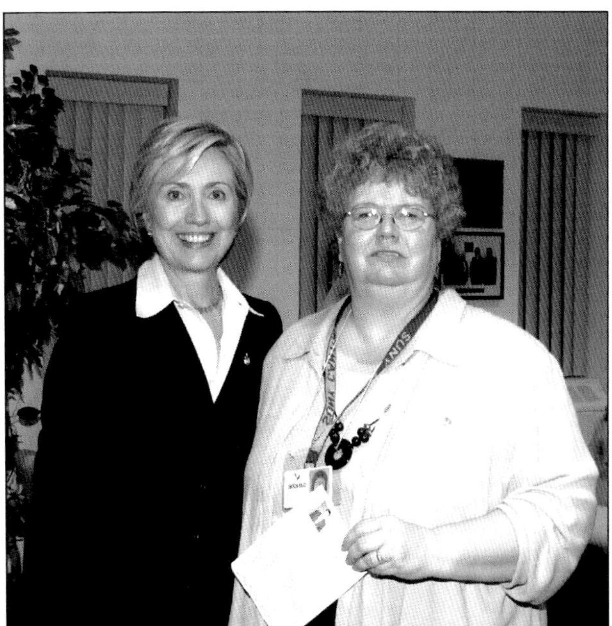

Senator Hillary Clinton has visited the region a number of times and has been to campus. Here she takes time from a busy day of activities for a picture with SUNY Canton's Deb Lowry.

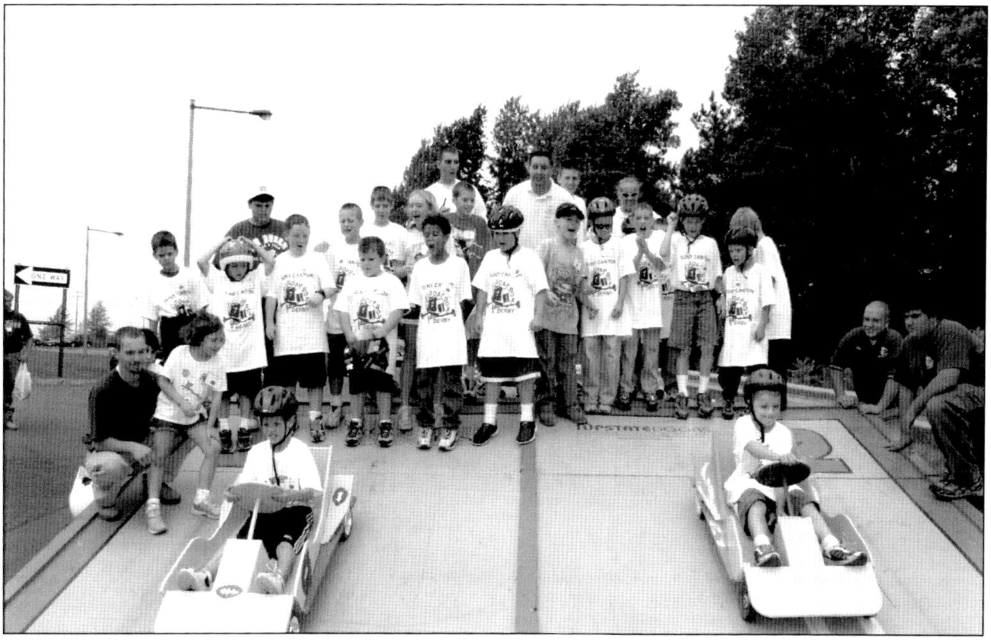

SUNY Canton's Fall Weekend event has been well attended over the years. Part of the reason is the varied and eclectic programs and events that appeal to a wide range of ages. In 2002, the soap box derby, with the assistance of the automotive technology students, attracted lots of interest and had a good turnout. Here two contestants are about to start.

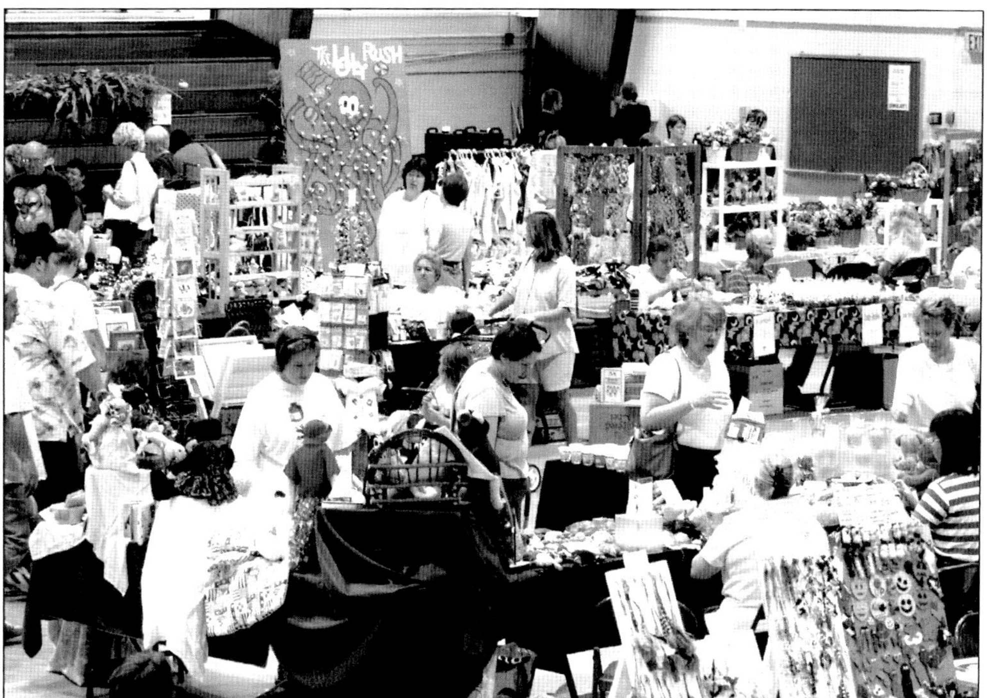

One of the favorite Fall Weekend events is the craft fair. It appeals not only to parents and alumni, but to the larger community as well.

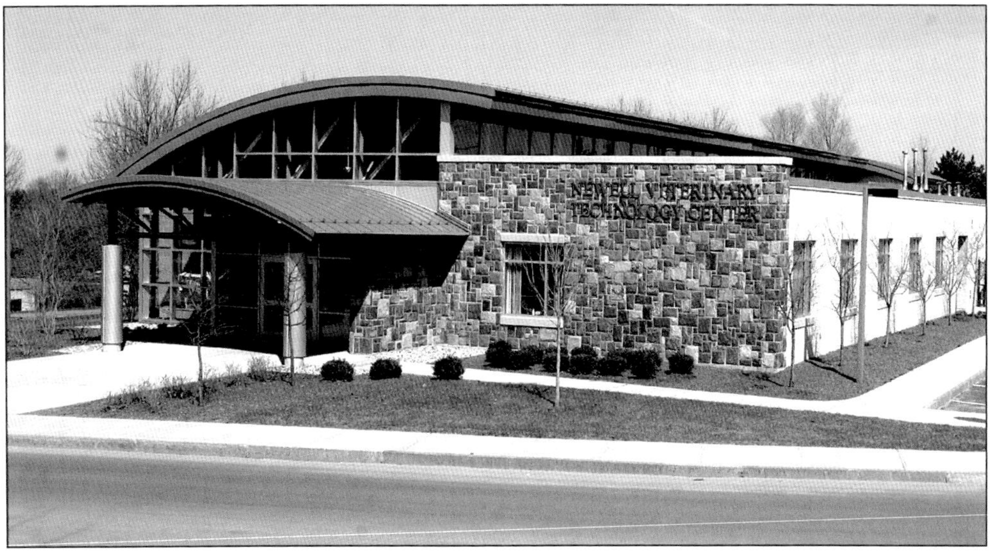

The Newell Veterinary Technology Center provided much needed space for one of SUNY Canton's more popular academic programs. The building was made possible through the generosity of Allan and Kate Newell.

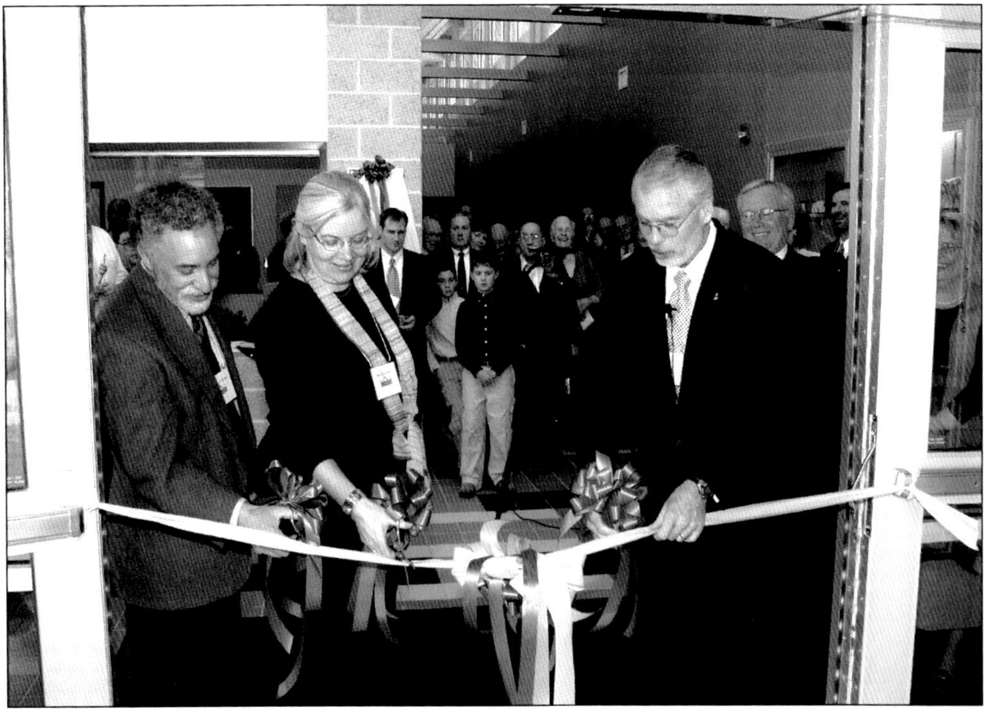

The Newell Veterinary Technology Center was dedicated on April 12, 2003. Pictured at the ribbon cutting, from left to right, are Allan and Kate Newell, with SUNY Canton president Dr. Joseph Kennedy.

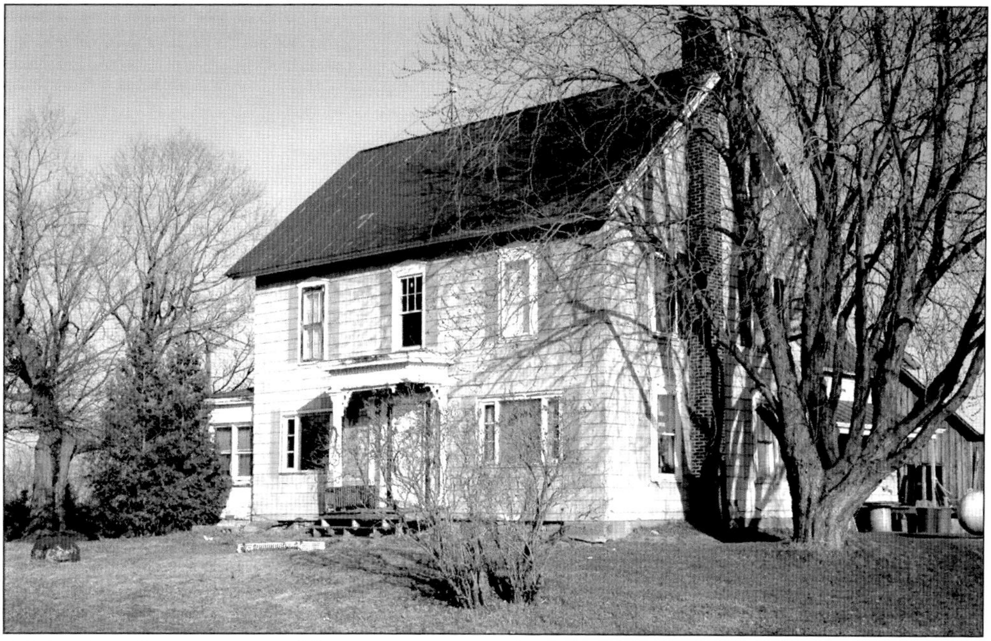

Of the four fraternities and four sororities, only three Greek organizations have houses. The ZAP house is located on Old DeKalb Road, a short drive from campus.

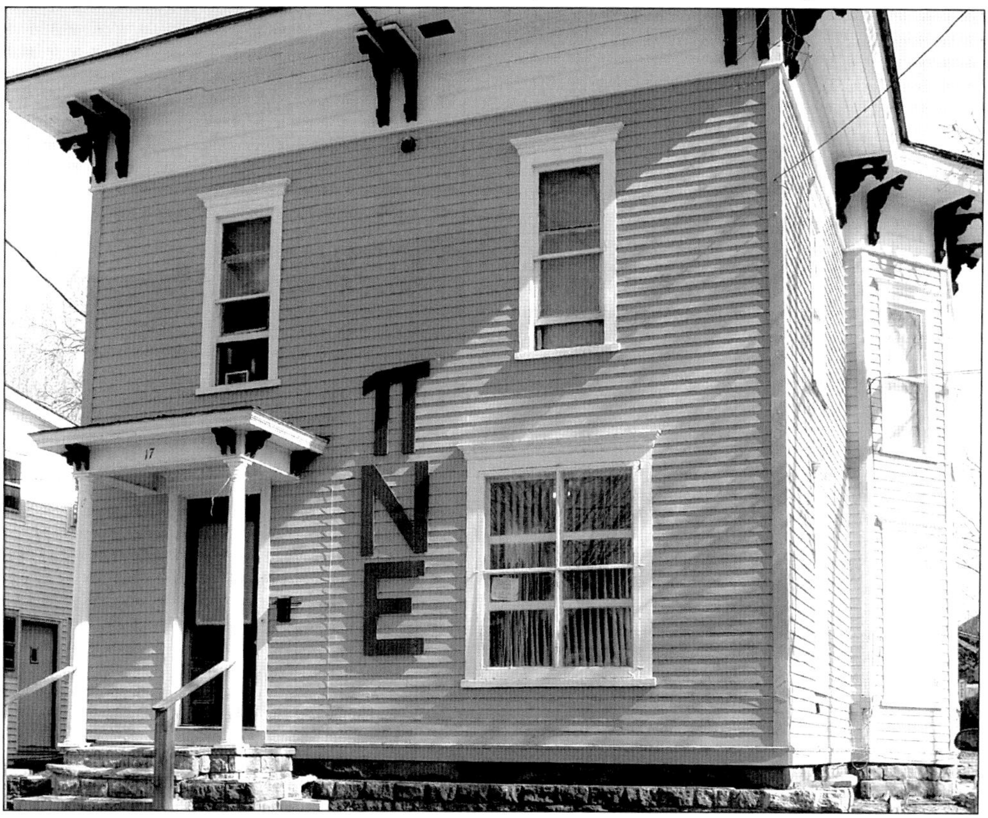

The Pi Nu Epsilon sorority house is located on Pine Street in the village of Canton.

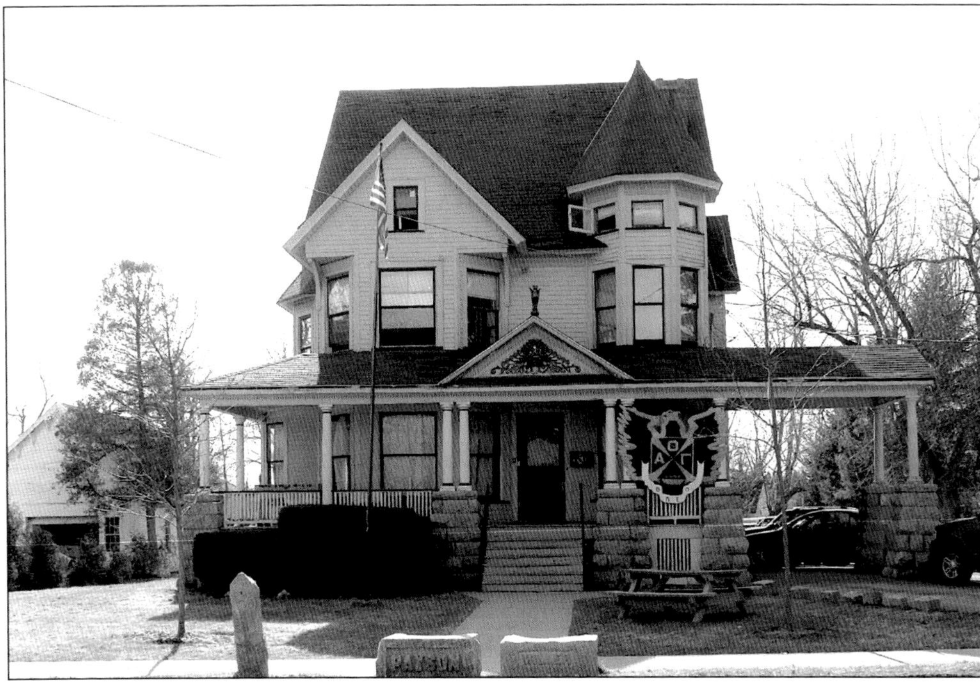

The Alpha Theta Gamma house is pictured as it has appeared in recent years. Note the stones located along the curb. One honors Dr. James Payson, who once owned the house and was an important person in the early history of the college. The other recognizes Richard Miller, who belonged to the fraternity as an advisor and later taught at the college. He is still an adviser for the fraternity. The stones were commonplace in the age before cars and provided a step for embarking and disembarking from horse-drawn carriages and wagons.

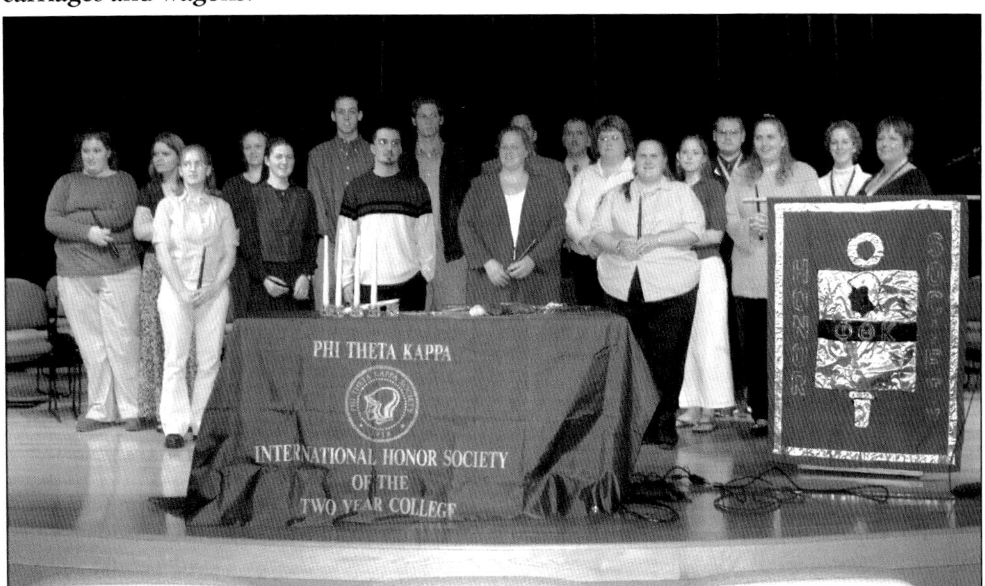

Phi Theta Kappa is the international honor society of two-year colleges. Here members are shown at one of their regular induction ceremonies.

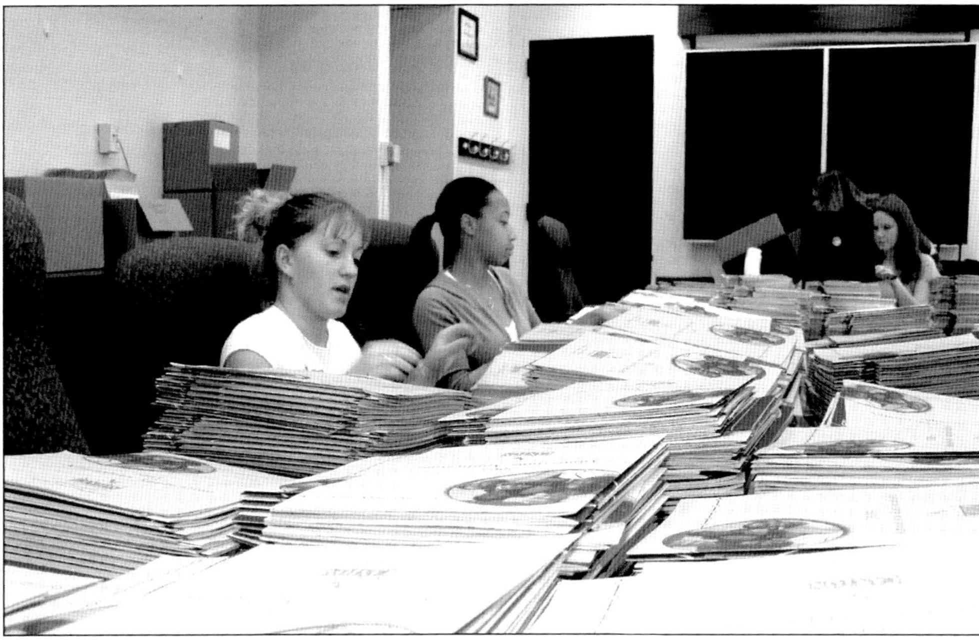

Student volunteers also make a difference on campus. Here students work on a massive mailing for the admissions office, helping to recruit another year's freshman class.

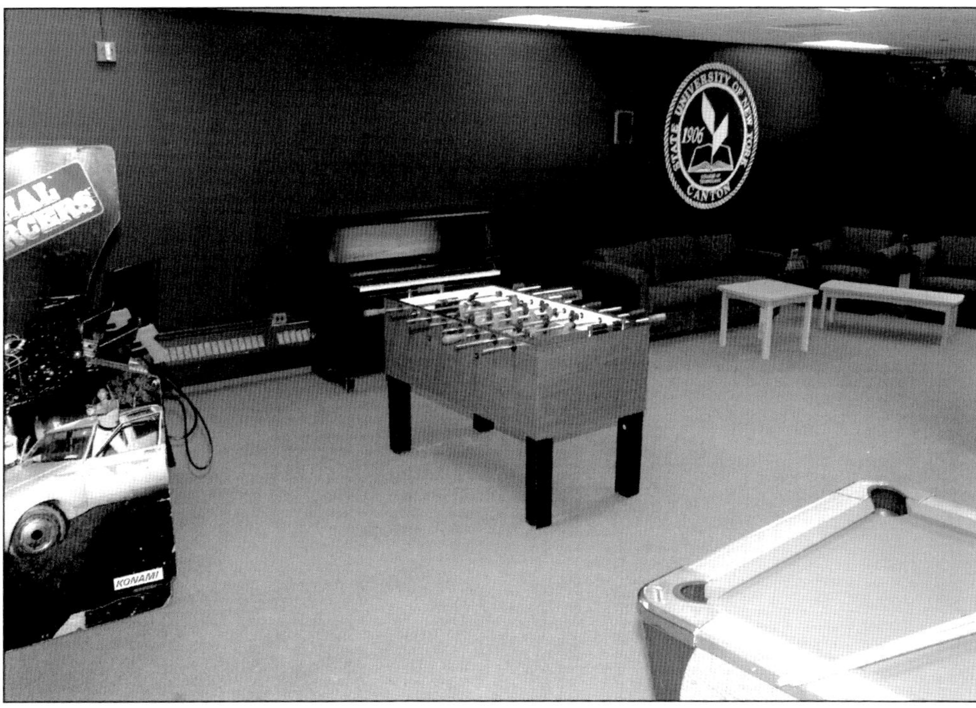

When Kingston Theater burned in 1997, the game room disappeared in the resulting reallocation of space. In 2004, this space was reclaimed from the textbook center to create a combination lounge and game room. It is popular, as nothing comparable exists off campus.

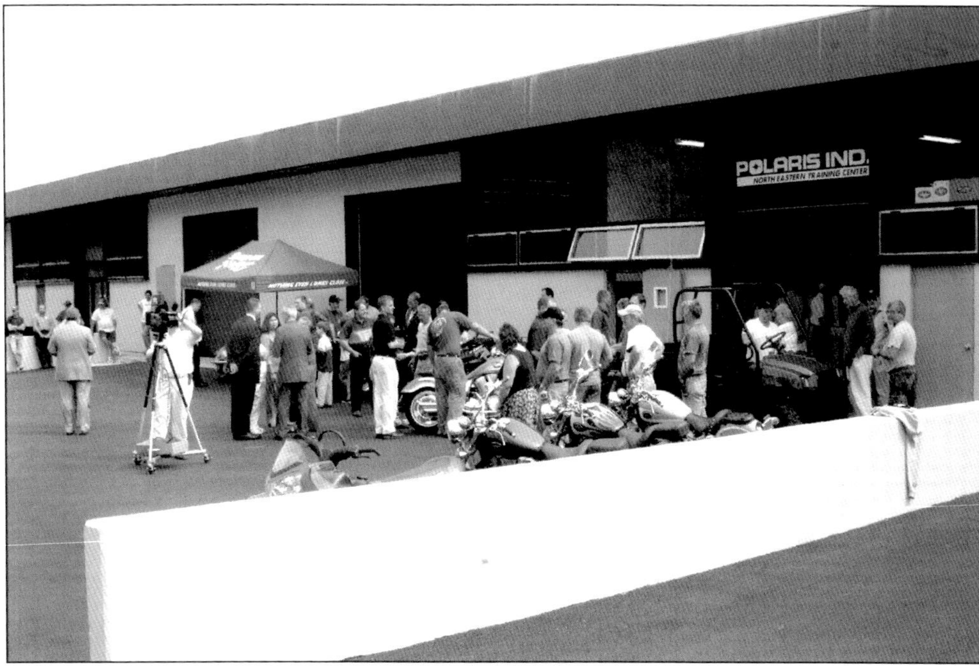

Another new and innovative program is the motorsports curriculum and the arrival of the Polaris Training Center in Nevaldine South. The group shot was taken on the day of the announcement.

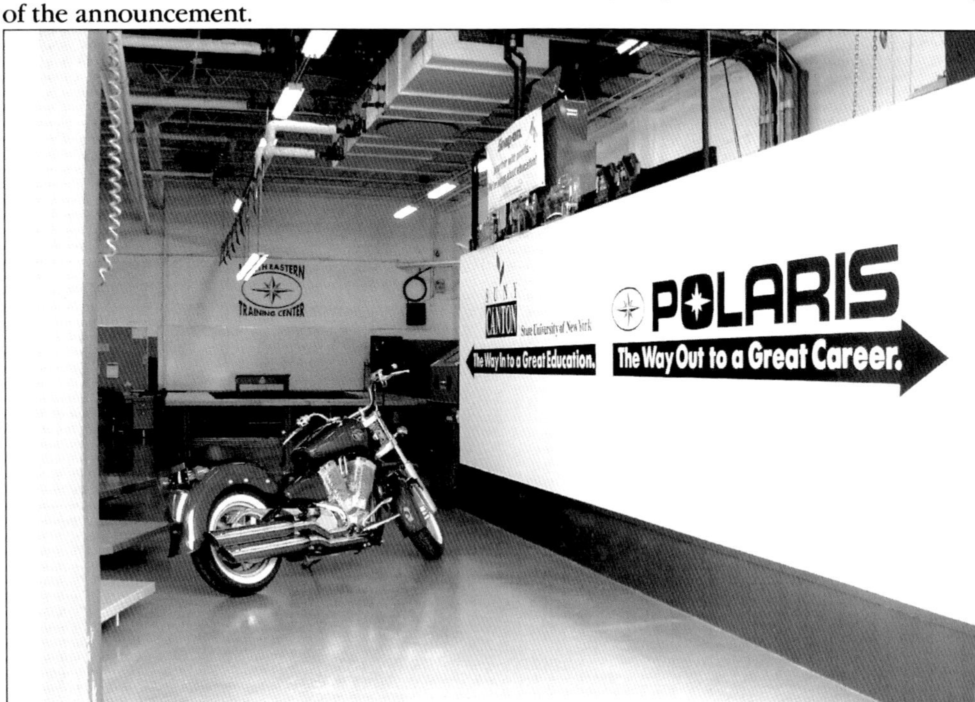

Inside Nevaldine South is the Polaris Lab, part of the Northeastern Training Center. The collaboration between industry and the college is providing high quality training opportunities for SUNY Canton students.

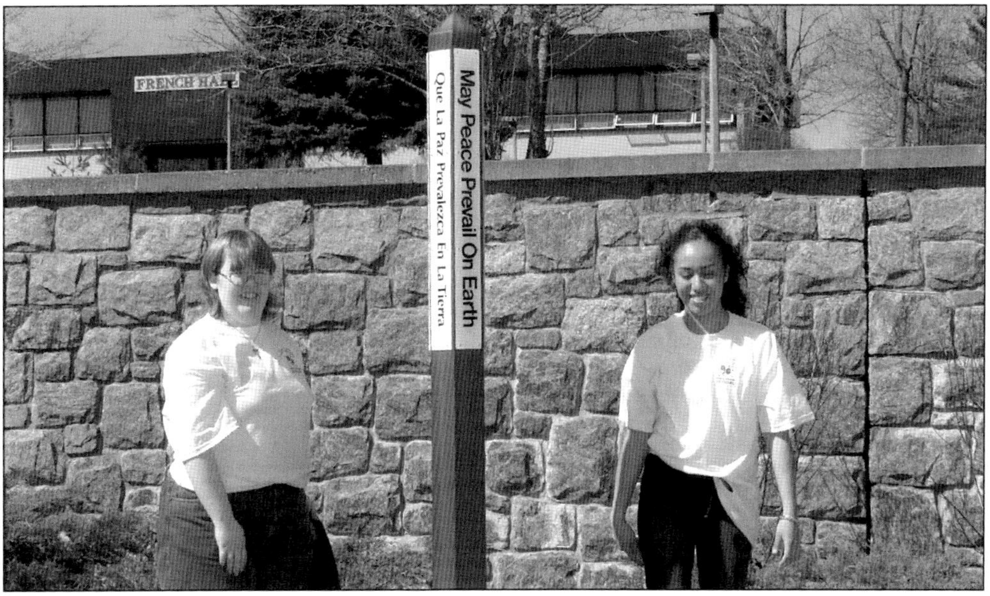

The Roselle Academic Plaza has become a center for campus activities, whether they are picnics, vigils, or social events such as the Spring Festival. The Peace Pole is located on the west side of the plaza, and its message appears in five different languages. Note French Hall is on the hill in the background.

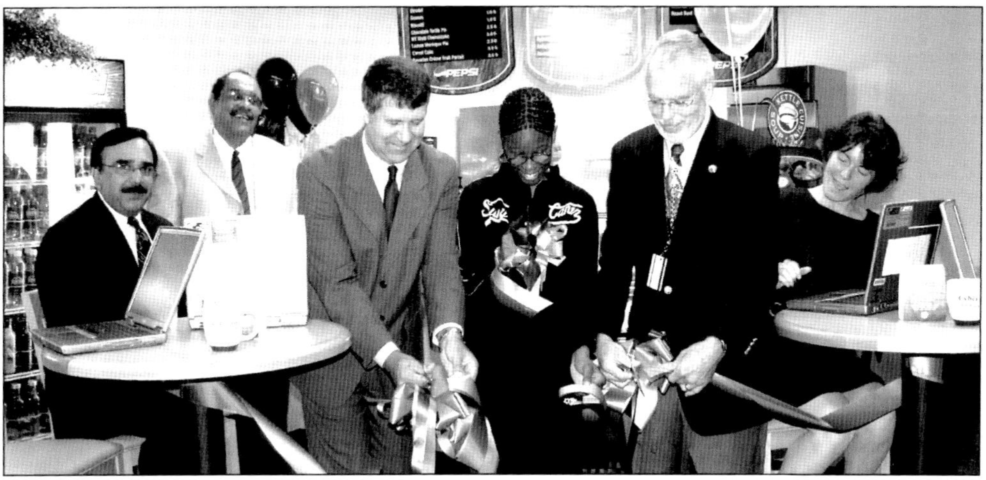

The new Cyber Café in Southworth Library was dedicated in September 2004 to a standing room only crowd. The official ribbon-cutting ceremony is pictured here. Pictured are, from left to right, the College Association's executive director Mike Perry, vice president Carson Smith, provost Dr. Jeremy Brown, student Enid Corbin, president Dr. Joseph Kennedy, and Sue Law. The Cyber Café has been a popular addition to campus eateries. Eight computers are available to surf the web in a relaxed setting. Note the laptops on both tables, which have been available for student use in the library since September 2004. Located where the writing center had been, the Cyber Café was the first major physical change to Southworth Library since the early 1990s. Most of the changes within the library have been less visible and focused on technology. In 1994, the Multilis online public access catalog and automated system was implemented. Nine years later Multilis was replaced by the ALEPH automated system.

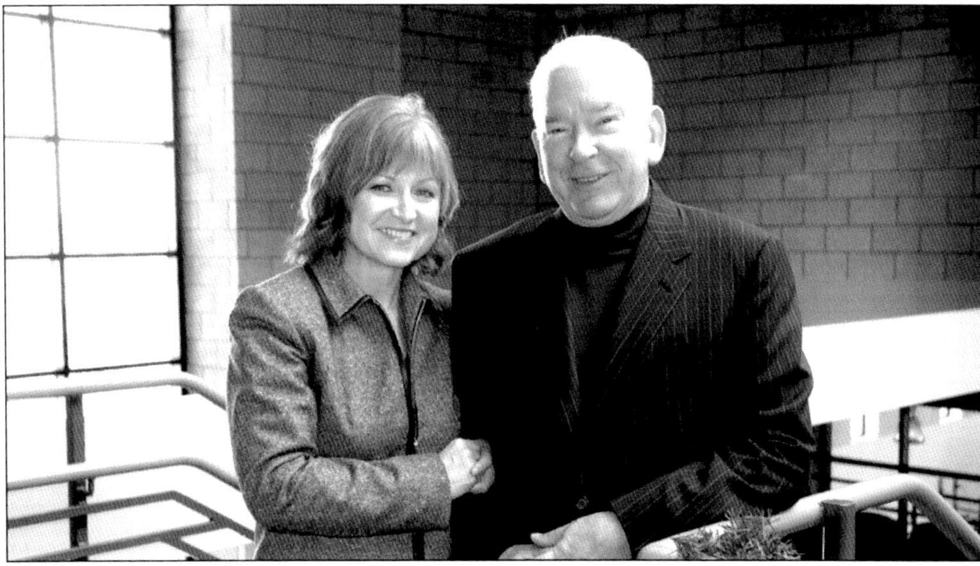

In recent years, as the overall level of state funding has decreased, donations to the college have been an increasingly important part of ensuring the college's future. Alumni have played a vital role. Pictured here are Joel M. and Carol Canino, who announced a major gift to the college in December 2004. Joel Canino was a member of the class of 1959. On May 13, 2005, SUNY Canton dedicated its School of Engineering Technology as the Canino School of Engineering Technology.

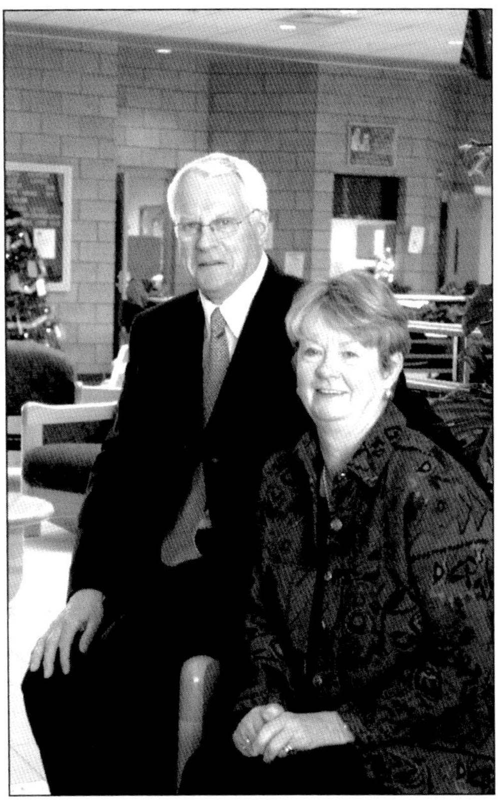

Another benefactor of the college is Morristown resident Ronald Woodcock, class of 1959. He is pictured here with his wife, Blanche, in the lounge of the Miller Campus Center in December 2004. The Woodcocks co-chaired the Canton College Foundation's Centennial Campaign.

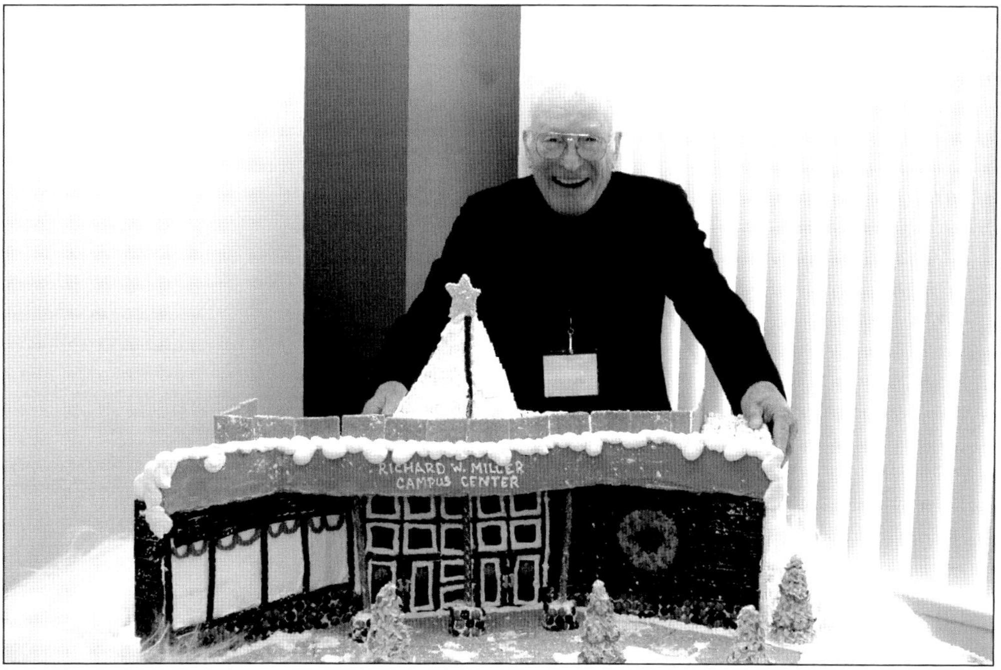

Professor Emeritus Richard W. Miller has been involved with the college in many different capacities—as a faculty member, and most recently as a donor. Here Professor Miller poses with a festive diorama of the campus center and plaza.

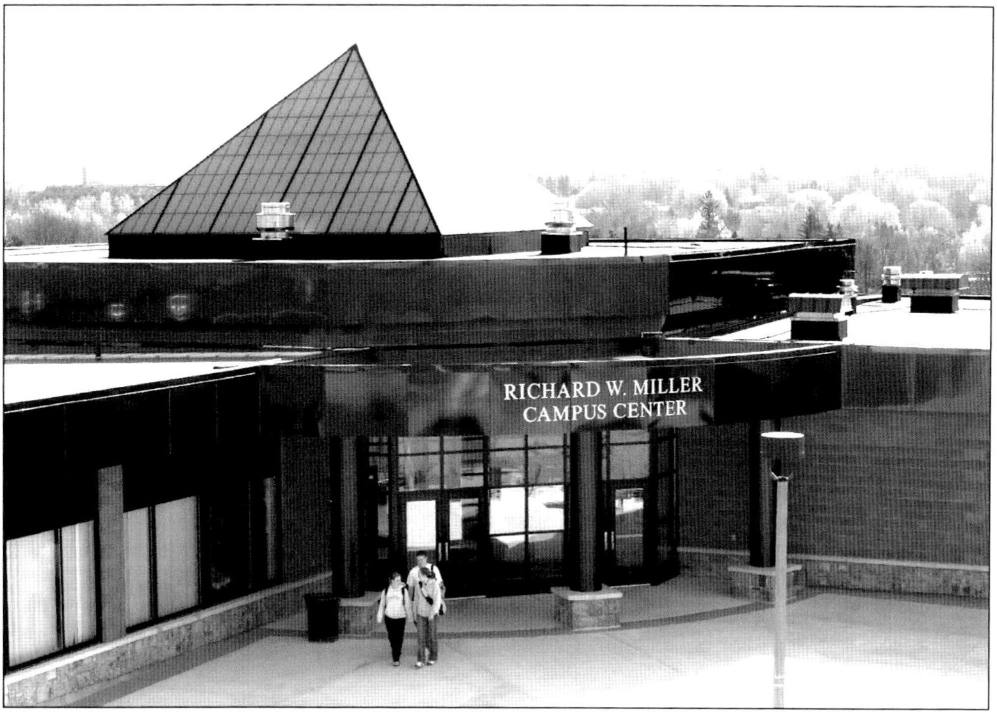

In recognition of Professor Miller's contributions, the campus center was renamed the Richard W. Miller Campus Center in 2004.

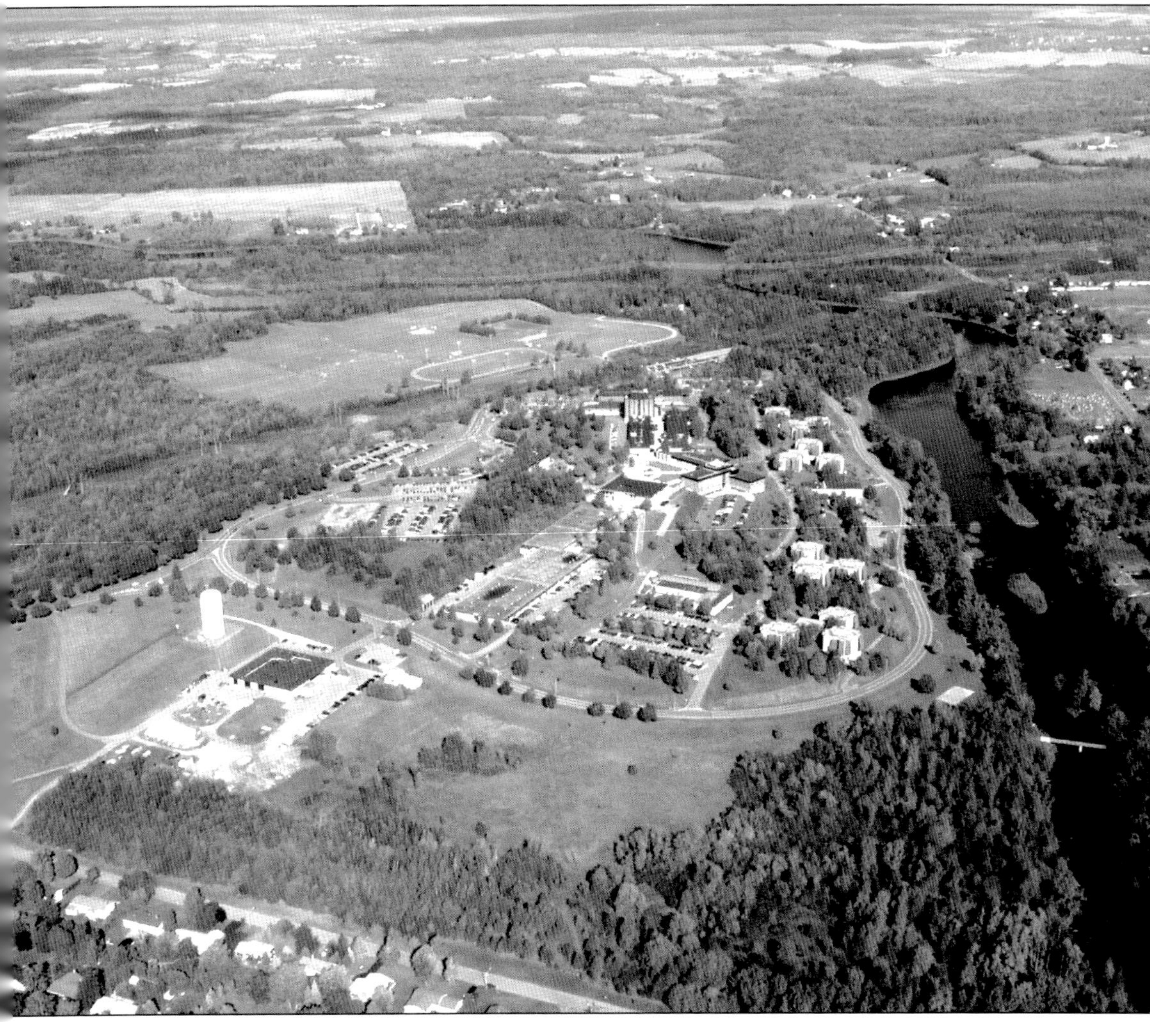

This aerial photograph shows the campus as it appeared on the eve of SUNY Canton's centennial celebration. Both the campus center (right center) and the Newell Veterinary Technology Center (lower center) are present. The athletic fields are the open space in the upper center of the photograph, just outside the Cornell Drive campus road.

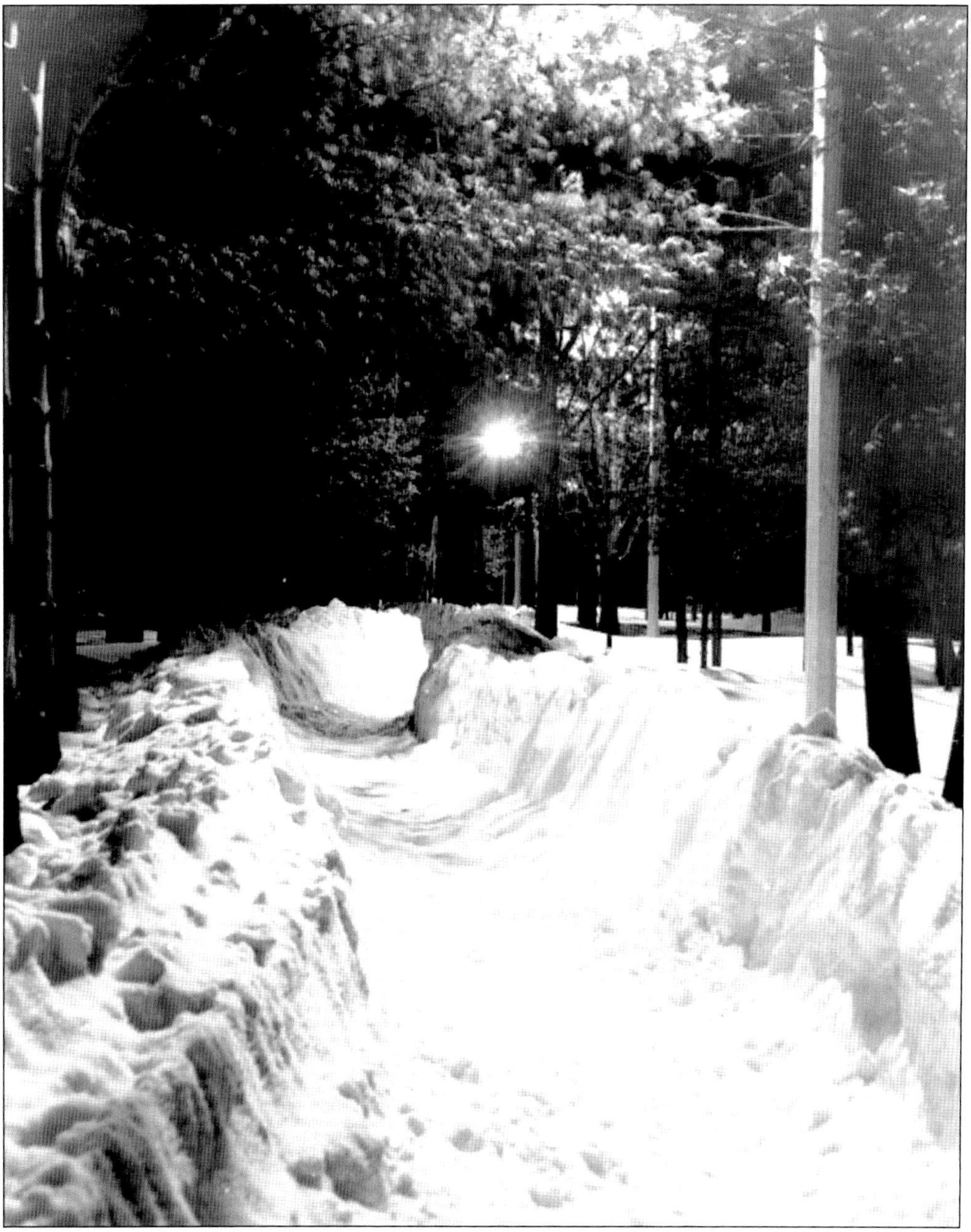

This older, undated photograph entitled "Footpath to ATC Campus on Bullis Island" first appeared in the *St. Lawrence Plaindealer*. While a beautiful photograph in its own right, it is also a fitting metaphor for SUNY Canton's development. What lights the way ahead is the confidence and strength that comes from enduring and meeting the challenges and changes of the past. (Courtesy of Vance Archives, St. Lawrence University.)

Bibliography

Howland, Camille. *Seventy Years of Change*. Ogdensburg, NY: Ryan Press, 1966.

Office of University Affairs and Development. *Sixty-four Campuses: The State University of New York to 1985*. Albany, NY: State University of New York, 1985.

Payson, James M. *A Brief History of the State School of Agriculture, St. Lawrence University*. s.l:s.n. Typescript, n.d.

Pink, Louis H., and Rutherford E. Delmage. *Candle in the Wilderness: A Centennial History of the St. Lawrence University 1856–1956*. New York: Appleton-Century-Crofts, 1957.